THE BOOK OF
SPORTS AND GAMES

EDITED BY

WALTER CAMP

AUTHOR OF "THE DAILY DOZEN"

WITH FOURTEEN DIAGRAMS AND SIXTEEN
FULL-PAGE ILLUSTRATIONS

NEW YORK

THOMAS Y. CROWELL COMPANY

PUBLISHERS

INTRODUCTION

In looking over the general subject of sports and games, I have been struck with the fact that very little in a comprehensive way has been offered to their followers. Single books there are on the subject of golf, tennis, football, and the various other games which have a large following of devotees, but very little is provided in the way of a compendium of all games.

In providing the course of daily exercises for the phonograph, known as the "Daily Dozen," I have had in mind the needs of the indoor man. Many of our months are shut-in months, and many of our office-workers have all too few hours of golden sunshine and fresh air. To all such persons, the daily regimen of exercise is absolutely essential to continued health.

However, for every month in the year there are certain outdoor sports, if only one will seek to find them. There are skating and hockey in mid-winter. Basketball, while an indoor sport, provides all the dash and freedom of many outdoor pastimes. With the coming of spring, the whole vista of such sports

Introduction

opens up to the enthusiast. The early golfer gets on his knickerbockers. Canoeing and rowing attract other adherents. Then come baseball, tennis, and all the rest, lasting well on to the time when snow falls again.

This book has been provided to give a general brief view of all the popular outdoor pastimes, together with certain indoor games which provide physical exercise during the shut in months. It is, of course, not the last word on the subject, as many of these games require much more extended playing rules than can be allotted in these pages. It does, however, endeavor to give the salient facts which the player will need to know in taking up any sport for the first time.

We cannot leave the subject without some comment upon the ethics of sport.

In the first place, play fair. Nothing counts more than that. Not only does the sport go out of the contest and the sun go behind a cloud, but the very chance of winning grows less when any other means are considered. The victory is only worth winning when it leaves no scar behind. Make the rules strict and then live up to them. Don't study to find where they can be evaded, but rather to insure their enforcement, and then you will have nothing to regret.

In your games try to give everyone a chance. Don't make them all games of strength. Don't make them all games of skill. Don't get so much enamored of any one that you cannot see the fun in another. But when you go in for a sport, follow it up and make the most of yourself. Don't be deluded, moreover, by the people who tell you to "play only for sport, never mind who wins." That spirit might come with the millennium, but I doubt it. A good, live American boy or girl has a right to win and to play to win, and if he is on a team or crew or nine, or if she be on a basketball team or golf team, or anything else, where upon individual effort depends somewhat the success of others, then that boy or girl must play to *win*. It is not a bad thing to feel a pleasure in success and a depression in defeat, so long as neither of these feelings lasts too long. They ought to come, and they will. They are part of the training and discipline, of the education and development, and without them life at school or college would lose a good deal of its savor. Of course, there are better things than winning, and there are a good many worse things than losing, but you don't need a preacher to tell you that, and it is generally only the lazy, careless, and indifferent who go upon the principle of never mind who wins or loses.

To those for whom there is an opportunity, I can only say: Take as much pleasure out of doors as possible. There is nothing that can compare with fresh air. No amount of gymnasium or indoor amusement can make up for the lack of the real benefit which comes from pleasurable sport out of

Introduction

doors. Don't stay indoors because it is cloudy or windy, or because the day seems disagreeable. We should naturally be out of doors, and it is only the exceptional case where, no matter what the weather is, one is not the better for being out every day.

Just one word more. Sports and games out of doors ought to teach you unselfishness. The narrow, cramped, confining four walls of a house ought to be forgotten, and with them anything small and contemptible. Growth of the body comes from out-of-door exercises and the fresh air and sunshine, and with it ought to come growth of the mind, not in the sense of book knowledge which the school and evening reading can furnish, but in the sense of greater breadth of view and wider horizon. This may seem like preaching, but everybody knows how much harder it is to be cross and mean and stingy when out of doors than when cooped up in the house. But just as you grow strong in body by these out-of-door sports through constant exertion, so the mind and heart, even though well disposed, should have the same amount of exertion along the right lines to make them broad and true. So I say, be generous to a fault, forget self and selfishness, and grow.

WALTER CAMP.

New Haven, Conn.
September, 1923.

CONTENTS

vii

ILLUSTRATIONS

Illustrations

BASEBALL

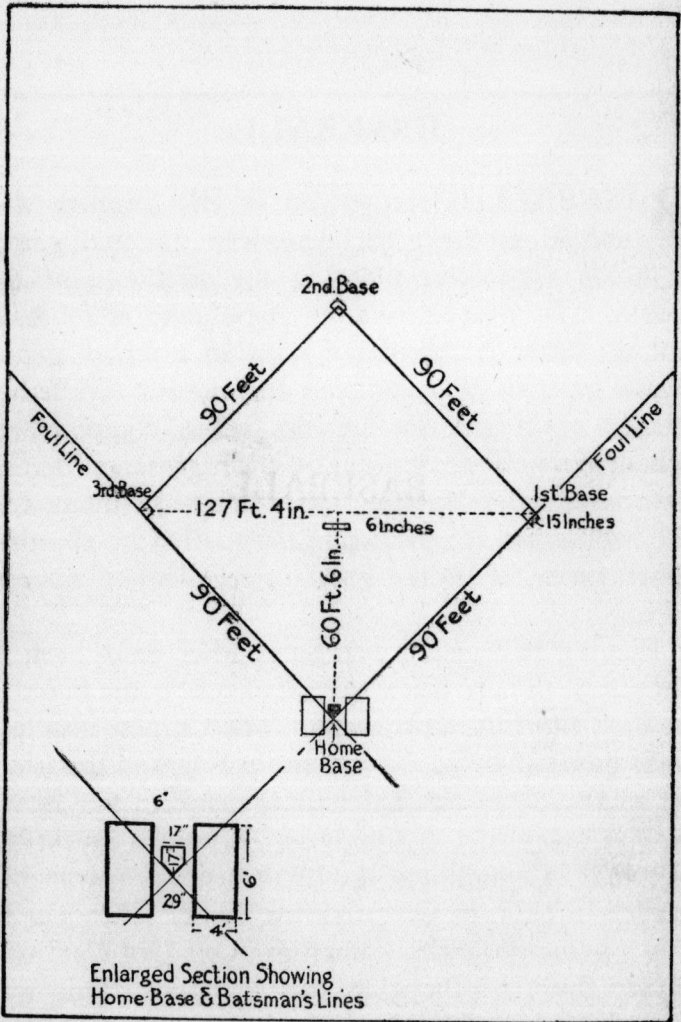

2nd. Base

90 Feet

90 Feet

Foul Line

Foul Line

3rd.Base

127 Ft. 4 in.

6 Inches

1st.Base

15 Inches

60 Ft. 6 In.

90 Feet

90 Feet

Home
Base

6'

17"

9'

29"

4'

Enlarged Section Showing
Home·Base & Batsman's Lines

2

BASEBALL

BASEBALL is recognized in this country and abroad as the great American national game. It holds a peculiar place in the affections of the public. Its nearest rival in popularity is football, but the latter is considered more of a school game, while baseball is a game of the masses. Whether played on a sand lot between teams composed of school boys, or professionally by high-salaried men before audiences running into the tens of thousands, the enthusiasm it can inspire is equalled by no other sport, unless it be the great intercollegiate contests of football.

Playing ball of one sort or another dates back to antiquity. There was a species of ball game popular in Egypt forty centuries ago. The Chinese also had their game of ball. Nowadays in England the nearest approach to our baseball is cricket; but as we play it today it is distinctly an American invention. Baseball in something like its present form was first played in 1839, in Cooperstown, N. Y. Previous to this a game generally known as "One Old Cat" was played by schoolboys in this country. This was played by three boys, each batting in turn, and scoring runs by going to a single base and back, without

Sports and Games

being hit or touched by the ball. Then came "Two
Old Cat," "Three Old Cat," and "Four Old Cat," ex-
tensions of the game using four, six, and eight players. Choosing sides came naturally next. A species
of "Town Ball" was played in Philadelphia, in 1833.

In 1843, organized baseball clubs began to appear,
with scheduled match games. One of the first of
these was the Washington Baseball Club of New
York. Two years later the first code of rules was
drawn up by the Knickerbocker Baseball Club of
the same city, and used in its matches with seven
other clubs of New York and Brooklyn.

In 1858 the National Association was formed,
which endeavored to take up the game professionally.
The first strictly professional baseball club was the
Cincinnati Red Stockings, which toured the country
in 1869 and defeated all comers. By this time the
game had evolved into baseball very much as it is
played today.

The National Association of Professional Baseball Players was organized in 1871 with a ten club
circuit. The National League followed in 1876, the
American Association in 1882, and the American
League in 1902.

There are now two "major leagues," the National
and the American, which play "World Series" games
to decide the championship. In addition to these,
numerous "minor leagues" flourish, such as the
American Association, the International League, the

Baseball

Western League, the Pacific League, the Southern League, and various State leagues.

The above resumé deals with the professional aspect of the sport. Amateur baseball, in its organized phase, is chiefly played by school and college clubs, and athletic associations. In 1879, a college circuit was organized which included Harvard, Princeton, Amherst, Brown, and Dartmouth; Yale coming in the next year. In 1887, an Eastern College League was established. Many colleges, however, arrange their schedules from year to year, and play independently of any league.

THE BASEBALL DIAMOND

Baseball may be played on any level field, but the size should be at least one hundred yards square. More is advisable if it can be obtained. In professional games the grounds are always enclosed. Upon this space is marked out a diamond (see diagram) with the sides measuring each ninety feet, and placed so that one corner is distant more than thirty yards or so from the end of the field. At this corner of the diamond is placed a white plate a foot square sunk level with the ground, and designated the "home plate." Canvas bags are placed at each of the other three corners, called bases, these bags being some fifteen inches square and called, beginning at the right as one looks into the field from the home plate, first, second and third bases, respectively. The lines from the home base to the first base and from the home base to third base are prolonged out into the field and are called "foul lines."

In laying out a baseball field proceed as follows:

With a steel tape-measure lay out the base lines and place the home plate and pitcher's box as shown in the diagram. If it is possible to do so, have the home plate due north and the pitcher's plate due south.

Remove the sod from the base lines between the home plate and first and third bases, also from first base to second base and from second base to third base. The sod may be removed from around the pitcher's plate. Fill in the base lines and the ground around the pitcher's plate if the sod is removed.

Mark lines of batsman's box, on each side of home plate, with whitewash, chalk or similar substance. Also foul lines, from home plate to first base and from home plate to third base, continuing out into the field beyond first and third bases.

Distance from home plate to first base, 90 feet; from first base to second base, 90 feet; from second base to third, 90 feet; and from third base to home plate, 90 feet. Total distance around the bases, 360 feet.

Distance from point of home plate to pitcher's slab, 60 feet 6 inches. Distance is measured from point of home plate, where the base lines intersect, and not from the front part of the plate.

Baseball

Distance across diamond, from home plate to second base, 127 feet 3⅜ inches; from first base, across diamond, to third base, the same.

Size of batsman's box, 6 feet by 4 feet.

Size of pitcher's slab, 24 inches by 6 inches.

Size of base bags, 15 inches square.

Home plate, 1 foot square, with the corners filled in on the portion facing the pitcher, where it will measure 17 inches across.

To obviate the necessity for ground rules, where space is limited, the official rules specify that the shortest distance from home plate to grand stand is 90 feet.

A simple method of laying out a ball field with a piece of cord is as follows:

First—Get a piece of rope or cord, with no stretch in it. Second—Measure off the following distances and make a knot at each distance: 60 feet 6 inches —90 feet—127 feet 3⅜ inches—180 feet. Third— Decide upon the location of home plate (north and south is preferable, to avoid the sun in the fielders' eyes); fasten the rope end to a peg at home and walk out straight to full length of rope; 60 feet 6 inches will be the pitcher's slab; 127 feet 3⅜ inches will be second base; put in spikes to mark same. Next fasten the knot at 180 feet at second; grasp knot at 90 feet and walk out to right of home until the rope is tight at all points; this will be first base; go to the left in same manner and you will have third base. This can be done in less than ten minutes. This method is good for use at picnics, outings or similar events.

OFFICIAL DIMENSIONS OF DIAMONDS FOR BOYS UNDER SIXTEEN YEARS OF AGE.

Distance between bases, 82 feet; home plate to second base, 115 feet 11½ inches; same distance across diamond from first base to third base; home plate to pitcher's slab, 50 feet.

IMPLEMENTS OF THE GAME

The ball must weigh not less than five nor more than five and one-quarter ounces avoirdupois and measure not less than nine nor more than nine and one-quarter inches in circumference.

The bat must be round, not over two and three-fourths inches in diameter at the thickest part, nor more than forty-two inches in length, and entirely out of hardwood, except that for a distance of 18 inches from the end twine may be wound around; or a granulated substance applied to the handle.

Players are also provided with uniforms, gloves, and reinforced shoes, to conform to certain requirements.

HOW THE GAME IS PLAYED

Two teams make up each contest, with nine players on each side. The fielders are known as the pitcher, the catcher, the first baseman, the second baseman, the third baseman, the shortstop, the left fielder, the center fielder, and the right fielder. None of these is required to occupy an exact position on the field, except the pitcher, who must stand with his foot touching the pitcher's slab when in the act of delivering the ball to the batter, and the catcher, who must be within the "catcher's space" behind the batter.

Each side has nine turns or innings at the bat, and by a turn is meant that that side continues batting until three men have/been put out. In case of a tie score at the end of the ninth inning, etxra innings may be played.

The batsman stands at the home plate, until he has hit the ball safely when he endeavors to make a circuit, or run of the bases.

Inside the diamond and in front of the home plate some sixty feet in a straight line is what is called the pitcher's position, where the pitcher stands when delivering the ball to the batsman. The catcher's position, not fixed by law but which he occupies by preference, is close behind the batsman. The men at the bat take their turn in regular order, and continue, as stated above, until three of them have been put out by the opponents. This is a signal for the retirement of the batsmen to the field, and the others come in to take their turn at the bat.

The officials of the game are either one or two umpires. In all important games two umpires are used—one stationed just behind the catcher, to judge balls, strikes, and put-outs at the home plate; the other out in the field to render decisions at first, second and third bases, and to judge all plays in this and the out-lying territory.

THE PLAYING POSITIONS

Batting. As every player must take his regular turn at the bat, the first thing one should take up is the batting, for there the average nine is far weaker in proportion than in any other department of the game. This is probably due to the fact that every American boy practices fielding from the time he can handle a ball, but his practice in batting is very limited. Drilling in batting takes time and requires close attention. There are several ways to conduct it, the most common being to have the substitute pitchers pitch to the candidates of the nine, letting each man take a turn at batting for a certain length of time each day.

The batsman should assume the proper position when at bat. Individuals differ somewhat in this respect, and a proper position for one man may not be the proper position for another, but there are certain faults which are detrimental to good hitting. The most common of these faults is that of drawing away from the plate. Sometimes it arises from the batsman having been hit with the ball and this makes him nervous, and he draws his front foot away from the plate as soon as the pitcher starts to deliver the ball. Anything in the way of an exaggerated position is bad; that is, if a man leans very far forward, or previous to the delivery of the pitcher holds his bat in some peculiar attitude.

The best position for the bat is just over the shoulder, and a man should make a slight motion preparatory to hitting the ball every time the pitcher delivers it. In other words, he should get himself in readiness to complete the swing if the ball proves good. The hands should not be at the extreme end of the bat, but an inch or two up from the end, and beyond that it is by no means a bad plan to shorten the bat still more until the man is practically sure to hit the average pitcher with fair certainty. The batsman should practice what is known as "free hitting," namely, hitting any balls that come within certain striking distance between his knee and shoulder. This prevents his being at the mercy of the pitcher who works the corners well, for a man who is trained to hit nothing except the ball that comes exactly over the middle of the plate, and who bats more according to the position of the plate than according to the ball delivered, is usually an easy man for the expert pitcher to deceive.

The batsman should also be taught to bunt the ball, that is, to block it with the bat, sending it just inside the diamond, and the practice of placing such hits is an excellent supplementary exercise. During part of the batting practice also the batsman should be taught to start off just as soon as he has hit the ball. It is absolutely essential that batsmen get off quickly after the ball is hit, for many times it makes a difference between a safe hit and an out.

The Pitcher. Practicing infielding should be supplemented with instructions the same as practice in batting. To begin with the battery, the main point nowadays is to have enough catchers and pitchers, so that they shall neither of them be overworked, especially the pitcher. A pitcher unquestionably is not at his best if he has pitched more than two games a week, and one really first-class game a week is enough if it is advisable to keep him at the top notch. Substitutes should be used freely, and the mainstay kept where he adds enthusiasm and does not run the risk of a lame arm. Especial care should be observed in the early part of the spring, for at that time men are very apt to get strains in pitching hard games, and these strains render them useless for the rest of the season.

Of recent years the game has come to center more and more around the pitcher. This does not mean to say that the pitcher is the whole game; far from it. Every nicely balanced club must look well to each position, as a single weak point is quickly detected by the other team and their attack directed thereto. For example, if a team plays well on the field but does not bat well in the box, it is only at the mercy of the opposing pitchers. The pitcher is in

Baseball

a sense the captain of the nine, although he may not be, and often is not the actual captain, but upon his coolness and judgment depends the success or failure of the game.

The veteran pitcher, Jack Coombs, has this to say in regard to the qualifications of a successful pitcher:

"Control is necessary to success in pitching. You must have it. The history of the game shows that many pitchers with control and plenty of brains were successful pitchers, although other men with more speed and curves than they had, were failures. They were successful because they could put the ball where they wanted to put it eleven times out of twelve.

"Next to control I would say head work. The use of the brain in pitching comes second in importance in my opinion.

"After that, a change of pace. By that I mean changing from a fast ball to a slow ball without giving the batter any way of knowing that change.

"Fourth, and last in the list of esential features of pitching, I put speed and curves.

"Now as to the kinds of ball you should pitch. You have probably read of pitchers having from ten to fourteen different ways to pitch a ball. I would advise young pitchers to use a fast ball and a fast curve and a slow ball and a slow curve. That will be about all you need. The spit ball and all the other freak deliveries are only different kinds of curves.

"When you are learning to pitch do not try to

master too much at one time. Go along slowly and patiently. Pick up little by little and be sure that you do everything right before you try to pick up anything else. Many boys who would have made good pitchers have spoiled their chances by trying to pitch too much, or rather to perfect too many kinds of deliveries at the same time. It does not pay in the long run.

"Most boys think that a good arm is all that is necessary in pitching. They believe that they must pitch solely with their arm. Do not do this. Learn to pitch with your body. Bring the muscles of your shoulders and the upper part of your body into play. Get them into action when you deliver the ball. If you do this, you will get more speed. Better than that, this system will give you a bigger and better curve. Also, if you use your body more than your arm it will not tire you. There are many pitchers losing games because they do not use their body enough. They simply use their arm, and the result is that the arm gets tired because it has to do all the work, and soon the pitcher finds his speed leaving and his curve not breaking right. The other team hits him hard and he loses the game unless he is taken out. Then sometimes he is not taken out soon enough to save the game.

"When you are pitching, find out the batter's weakness. You can do this by pitching different kinds of balls to him. Practice will teach you to find out

Baseball

what he likes to hit and what he does not like to strike at, by the way he goes after the ball. Always study the batter carefully.

"After you discover where the batter's weakness lies, do not pitch him constantly the kind of balls he is weak on. Change your tactics. Let him think that you will pitch to his weakness, but cross him with the sort of ball that he does not believe you will dare to pitch him.

"Much of the pitcher's success lies in outguessing the batter. That is, pitching the kind of balls to him that he is not looking for. If a batter knows that you know his weak point, he may get an idea that every ball you pitch to him will be at his weak spot. He will be prepared for it. And just when he thinks you are about to give him the kind of ball he is weak on, give him something else. Always try to pitch the kind of ball the batter least expects."

Success in pitching is the same as success in anything else. All successes are achieved alike and with these two factors—persistency and confidence. Keep on trying constantly and keep your nerve. Realize that you will be able to accomplish a certain thing, set your goal, and keep on trying until you accomplish it.

The Catcher. The catcher does not require the same amount of tender attention in training as the pitcher, but he too should be well looked after, and not used too much. Particularly is it well to see that

15

the catcher does not, in practicing his throw to the
bases, keep at it too long. A few good throws with
the men will keep him in shape and do better than to
have him throw until his arm is tired. He should
practice throwing not only to first, but to second and
third as well, and particularly with the batsman
standing in front of him striking at pitched balls.
The great thing for the catcher to study is getting
the ball away quickly, and without unnecessary motion either of the feet, arms, or shoulders.

The catcher, next to the pitcher, is the determining
factor in many a hard-fought game. He it is who
signals to the pitcher what kind of a ball to deliver.
The signal is usually given by means of the fingers
or hand upon the mitt, and the pitcher should not
send over any other ball, without making sure that
the catcher understands the change in plan. A
smoothly-working "battery," as the two are called,
forms the backbone of a nine.

The First Baseman. The first baseman can be
used more freely than any other man on the nine,
and the aim of his instruction should be to see that
he covers as much ground as possible in filling his
position; and, second, that he is able to extend himself in all possible directions in meeting the balls
when thrown to him. That is, he should learn to
step forward so as to get a ball which is liable to
come to him on a bad bound, or to step back slightly
so as to get on a better bound a bad throw which is

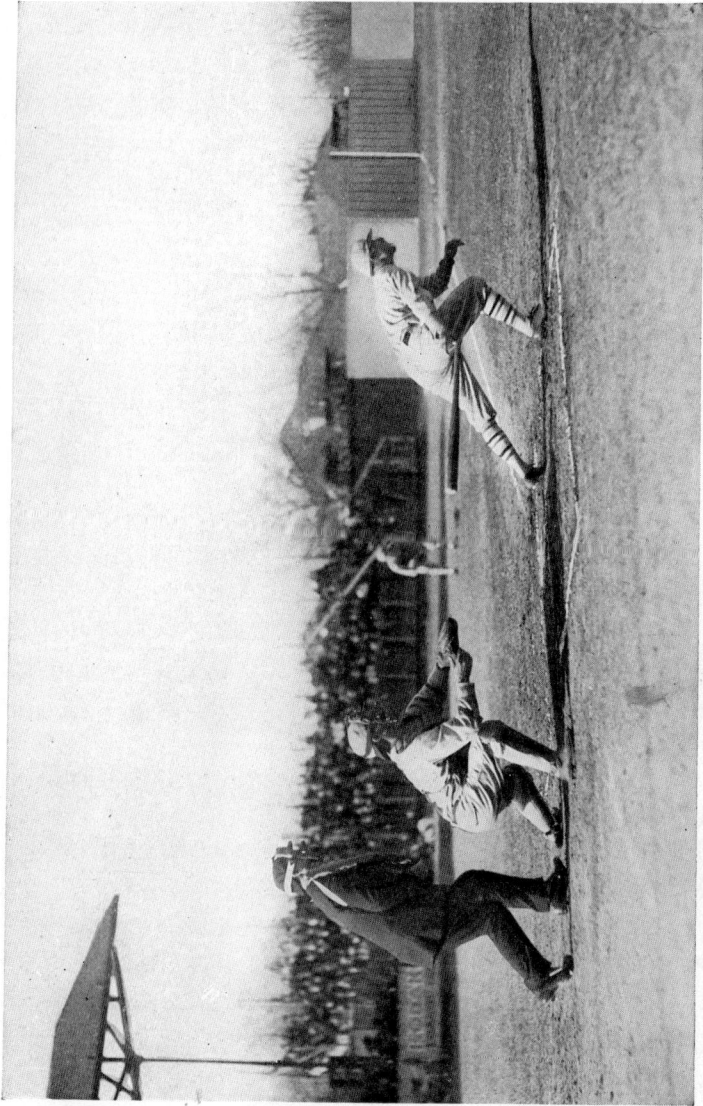

BASEBALL

A practice game between the New York "Giants" and the Chicago "White Sox," at San Antonio.

too far away from him to be trapped. He should also try reaching from side to side, keeping his foot on the base, and in fact, all possible motions which will enable him to save wild throws. He should, besides all this, have practice in putting the ball on a man when receiving it from the pitcher. This is important.

The Second Baseman. The second baseman's work is in covering ground and in catching balls from the catcher and pitcher and putting them on the base-runner. He should be encouraged to play a pretty deep field game and cover all the ground he can on his side of the diamond. He should also practice quick throws, for by thus playing a deep field he may get what would apparently be base hits, and by being able to throw them quickly to first, put the runner out.

The Shortstop. The shortstop's work is similar to that of the second baseman, except that his throw is longer and must be better timed. The shortstop who now plays the most up-to-date game plays very deep so that the third baseman can take short balls in front of him, and between the two they can close up as much as possible the gap, and prevent its coming between third base and short.

The Third Baseman. The third baseman has one of the most difficult positions in the infield, for he has opportunities to get hard hits along the third base line which require him to get quickly toward the base and then recover himself for his throw to first. This is one of the most important points of a third baseman's work, and should be practiced a great deal. Especial attention should also be paid to running in on short hits and getting over in front of shortstop on high-bounding balls.

The Outfield. In the outfield—right, center, and left fields—the practice is simpler, and consists in catching flies, stopping grounders, and at the same time practicing throwing from the out-field to home plate and the various bases. The outfielders, like the catcher, ought not to do so much throwing as to get their arms tired, but they should have plenty of work in catching batted balls, especially of a varying kind, such as high fly balls, long-line hits, and grounders which come out from over the infield.

Base-Running. There is one more important feature of coaching a nine which requires judgment, and that is the base-running. It is difficult to practice save in games, but there is an opportunity to do some work by having one or two men run the bases while the rest of the nine field. The main points about base running are everlasting vigilance coupled with plenty of daring and judgment as to chances. The secret of its success consists in quick starting, getting away to first sharply when the ball is hit, getting a long lead from the bases, and being able to recover, reaching with the foot or hand for the bag and sliding. This latter can be practiced both indoors and outdoors, but a man never ought to get sore or lame at it, especially within a week of a big match. One of the cardinal points for base-runners to remember is always to draw the throw of the fielder, if possible, by making a pretended start toward the next base, then if the throw goes wide, the base-runner will get the base, whereas, if it is accurate he has plenty of time to return to the base he was occupying.

THE PROFESSIONAL GAME

Professional ball playing does not differ in its essentials from college or high school playing. It simply means that the player has graduated up to a big position in the sport and that he must specialize in this work just the same as in any other line of business. The professional baseball player strives to keep his body at the highest point of efficiency. Even in winter, he does not dare relax and get logy; as he knows full well that the work in the spring training camp will be all the more arduous. We read only recently of a famous batter, who reported to his Southern training camp weighing about twenty pounds too much, and this proved to be a deterrent factor in his work for several weeks.

Professionals generally report for duty the latter part of February. All of the big league clubs maintain Southern training camps, in which for the first week or two practice is light to avoid overstraining the muscles which have been idle during the winter.

Sports and Games

Then the work gradually stiffens up and includes practice games with other league clubs in the vicinity. On the way North these practice games continue. The club aims to travel easily with small jumps and get in practice almost daily, if possible. It thus reports to its home grounds early in April in the pink of condition. After the season opens, games are held continuously except for days of rain or travel, until the close of the season, which is usually early in October.

Coaching a baseball nine has now become developed to such an extent that it is an art, and a set of players drilled by a good coach through one season are usually improved to a point of efficiency at least twenty-five percent in advance of other equally good players who lack this guidance and co-ordination. For this reason, it is not advisable to change managers or coaches any oftener than absolutely necessary.

DEFINITIONS

Diamond—The boundaries of the infield.

Ball—A pitched ball which does not come within required distance of the batsman.

Foul Hit—A legally batted ball which falls or goes outside the diamond or foul lines.

Balk—Any false motion on the part of the pitcher which is calculated to deceive. (The playing rules define 14 varieties of balk.)

Baseball

Dead Ball—A ball delivered to the bat by the pitcher, not struck at by the batsman, that touches any part of the batsman's person or clothing while he is standing in his position.

Block Ball—A batted or thrown ball that is touched, stopped or handled by a person not engaged in the game.

Fair Hit—Any legally batted ball that first falls on fair territory inside or beyond first base or third base, even though it afterwards rolls into foul territory.

Bunt Hit—A legally batted ball, not swung at, but met with the bat and tapped slowly within the infield by the batsman. If the attempt to bunt result in a foul not legally caught, a strike shall be called by the umpire.

Strikes—(1) A pitched ball struck at by the batsman without its touching his bat. (2) A fair ball legally delivered by the pitcher at which the batsman does not strike. (3) A foul hit ball not caught on the fly unless the batsman has two strikes. (4) An attempt to bunt which results in a foul not legally caught. (5) A pitched ball, at which the batsman strikes but misses, and which touches any part of his person. (6) A foul tip, held by the catcher, while standing within the lines of his position. When the batsman strikes at a pitched ball and misses it, a strike is called. When the batsman fails to strike at a pitched ball which passes over the plate at the

legal height, between knees and shoulder, a strike
is called. A foul tip caught by the catcher is a strike.
If after two strikes a foul tip is batted and muffed
by the catcher, it is not a strike. A foul hit, whether
a fly or a ground hit, bounding to any part of foul
ground, is a strike unless the batter has two strikes.
After two strikes the batter may foul the ball without penalty unless he bunts or is caught out on a foul
fly or on a foul tip. All bunts rolling foul are strikes.
If the batsman strikes at the ball and misses it but
the ball hits him, it is a strike. If the batsman, with
either of his feet out of the batsman's box, hits the
ball in any way it is an illegally batted ball, in former days called a foul strike, and the batsman is
out.

Put-Out—Any successful play on the part of the
nine out in the field which retires an opposing player,
such as a caught ball, or a runner touched off of base,
or prevented from reaching base safely.

Forced Play—A force-out can be made only when
a base-runner legally loses the right to the base he
occupies by reason of the batsman becoming a base-
runner, and he is thereby obliged to advance.

Play—An order of the umpire to begin the game
or to resume it after its suspension.

Time—An order of the umpire to suspend play.
Such suspension must not extend beyond the day.

Game—An announcement of the umpire that the
game is terminated.

Baseball

Inning—The term at bat of the nine players representing a club in a game and is completed when three of such players have been legally put out.

Time at Bat—The term at bat of a single batsman. It begins when he takes his position, and continues until he is put out or becomes a base-runner.

Home Run—A complete circuit of bases on a single batted ball.

Base Hit—A fairly batted ball which cannot be returned to first base in time to stop the runner. Also called a "safe hit."

Sacrifice Hit—A hit by a batsman which is calculated to put himself out, but which results in advancing a runner on the bases.

Error—A misplay either in judgment or in actual handling of the ball, which results to the advantage of the opposing side.

Stolen Base—A base secured by a runner, after reaching first, which is obtained while other plays are proceeding, or despite the attempt of the opposing side.

BASKETBALL

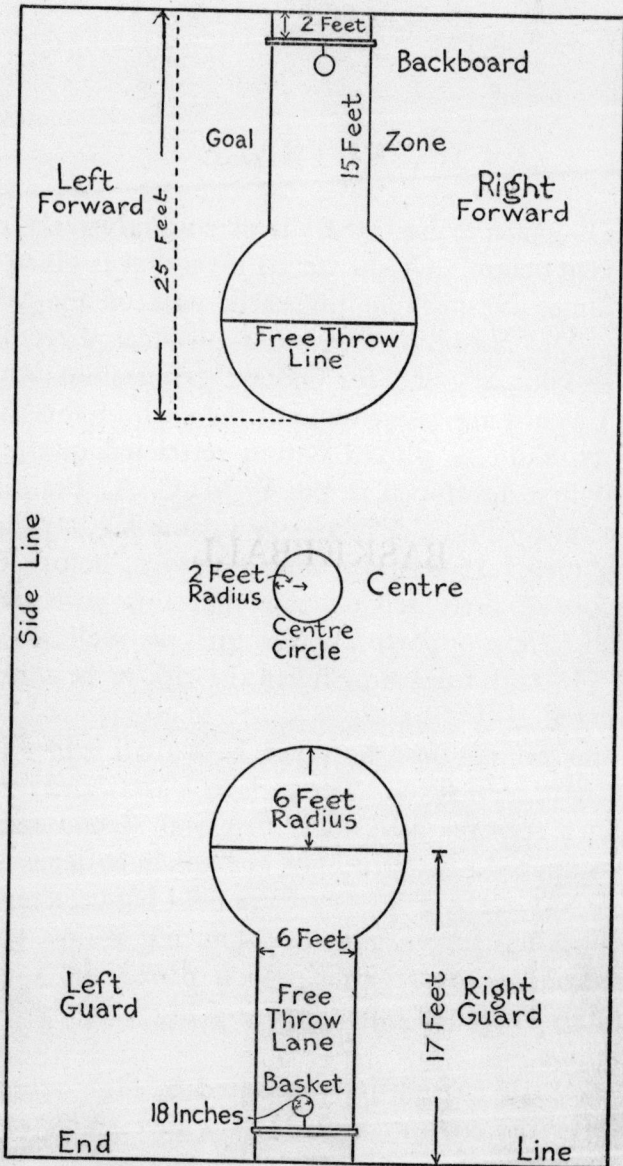

2 Feet

Backboard

Goal

15 Feet

Zone

Left
Forward

25 Feet

Right
Forward

Free Throw
Line

Side Line

2 Feet
Radius

Centre

Centre
Circle

6 Feet
Radius

6 Feet

Left
Guard

Free
Throw
Lane

17 Feet

Right
Guard

Basket

18 Inches

End

Line

BASKETBALL

THE game of basketball is of comparatively recent origin. Credit for its invention is given to Dr. James Nasmith in the early part of the year 1892. Dr. Nasmith, like other physical directors, was seeking a game for indoor gymnasium work which would also offer some of the dash of football, and yet could be played within restricted quarters. It was first developed in the Y. M. C. A. Training School at Springfield, Mass., as a game for boys and young men. It was not long, however, before the directors of girls' schools saw that this new game offered a fine opportunity for girls as well as for boys. In fact, for a time it ran the risk of becoming feminized.

At the present time, however, basketball is in equal favor with both sexes. The girls at Vassar and other women's colleges have their first and second teams just as they do in Princeton and other colleges for men. Naturally, contests are not held between teams of opposing sexes, but the women's teams have brought their own game, which differs in a few essentials from the other, up to a high standard of perfection.

Basketball is peculiarly adapted to high schools. All over the country such high school teams exist, and the record of their contests finds much space in the local newspapers. Even the metropolitan dailies have given large space to achievements such as the sensational record of the Passaic (N. J.) High School team which in the early part of 1923 had won over one hundred straight victories over all opponents. The men's colleges hold their intercollegiate contests in this sport just as they do in football and baseball. There is an Eastern Intercollegiate League consisting of leading colleges along the Atlantic seaboard; also a Western Conference, one for the Missouri Valley, another for Ohio, and another for the Pacific Coast. In addition to these there are Amateur Athletic Union Championships which include picked teams from the Y. M. C. A. and Athletic Clubs generally.

The following description of the game is condensed from the National Basketball Rules for 1927-28. The complete and unabridged rules are issued by the Joint Rules Committee representing the Amateurs' Athletic Union, the National Collegiate Association, and the Young Men's Christian Association.

The game of basketball is played by two teams of five each, the ball being passed from one player to another, by hand. The ball is never kicked. The purpose of each team is to score as many points as possible by tossing the ball into its own basket, and at the same time prevent the other team from securing possession of the ball or scoring.

Basketball

The playing court is a rectangular surface free from obstructions, 90 feet in length by 50 feet in width. Where space does not permit this size court a minimum dimension of 60 feet by 35 feet is allowable.

The court is marked by well-divided lines not less than 2 inches in width, which at every point are at least 3 feet from any fixed obstruction. These are known as side lines. The court has a center circle with a radius of 2 feet and is marked as the name indicates in the center of the court. At either end of the court there is a "free throw lane." From points 3 feet on either side of the center of the end line two lines are drawn perpendicular to the end line and 15 feet long. These are capped by the arc of a circle whose radius is 6 feet. Parallel to the end line, to form a diameter of this circle, is drawn the "free throw line"—not over an inch wide. When a foul is committed by one team, a member of the opposing team makes the free throw from within this semi-circle.

Backboards must be provided, the dimensions of which are 6 feet horizontally and 4 feet vertically. These backboards are painted white and made of plate glass or wood, or a cement or stone with smooth plastered surface, or any other material that is permanently flat and rigid.

The backboards are located in a position at each end at right angles to the floor and parallel to the end lines. Their centers lie in the perpendiculars erected at the points in the court 2 feet from the midpoints of the end lines. The face of the backboard shall be 15 feet from the far edge of the free throw lines.

The backboards are protected from the spectators to a distance of at least 3 feet behind and at each end.

The baskets are nets of cord or other material, suspended from metal rings 18 inches in inside diameter. The nets are so constructed or tied as to check the ball momentarily as it passes through the basket.

The rings are rigidly attached to the backboards at a point 1 foot from the bottom and 3 feet from either side, supported by a horizontal arm which if extended would pass through the center of the rings. The rings are placed in such a position that they lie in a horizontal plane 10 feet above the floor and so that the nearest point of the inside edge is 6 inches from the playing surface of the backboard.

The ball used in the game is made of rubber bladder enclosed in a leather outside case. The ball when inflated should be not less than 30 inches nor more than 32 inches in circumference and should weigh not more than 23 ounces. The object of the game is for a team to obtain control of the ball and finally toss it by hand up into the basket previously described. Each of the two teams playing strives to carry out this maneuver and at the

© *E. Galloway*

BASKETBALL

A close try for a goal. Basketball has the advantage of being adapted to either indoors or outdoors.

same time prevent the opposing team from scoring upon them.

The team as it appears upon the floor consists of five players; therefore, with two teams engaged there are not more than ten players upon the floor at a given time. If a player gets injured or incapacitated in any other way, a substitute may be provided.

The officials of the game consist of a referee, umpire, two time-keepers and two scorers. Their duties areas follows:

The referee shall put the ball in play; shall decide when the ball is in play, when the ball is dead, to whom it belongs and when a goal has been made. He shall call violations and fouls, shall administer all penalties, shall recognize substitutes, and shall order "time out" when necessary. He shall announce each goal as made, indicating with his fingers the point value of the goal. He shall also publicly announce the score at the end of each half. This final announcement terminates his official connection with the game.

The referee shall forbid a player to continue in the game, who has made four personal fouls, or who has committed a disqualifying foul.

The referee shall have power to call fouls for unsportsmanlike conduct on the part of players or spectators, or to make decisions on any points not specifically covered in the rules.

Neither the referee nor the umpire shall have

authority to set aside or question decisions made by the other within the limits of their respective duties as outlined in the rules.

If the referee and the umpire make approximately simultaneous decisions on the same play, and the decisions involve different penalties against the same team, the one drawing attention to the graver of the two shall take precedence.

The referee and the umpire shall have power to make decisions for violations of rules committed either within or outside the boundary lines; also at any moment from the beginning of play to the call of time at the end of the game. This includes the periods when the game may be momentarily stopped for any reason. Fouls may be called on any number of players at the same time. The official calling the foul shall designate the offender. A personal foul shall be indicated by the official raising his own hand over his own head.

The referee shall call "time out" in case of injury to players. The umpire may stop the game by blowing his whistle in case of injury to a player which the referee does not see, but "time out" is taken only upon order of the referee.

The referee shall inspect and approve all equipment, including court, baskets, ball, backboards, timekeepers' and scorers' signals.

The umpire shall call violations and fouls committed by any player, but he shall pay particular attention to the players in the back field away from the ball. The referee shall request the umpire to assist in out-of-bounds decisions and to co-operate in enforcing the rule against coaching.

The scorers shall record the goals made and the fouls committed; shall distinguish in their records between personal and technical fouls; and shall notify the referee immediately when the fourth personal foul has been called on any player. Their records shall constitute the official score of the game. They shall compare their scores after each goal and any discrepancy shall be at once referred to the referee. If they fail to notify the referee at once, the latter shall decide in favor of the smaller score, unless he has knowledge that permits him to decide without reference to the scorers. The scorers shall be provided with a horn with which to signal the referee when a substitution is made.

The timekeepers shall note when the game starts; shall deduct time consumed by stoppages during the game on order of the referee; and shall indicate with a gong, pistol, or whistle the expiration of the actual playing time in each half or quarter. Upon the sounding of the timekeepers' signal play shall cease instantly, except that if the ball is in the air on a try-for-goal when the timekeepers' signal is sounded, play shall continue until the ball has entered or missed the basket. The timekeepers' signal terminates actual playing time in each half.

Sports and Games

The officials shall blow a whistle whenever necessary to make a decision.

PLAYING REGULATIONS

The game is started by the referee, who tosses the ball up between two players of opposite teams. The game consists of two halves of 20 minutes each, with an intermission of 10 minutes between the halves. This is the time of actual play. These times may be changed by mutual agreement of the captains. When a foul is committed simultaneously with, or just previous to the sounding of the timekeepers' signal, time shall be allowed for the free throw.

Captains are notified three minutes before the termination of the intermission between the halves. If either team is not on the floor ready for play within one minute after the referee calls play, either at the beginning of the second half or after time has been taken out for any reason, the ball shall be put in play in the same manner as if both teams were on the floor ready to play.

The visiting team shall have choice of baskets in the first half. For the second half the teams shall change baskets.

The ball may be thrown, batted, bounced, rolled, or dribbled in any direction.

The ball is put in play in the center circle:

1. At the beginning of each half, or quarter, and of each extra period.

Basketball

2. After a goal has been made.

3. After an illegal free throw has been made.

4. After the ball has lodged in the supports of the basket.

5. After the last free throw following a double foul. In the following manner:

Each center player stands with both feet within his half of the center circle, with one hand in contact with the middle of the small of his back. This position must be maintained until the ball has been tapped by one or both players. The other players may take any position upon the court they may desire, provided they do not interfere in any way with the referee or the center players. The referee shall toss the ball upward in a plane at right angles to the side lines between the center players, to a height greater than either of them can jump, and so that it will drop between them.

When the referee puts the ball in play in the center, he shall blow his whistle when the ball reaches its highest point, after which it must be tapped by either one or both of the center players. If the ball touches the floor without being tapped by one of the jumpers, the referee shall put it in play again in the same place.

When the referee tosses the ball up between two players elsewhere than in the center, the players shall assume the same position in relation to each other as when jumping in the center.

35

Sports and Games

A game is decided by the scoring of the greater number of points in the playing time.

A goal made from the field counts 2 points; a goal from a free throw counts 1 point.

If the score is a tie at the expiration of the second half, play is continued without delay or change of baskets for an extra period of 5 minutes, or as many such periods of 5 minutes as may be necessary to break the tie. Each extra period is considered a continuation of the second half, but at the beginning of each extra period the ball is put in play at the center.

Any team refusing to play after receiving instructions to do so from the referee forfeits the game. The score of a forfeited game is 2-0.

VALUE OF TEAMWORK

Basketball, like baseball and football, is an excellent example of the benefits of teamwork. Its success is absolutely dependent upon the co-ordination of the team-mates. They must learn at the outset to play together—to subordinate desires for individual glory to the best interests of the whole team. To illustrate: a player (A) has the ball and can throw for goal, or can pass the ball to a player (B) nearer to the goal and having a better opportunity to cage the ball. Individual interest will lead (A) to throw for the goal. He may take it, and thus win for himself credit for a brilliant play. This is one of the

36

faults of beginners and always of selfish players. If (A) looks mainly to the interests of the team, he must forego his own chance for prominence and must play the ball to (B), who may secure the popular applause, much of which in this case really belongs to (A). In case (A) throws directly for the goal and makes it, he is not thereby justified in the play; on the contrary, he should be censured by the coach or captain. In the long run such a player, who puts his own interests above that of the team, will prove a detriment to the team.

The single instance given is but a simple illustration of what characterizes basketball. A team of moderate players, but who play well together, who play a strong team game, will defeat a team of experts who play each one for himself. This has been repeatedly demonstrated.

BOATING

ROWING
      CANOEING
            SAIL BOATS
                  MOTOR BOATS

ROWING

ROWING is the oldest of the organized college sports, and has also been taken up by other athletic organizations. Almost a century ago, the two English universities of Oxford and Cambridge began to hold annual rowing contests. Since 1841 they have held 76 such contests, up to 1927, over a four-and-one-fourth mile course, and it is interesting to note that Oxford has won 40 and Cambridge 35, and one race is recorded as a dead heat. That must have been a gruelling contest!

In America, the earliest college boat club was formed at Yale, in 1843; and in the following year another was organized at Harvard. In 1852 the two college crews met for the first time, the race being for two miles on Lake Winnepesaukee. Harvard won. Three years later the course was changed to the Connecticut River at Springfield, and lengthened to three miles. Since 1878, the course has been over the Thames River, at New London.

In 1896, an Intercollegiate Rowing Regatta was instituted upon the Hudson River at Poughkeepsie, and has since become an annual feature. The distance has varied between two and four miles. Of recent years, both distances have been rowed. The colleges competing have included Cornell, Washington, Columbia, Pennsylvania, Syracuse, Wisconsin, Georgetown, and the Navy.

During the early years of this sport Princeton did not compete, as it had no watercourse. The generosity of Andrew Carnegie in providing an artificial lake near the campus enabled this university to organize a competing crew. Dual and triangular regattas have been held with other crews, chiefly Eastern; although Wisconsin and California have been represented in some meets.

Colleges have met outside crews as well in the exceptionally interesting American Henley Regattas, held annually at Philadelphia, usually in the latter part of May. Here we find Princeton, Pennsylvania, Yale, Navy, and perhaps three or four other colleges represented, alongside of crews from other clubs.

Indeed, colleges by no means have a monopoly on this very healthful sport. Each year the "World Almanac" prints a long list of amateur rowing contests, such as the "Golden Jubilee and National Championship Regatta of the National Association of Amateur Oarsmen of America" (certainly a mouthful!), the American Henley already spoken of, the People's Regatta, and the Gold Challenge Cup Race. Races include single gigs, single shells, double shells, quadruple shells, four-oared gigs, four-oared shells, and eight-oared shells.

Rowing, like other sports, was interrupted by the

Rowing

World War, but great interest was shown in its re-
vival. In 1920, a veteran crew from the U. S. Naval
Academy, at Annapolis, defeated a picked crew from
England, at Brussels, for the Olympic championship.

ROWING REQUIREMENTS

Rowing is a sport which requires a great deal of
steadiness of purpose, because, unlike other sports,
daily practice does not consist in contests, but in
practice without the stimulus of rivalry save that of
securing a place in the boat. It is true that of late
years, college crews have been trained to contest
more freely than in the old days, and occasional
brushes between first and second crews, or with class
crews, enliven the somewhat dull routine of preparation. But, for all that, there are weeks and months
of training and long days of hard work when no
enthusiastic crowd assembles to watch and inspire
them by their presence. For this reason probably,
more than any other, coaching has been longer recognized in rowing than in the other sports. It is necessary that all the men in the crew row together, and
some of the best practice consists in early rows of
many miles, in which the mere fact of sitting behind
another man and watching him tends to make all
the men more uniform in action. Many a man becomes discouraged in rowing, but those who per-
severe eventually reap reward for all their work.

Sports and Games

A certain adaptability is regarded as essential, and as in any other contest requiring skill, it is probably true that some men have the knack of imitating others and following instructions more than others, and these are men who are considered adaptable as oarsmen. As far as the build of a man goes, it is not essential that he be a giant, either in stature or strength. Other things being equal, it is probably desirable to have an eight-oared crew with four powerful men in the waist of the boat, but winning crews have had men who would hardly answer that description. It is also desirable that the men sit as nearly uniform as possible, that is, from the hips to the shoulders; the height is something the same. This makes it more simple to have every stroke of the same length. Endurance is an essential, and that, too, whether in a mile race or a four mile race, for the effort is adapted to the distance, and a crew is expected to row themselves out by the time they pass the line unless they have a marked lead.

For the organization of a boat club some proper piece of water is essential. It may be a river, it may be tide-water, and it may be a still-water lake. Of all these, probably a still-water lake is the most satisfactory, because it is possible there to get exact measurement of the work of various crews, and to tell by actual times over a measured distance the advantage of certain measurements in men, rigging or stroke, and this naturally gives the coach or captain a more definite idea of the value of any change. But for all that, any course where a mile or even three-quarters of a mile of good water can be obtained is good enough to support a crew.

Of boats there are an infinite variety, from a single scull up to the eight-oared shell. The boats most commonly used are single-sculls, pair-oars, six-oared shells and barges, and eight-oared shells and barges. A shell, it should be understood, is a more delicate, cranky piece of work than a barge, and men or boys rowing for the first time should begin in broad boats of almost any kind, and gradually work their way up until they can row in a barge, and from that they can graduate to a shell. One of the essentials in any boat club is to take care of the equipment. These fragile boats which are used for racing can not be bumped up against a wharf or grounded in the middle of a bar, while the men are sitting in the boat, without damage that can hardly be repaired. Old boats should be used for early practice, and every boat when not in use should be shelved, that is, hung upon a number of brackets, bottom up, four to six of these brackets being necessary for the ordinary eight-oared shell, as they must be near enough together to prevent sagging. The boat should be kept well varnished, with bolts, out-riggers, screws, locks, and stretchers all kept in good order. The boat should be wiped when taken from the water, both inside and out. Before the race it is customary to rub down the boat with pumice stone and grease it with oil or some similar substance. The customary eight-oared racing shell weighs in the neighborhood of 230 to 270 pounds. The cedar boat weighs something more than the paper boat, and while a paper boat is stiffer at the outset, it is claimed that the cedar boat holds its stiffness longer. The length is about sixty feet, and the depth some nine inches, and the breadth from twenty-two to twenty-five in the middle, and varying down to a foot and a half at the ends of the cock-pit. The oars weigh about seven or seven and one-half pounds apiece, and are about twelve feet long.

In launching a boat the crew take it from the rack, carrying it usually keel up to the edge of the float, four men being on each side of the boat, and when the edge of the float is reached, one set of four men hold the boat, or rather they lift it above their heads while the men on the side next the water come under. Then all eight lift the boat out on to the water.

ROWING TERMS

There are certain rowing terms which should be understood, as they are used in coaching and in descriptions generally.

"Ready All" means the eight oars are put back to the full reach, the knees of the men being bent, the slides all aft, and the arms extended.

ROWING

Coaching two college crews on a practice spin.

Rowing

"Give Way" is the order for the men to swing up from the ready position after the beginning of the stroke.

"Way Enough" means stop rowing, and this order should be given when the oars are in the water, and not when they are on the recovery, except in the case of critical moments.

"Hold 'er all" is an order instructing a man to keep the oar buried at right angles to the side of the boat, the plane of the blade parallel to the surface.

"Back water" is the reverse of rowing.

"Catch" is when the oars take the water on the stroke and the shoulders swing up.

"The Finish" is when the oars leave the water at the completion of the stroke.

"Recovery" is the set of movements made by an oarsman from the time of the finish until he reaches the position of catch again.

"Bevel of the Oar" is the angle it makes with the water when being dipped.

"Time" indicates the unison of the crew.

"Bucking" or "Meeting" the oar is letting the body come toward the oar at the finish when the arms are pulled in.

"To slump" is to settle down with the upper part of the body at the finish of the stroke.

"Rushing the slide" is to moderate the sliding seat instead of keeping it under control with the feet on the stretcher.

Sports and Games

"To swing out" is to fail to keep the body in line over the keel.

To "Get in late" or to "Get out late" is to make the stroke after the rest of the crew.

"Short on catch" means not reaching far enough toward the bow with the oar at the full reach.

To "miss water" is to row the first part of the stroke in the air.

HOW TO MAN AND ROW A BOAT

Rigging is a most delicate matter, and only those who follow the sport very closely or who are professional boatmen understand about it. It consists in getting a man so fitted as regards his seat, out-rigger, stretcher, oar and slide, as to do his work at the maximum of efficiency, and at the same time keep with the rest of the crew.

The stroke means the entire movement of the oarsmen in sending the shell through the water by a certain repetition of acts, consisting of repeated pulling of the oars in the water. There are two parts to the stroke—the stroke proper, that is from the catch to the finish, and the recovery, from the time the oar comes out of the water on the finish until it again enters it on the catch. The stroke itself consists of three parts, the catch, the pull through, and the finish. The recovery consists of the feather, the carrying of the blade back over the water, and the turning of it up for the catch. While he is making the stroke the

48

oarsman swings up with his shoulders, pushes out his legs until his knees are nearly straight and finally brings the oar to the body with his arms. During the recover these movements are reversed. He first gets his hands out, then bends his knees, his shoulders come forward, and he is ready for the next stroke.

Over the method of performing these acts, there has been more discussion than would fill twenty books the size of this one. There have been advocates of the fast stroke, of the slow stroke, of the long stroke, and the short stroke. There are schools of rowing, and have been ever since college racing was taken up. No one has yet satisfactorily settled all the points connected with rowing, and even one of the simplest —the question of the wide or narrow blade—is a point upon which oarsmen still differ radically. But there is one point upon which all are agreed, and that is harmony. That the men in a crew must row as nearly alike as possible in order to get speed out of the boat, and still more, that every man must do a certain part of the work at least in perfect time with his companions. Upon these two points it is impossible to go astray. After that one may follow all sorts of schools and never row well, when a crew, entirely lacking in knowledge, but having rowed together for a long time, may turn out fast.

An oarsman about to row, having taken his oar in hand, proceeds to embark.* This he should do by

* From the "Athletic Guide," Spalding's Athletic Library.

laying the blade of his oar in the water, if on the outside, or on the float if on the shore-side oar, and then stepping into the boat with his face to the stern, putting one foot on the keelson, lengthwise—not athwart it, for fear of forcing his toe or heel through the boat—and, stooping, should let himself down gently on the seat by placing a hand on each gunwale. He should next ship his oar, placing the handle in the rowlock outside. He should sit square and exactly opposite the handle of his oar, not askew. The body should be erect, with the shoulders slightly thrown back and the elbows close to the flanks.

The oar should be held firmly yet lightly in both hands, the outside one close to the end of the handle —but not at the end, capping it—with the fingers above and the thumb underneath it, although some men prefer the thumb of the outside hand in the same position as the fingers—and the inside hand, or that next the loom or body of the oar, from one and one-half to two inches, though not more than two and one-half inches away from, but grasping the oar more convexly than its fellows, the thumb underneath; bearing in mind always that the mechanical power of the outside hand is the greater in the bare pulling, and the inside hand mainly guides and manipulates the oar. If the inside hand is held too low, a good deal of force is lost, the arm is bent, the shoulders are not squared and the beginning of the stroke is weakened. The forearms should be below the level of the handle, and the wrists dropped and relaxed, the oar being now quiescent, at right angles to the keel of the boat, and feathered. The divers positions of the two hands and wrists enable the oar to be wielded with greater facility than if alike, and permit of both arms being stretched out perfectly straight, not crooked or bent—when getting forward.

In rowing the stroke, the body should be inclined forward, with the backbone perfectly straight, the stomach being kept well out and down between the legs, the chest forward and raised as much as possible; in fact, the position of the trunk will be like that of a soldier at drill, except that in rowing, the great secret is to keep the stomach out, whereas in drilling it must be kept in.

The shoulders should not be allowed to come too far forward; neither should one be advanced before the other, nor should one be higher than its fellow. The arms should play freely in the shoulder joint, as stiffness here and at the hips is a real hindrance to the best form. They should be perfectly straight from the shoulders to the wrists, and they should be treated in the first part of the stroke as mere connecting-rods between the body and the oar. If they are crooked, immediately the weight and strength are thrown on the handle of the oar, and thus the first part of the stroke is lost. The inside wrist, however, must be somewhat raised and the outside one bent slightly round, in order that the knuckles may be parallel to the oar, as the oar must be firmly grasped with both hands, otherwise the beginning of the stroke will be weak. But it must be kept nearly flat, though pressed down the least bit in the world; in other words, it must show only the natural hollow.

The hands should hold the oar firmly, not with the tips as usual, but with the whole of the fingers well round the oar, and each separate finger—not merely the first two—must feel the oar distinctly. The knuckles of the thumb must not be more than one and one-half or two inches apart at most, for if kept too far off one another, the inside arm is sure to get bent and the inside shoulder thrown back. The head must be held up, the eyes looking in a direct line astern, and the feet must be firmly planted against the stretcher. In reaching forward, the hands should be shot out straight from the body without the least pause, a peculiar way of doing this, but impossible to describe, though easily discernible, being the mark of first-class oarsmen.

Almost as soon as the oar has passed the knees, the wrists should be raised to bring the blade at right angles to the water preparatory to dipping it, the fact of delaying this motion often resulting in not putting the oar in square. The body of the oarsman and the sliding seat are then drawn forward concurrently by the aid of the stretcher boots in readiness for taking the stroke. Care must, however, be taken not to lower the hands too much, as this practice leads to chopping and cutting the stroke.

Men differ slightly in their length of reach, but every one ought to be able to get the handle of his oar over his stretcher, and when there, he should raise his hands straight up at once, as, if not raised at once, the result is a hang, and if not straight the stroke is cut. The oar should then be instantaneously covered up to the shoulder, but no further, and immediately it is in this position the stroke should commence. The rower should "knit himself up," as the Irish call it, he should then spring like a bow when the string is loosed, and bring the muscles of his back and legs into play, as far as possible raising his weight off his seat, thus using his whole strength and weight at once and together. The motions at the end of the feather and at the beginning of the stroke are, however, so simultaneous and take place so rapidly that it is very difficult to analyze them.

It is in this part of the stroke that five minutes' looking at a good oarsman rowing is worth more than any number of words: in fact, no words really convey what is wanted. A coach may tell his pupil to "hit" the water, to "smite" it, etc., which may convey to the mind of a man who knows how to row what is required, but which can never impart the idea to a tyro. Catching the beginning properly, like swinging, must come from inspiration. It will, however, assist a crew immensely if the coach will get the boat and row a few short spins at a slow stroke, employing all his power at the beginning and making the crew follow his example, but he must be a strong man, as he will have the whole weight to lift at the commencement of the stroke.

Having thus learned to catch the beginning of the stroke with his body only, the rower should finish it with his arms and shoulders, taking care to send his elbows close past his side, and to drop his shoulders well down and back, keeping his head up and his chest out. In the next place, the whole strength of his arms and shoulders should be put into the finish of the stroke. This may seem to be recommending the fault of rowing the stroke out to the end, but it is really not so. This fault arises either from the beginning of the stroke having been shirked, from not using the full force of the body, or from not bending the arms soon enough. If this happens, the body has to be kept waiting until the arms come up to it, and hence an unseemly jerk. It is very difficult to determine the exact period at which the arms are to be brought into play, but it ought to be done about the time that the body is perpendicular. Thus the full weight and strength of the rower would be applied, and the oar will be dashed through the water in the way that marks a good oarsman.

The oar should be brought straight home to the chest, the root of the thumbs touching the body about an inch or less below the button of the breast bone where the ribs branch off. Thus every inch of water is made use of. When there, the hands should be dropped straight down and then be turned over and shot out again close to the legs, and the body should follow without the least pause. If this be not done the oar will be feathered under water, and the boat buried; water will be thrown on to the next oar and the recovery impeded. In effecting the recovery, the slide is an important agent; but before the forward sliding movement takes place, the body should be swung evenly forward from the hips, not with a jerk or plunge, or quicker at one time than another, but freely and easily, as if the hip joint worked well and not stiffly. Much benefit may be derived from watching two or three of the best oarsmen that can be found, observing them carefully, forming an ideal model, and then endeavoring to copy it.

Two or three points should particularly be borne in mind: First, that when the hands are raised at the commencement of the stroke, and the oar, ipso facto, struck down below the surface, the whole of the power should be brought to bear at the moment of the oar's contact with the water, so as to create the greatest effect in the first or vital part of the stroke, one of the most important and too frequently broken laws of rowing; secondly, that the pull home to the chest should be in a perfectly straight line, thus causing a horizontal stroke through the water, which is another law frequently disregarded; thirdly, that the finish of the stroke should be as quiet and easy as it is possible to make it, but without lessening the force applied, which naturally diminishes, because at the first part of the stroke before the rowlock, the oar is at an acute angle to the boat, and after that at an obtuse angle. Here it is that one so often sees the stroke wind up with a jerk, as if to make some use of the little strength remaining in the human frame, the oar flirted out of the water, the elbows dug sharply back in an awkward and ungainly manner, and the body harshly and suddenly jolted forward.

Next in importance are the movements described by the oar itself, starting from a state of rest, i.e., feathered and at right angles to the keel of the boat.

When the forward reach is taken, the blade of the oar should travel backward in the air, horizontally, at the distance of a few inches from the surface of the water—of course, depending upon the state of the surface, whether smooth or rough—until dipped for the stroke. As regards this dip, it is imperative that the blade descend to the proper depth before any force is applied, otherwise the stroke will be cut. To effect this the hands must be raised sharply, and the stroke must be instantaneously commenced. When on the feather, the oar passing the knees should be gradually turned before immersion, the feather concluding and the stroke beginning at once, with no interval whatever. Hence it will be perceived that the line described by the end of the blade, about which there are numerous theories and a variety of opinions, will be nearly parallel with the water until entering it, when it will immediately be dipped with a powerful scoop.

Then the entry of the oar into the water can not be too sudden or too decided, so that it be not a chop and a splash; and for this purpose the muscles of the arms should be gathering themselves together as the hands reach forward. It is a well-known and indisputable law that the greatest power can be applied in the first half of the stroke; that is to say, before the oar comes level with or abreast of the rowlock, and that the further aft it goes subsequently to passing that point, the more the power decreases. Such being the case, it is only an act of common-sense to endeavor to do as much work as possible when it will tell the most, and when it contributes to lift a boat lightly along the top of the water. On the other hand, if the application of the strength is deferred until the last part of the stroke, it is brought to bear when it is of least service; a great and useless expenditure of power ensues, and the boat, instead of being assisted over the water, is driven down and buried in it, her way being therefore checked. The same result ensues from men letting their weight rest on the seat, instead of letting the weight rest on the stretcher and handle of the oar—in a word, from rowing with the arms unassisted by the body, instead of using both.

We now come to the position in which the blade is immersed, and I would observe that this is a most important point. It is said that the blade should descend at right angles to the water. In this opinion I can not altogether coincide, although even such a position is far superior to an entry with the back of the blade forming an acute angle with the water, and the front of the blade an obtuse one. In either of these cases, however, there is something wrong with the thowl rowed against, with the side of the loom which bears against the thowl, or with that on which the oar rests when traversing the water. The proper position is for the front or hollow of the blade to be looking slightly downward upon (not along) the surface; its entry is consequently less than a right angle. This enables the oar to take full and square hold of the water at once; it prevents its running down too deep, and, if firmly and scientifically manipulated, it obviates splashing. At the same time the oar ought not to be turned over too much, as otherwise it will not enter the water easily and will be apt to twist in the hand, besides straining the wrist; but no effort should be made whatsoever to force it over.

The depth to which the oar descends through the medium of this peculiar catch, is to the shoulder or upper end of the blade. In this position it must continue until the hands are up to the chest—not stopping at a distance of a foot from it—when the stroke is concluded, and the feather commences. In the traverse through the water the blade of the oar should be barely covered, and no more—this is an accepted rule—and with the unusually light boats used at the present day strict attention to this principle must be paid. When bringing the stroke to an end, the blade of the oar by a sudden movement—caused by dropping the hands and turning the wrists—is feathered or brought into plane with the surface of the water, from being at right angles to it.

This action should take place at the moment when the oar leaves the water, and the lower end of the blade, by being turned suddenly cleanly aft as the loom rotates in the rowlock, throws the water astern in a little eddying whirlpool, and the whole business of the stroke is completed. The appearance of this whirlpool should be carefully studied, as it is a pretty good criterion of how a man is rowing, and if a coach happens to be pulling himself, as is occasionally the case, it is one of the only guides he has in judging how his pupils are rowing behind him. It is almost impossible to describe the look it ought to wear, but plenty of small air-bubbles should keep rising, as in a soda-water bottle, long after the swirl has left the oar; the smaller eddies should be deep and well marked. Very light rowing makes a splash that soon subsides and deep rowing shows no air-bubbles.

The foregoing component parts of a stroke, and its succeeding feather, it must be admitted, are numerous, and to a certain extent apparently incompatible, but yet they are so blended in the work done by an expert oarsman as to seem but one action. Each, however, may be fully and correctly performed, and the sum of these separated actions is consequently also perfect.

In conclusion, I will briefly recapitulate the main points in good rowing. They are as follows: First, a full, fair reach-out over the toes, with both arms perfectly straight; secondly, a square hold of the water at the dip of the oar, with an application of the whole power at the moment of immersion; thirdly, a firm stroke of medium depth, pulled straight through the water, without wavering and without vibration, yet always kept long and duly light; fourthly, a graceful, easy finish, with a clear turn of the water off the after-ledge of the blade— the feather being light, moderately low and rapid— and an instantaneous movement when the oar completes the feather, and descends under the water. Then comes the most delicate and important of all —the recovery—the stealthily creeping forward on the slides so as not to check the forward progress of the boat, and the final assuming once more of the position from which to start the next stroke.

CANOEING

THE most popular of all light water craft is undoubtedly the canoe. Its light weight and easy
management, no less than its trickiness, make a very
definite appeal to young folks of both sexes and to
campers and outdoor enthusiasts generally.

The canoe has its enemies as well as its devotees.
Your anti-canoeist will tell you that the canoe is
unreliable, unmanageable in choppy water, tricky
even in smooth water, headstrong and otherwise
troublesome. These indictments may all be true, yet
their presence lends charm to canoeing for venturesome youngsters. Expertly handled most of such
objections disappear. At the same time, there are
many advantages which commend the canoe for a
variety of uses.

First, it is light and easily propelled over the water
and can be portaged around rapids, rocky points or
other non-navigable places.

Second, it is much more adaptable for light general use around a camp than is the row-boat. For
some reason most row-boats are made extremely
clumsy and unattractive. Your canoe is the embodi-
ment of grace alongside of this patient, unemotional
beast of burden.

Third, the canoe lends itself easily to water stunts of all sorts and especially to light sailing, of which more further on.

BUILDING A CANOE

Many boys and young men have been seized with the ambition to build their own canoes; many in fact have succeeded; but where one has succeeded, scores have failed. To build a canoe properly requires not only the best materials but a knowledge of carpentry and of navigation of no mean order. The Indians used to make their staunch canoes out of birch bark, and our large museums still contain examples of their work. Nowadays, however, it is really cheaper to buy one. The writer knows of two boys who undertook to build a canoe one summer and who spent nearly ten dollars apiece for material alone, to say nothing of their labor, when for a reasonable sum the two together could have purchased for joint use a much more seaworthy craft.

In building or buying a canoe, the first question which is raised is, shall it have a keel? This vexed question has been argued ever since we succeeded the Indians in building boats and it is as far from settlement as ever. Arguments in favor of the keel show that it lends staunchness and durability to a craft. When lifting a canoe over a log or other obstruction, especially if the craft is heavily loaded, your keelless canoe is liable to buckle or become warped under the strain. A keel prevents the bottom from becoming seraped when being hauled over stones, rocks or other obstructions. It provides a support for the mast if the latter is stepped down into the boat. Those who do not like keels say that to add one increases the draft of the boat by an inch or more and this increases the likelihood of the canoe sticking when going over a shallow bit of water. When portaging, the keel adds that much to the weight. Some argue also that the keel detracts from the grace and ease of the vessel.

Still others have adopted a compromise practice of running a thin strip of hardwood such as spruce or maple about half an inch thick and two inches wide from stem to stern down the center of the outside of the keel. This strip shields the canoe from a great many bumps, bruises and scrapes and adds considerable rigidity without increasing the weight or the draft appreciably.

SIZE AND WEIGHT

Says Warren H. Miller in "Canoeing, Sailing, and Motor-Boating": "In picking a canoe, the safest and fastest model has quite a flat bottom, with a sharp, round turn to the bilge. The tippy ones are those deep and round on the bottom with no bilge, having no more stability than a barrel. The flat bottom draws but little water, slides over the stream like a duck, and makes her a prime sailer because she is so staunch. The dimensions of my canoe, a faster canoe by hours than many another model which she has raced down stream, are: length, 16 feet; beam, 33 inches; depth amidships, 12 inches; depth bow and stern, 24 inches; width of camparatively flat bottom, 24 inches. The cheaper type canoe, one of which is owned by my boys, has the following dimensions: length, 15 feet 6 inches; beam, 31 inches; depth amidships 12½ inches; depth, bow and stern, 22 inches; width of comparatively flat bottom, 16 inches. This latter canoe is much more tottly than mine, hard to sail, and nowhere so staunchly built. Each canoe weighs about 60 pounds."

LEARNING TO PADDLE

The novice should approach his canoe carefully and by easy stages, much as one would approach a skittish colt. First, study your craft and learn its center of gravity and how to adapt yourself to changes of current and wind. Take your first lesson in shallow water and with a bathing suit on, so that if the craft shows a tendency to tip you will be quite ready for it and will really not care whether it tips or not. Learn by experiment how far over the canoe will luff before anything serious happens. Later, as your confidence grows, you will be able to adapt yourself automatically to its whims and caprices, much as a bicycle rider learns to swing with the swaying of his machine.

Canoeing

However, no matter how expert you get in the management of your canoe, do not treat it as a place to skylark in. A staunch and solid row-boat will permit a certain amount of liberty where a canoe may resent it. We have seen foolish young people out in a canoe changing positions, shifting paddles recklessly, and in other ways inviting trouble, and more than once the trouble has occurred. How many tragedies could be summed up under the one word, carelessness!

Learn to paddle in still water where there is little or no current, preferably a canal, pond or lake. Begin by sitting in the bow of your craft while a more experienced canoeist is sitting in the stern— both of you with paddles in hand. You will soon learn that the oarsman in the stern will be able to steer the craft and steady you through his point of vantage. Learn to take long even strokes and time your work with his.

The beginner or amateur oarsman is easily located by the onlooker on the shore. He usually reaches too far ahead for his stroke and digs down too deeply with his paddle. Don't waste your energy scooping up water. You only lose your reserve strength in fighting it. Put your shoulder, arm and wrist into a light easy stroke in which the paddle is not buried too deeply into the water, then propel your craft forward. Put your strength into the stroke just as your left wrist passes your left hip, in paddling on

65

that side, and while your right hand is thrusting the top of the paddle forward. In other words, at this moment it becomes the fulcrum of the lever. The moment the paddle reaches an awkward incline in the rear for you, lift it out cleanly without spattering or making unnecessary noises, lift forward cleanly and again insert it just ahead of you in the water at the point where you can control the whole motion easily. You will find after a lot of practice that there is a certain rhythm in this motion, which prevents it from tiring you if you are at all seasoned, and by occasionally changing from side to side you can paddle for a long time without undue fatigue. Remember always, don't fight the water but insert the paddle almost with a caressing motion. We have seen two expert paddlers pass by within twenty feet of the shore and so noiseless were they in their strokes that we did not know they were going by, until the eye itself beheld them. The Indians usually prided themselves upon their silence in the water, and their ability to surprise their enemies or the wild game which they were stalking.

After you have become thoroughly familiar with the stroke from the bow end of the canoe, it is time to try the stern stroke, and again for the first time or two it is well to have an experienced man in the bow to coach you. You will find that the canoe responds far more quickly through the stern stroke than through the bow stroke. If the paddler in the

Canoeing

bow is weaker than you, you can easily correct his
paddling and steer a straight course by accommodat-
ing your stroke to his own. Don't hurry him but
insist always on a modulated and quiet stroke. The
easiest way for you to correct his wrong course is
by a slight turn of your paddle at the end of your
stroke. This twist of the paddle is constantly used
by canoeists when paddling alone. They soon become so expert in this particular that they never
shift paddles from side to side for the sake of steering the craft but only when it becomes necessary to
ease up one set of muscles. We have watched canoeists paddle for an hour at a stretch steering their
canoe in all sorts of directions and without shifting
the paddle from the chosen side. The trick of this
is to bring your paddle back with an easy sweep and
then just at the end of this stroke twist it with your
hand and wrist over to the right or left as may be
desired. If a short turn is needed, the paddle is held
for a moment deeply embedded in the water until
the prow of the canoe swings in the direction desired.
The only objection to this sudden shifting is that it
is equivalent to backing water and retards the speed
of the canoe.

Where there is a slight current, the canoeist will
have to adapt his paddling to its vagaries. For example, in paddling down stream, the stroke is quite
different from the one that would be used in turning
or in driving the canoe upstream. If there is a slight

current crossing the bows it further complicates the steering when one is alone in the canoe. Experiment alone can determine what is the best stroke to use under such varied conditions. The principal thing to remember, however, is not to dig the paddle too deeply into the water, not to hasten the stroke unduly, and above all not to lose one's head. If the craft does not respond at once to one type of paddling and steering, try another.

Ofttimes a craft that is very cranky and unmanageable, when paddled one way, will respond instantly when paddled in another style—due to course riffles or breezes. Sometimes the fault is due to the way one is seated in the craft. Most canoes nowadays are built with two light seats, the one in the bow being placed just far enough back to allow the paddler leg room. The stern seat is placed so far back in some instances that there is danger of tipping it when the craft is otherwise empty. A seat that can be slid forward on such occasions is vastly preferable, as it gives the canoeist an opportunity to balance his canoe. Some canoeists in choppy waters, when alone in their boat and it proves unmanageable, kneel down in the bottom of the canoe about halfway between the stern and the center, thus keeping the craft well balanced and the load well down.

River paddling is in a class by itself—especially in rapid water which is full of kinks and which you have to know and adapt yourself to instantly. If

© Underwood & Underwood

CANOEING

Contestants in a race show how to fall out of a canoe and get back in again.

Canoeing

you are the bow man, never embarrass the stern man by striking at rocks or other obstructions with your paddle. You will do no good whatever, and may upset the canoe. The water always takes care of the bow, while the stern is your chief concern. Sing out "Rock ahead" to the stern man and be sure that he sees it, and then leave it to him. His stunt is to back paddle the stern away from the obstruction, and allow the current to swing the bow clear, as it is flowing faster than the canoe is going. The bow man's hard work is in going around bends. The river tends to swing the canoe into the main eddies, which you must keep clear of, cutting across in the still water. If you want hard work going down stream, allow your canoe to follow the deepest and fiercest channel. The bow man therefore must anticipate the current and get his bow headed out of the eddies and into the quiet part of the bends, while the stern man puts in his strength and shoves her ahead.

IF THE CANOE UPSETS

In many Scout camps lessons are given in righting an upset canoe in deep water. The boys of course in such lessons are in bathing attire and are expert swimmers. They are taught how to handle such a craft under all sorts of conditions. Four boys, for instance, will be in one canoe which at a given signal is turned over. It is the job of all of them to turn the boat back, and although it is full of water it will not sink entirely. Then the bulk of the water is cleared out of the craft by a process of rocking. In other words, the boat is rocked violently back and forth so that one-third to one-half of the surplus water is splashed overboard. Then one boy climbs up across the stern lying flat across the gunwales so as not to allow the canoe to tip further. The other boys meanwhile hang on but only by their finger tips and with their bodies so far down in the water that very little weight is exerted upon the craft itself. The first boy then scoops out all the water that he can with his hands throwing it out ahead of him as he works himself down the boat and crouching well down within it. Then at a given signal he assists first one and then another of his comrades to climb aboard.

It goes without saying that the worst possible way to try to climb in a canoe is by seizing the side nearest you. This only causes the canoe to turn over and over in your direction, and you are lucky if it does not swamp you. If you are alone in the canoe when it capsizes, get yourself clear of it, then as it comes to the surface if keel side up take hold of it by either stem or stern but never by the side. If at all near to the shore you can swim using mostly leg strokes and pushing your canoe to shallow water. If help is anywhere within reach, it is better to hang on quietly until such help arrives—that is, until you

Canoeing

become expert in handling your canoe. If away from the shore and by yourself, try to clear the water out of your boat first by quickly flipping the boat right side up and then by rocking or shoving the water out of it. The rocking process is accomplished by getting hold of the stern of the canoe and alternately raising and depressing each arm as each holds on to the canoe. This serves to rock out enough water to give you a few inches of freeboard so that the boat will then sustain your own weight if you are careful. Now climb aboard over the stern and scoop out water with your hands. To "shove" water out requires some skill and strength. Again you work from the stern, giving the boat quick jerks towards you, then away from you, and so back and forth, each time precipitating a quantity of the water out over the bow or stern. Keep this up until the boat is half empty, then climb carefully aboard over the stern and scoop out the rest with your hands.

In rough water it is not advisable to try to bale out a canoe after once overturned unless one is a strong swimmer and is perfectly sure of himself. If there are more than two persons in such a canoe, their best plan is to hold on to the canoe and trust to help from the outside. The best place to hold, as stated before, is at the two ends and it is surprising how much even a submerged canoe will sustain if the two persons will keep well down in the water and hold lightly with their hands and not struggle. If it is

71

possible to kick off the shoes and throw off the coat, one's chance of managing the canoe is so much the better.

When approaching rough water or in navigating rapids old canoeists often tie a stout piece of cord or small rope around the paddle and to some part of the canoe. This prevents the paddle from floating away and leaving the canoeist still more at the mercy of the wind and wave; for no one is more helpless even though the canoe is regained than a canoeist without a paddle.

In navigating rough water, both paddlers kneel in the body of the boat and manage it in this way, at the same time giving the craft stability. A medium load makes the canoe ride more steadily than if it is empty, but the center of gravity should be low.

When approaching riffles, shallows or eddies which indicate rough water or hidden obstruction, the man in the bow should keep on the alert every moment and should warn the man in the stern well in advance. Sometimes such obstructions require instant decision and a cool head in order to avert disaster. If you are in a swift current that is carrying you down toward rapids or rocks, do not try to fight it or use up your energy needlessly, and above all things don't try to send the boat over such rocks by use of the paddle, as it is liable to snap off in your hands and leave you powerless. Guide the canoe into the water of such a channel and try to clear such

Canoeing

obstruction as closely as possible rather than giving it a wide berth. By taking the latter means you are liable to strike some other obstruction on the other side; whereas the current will probably aid the paddler to round the dangerous point.

If a fallen tree lies directly across the current and the latter is not too swift, then the best plan to follow is to steer the craft so as to pull up alongside of this obstruction; but never attempt to paddle across such a log unless perfectly sure that there is enough water to allow for the draft of the boat. It is the easiest thing in the world to break a canoe in two or to bend its back seriously by trying to slide across with a man in each end of the vessel. Pull up alongside as gently as possible, then climb out on the log even though you subject yourself to a thorough drenching, and lift the canoe sidewise across the obstruction. If the canoe is heavily laden, the alternative is to lighten it of some of its contents before trying to raise it out of the water, as here again you will be liable to strain the craft.

PORTAGING

After all, the safest plan when rapids, rocks or other obstructions are encountered, is to portage around to smoother waters. One may be able to navigate nine-tenths of the bad piece of water successfully, only to stove a hole at the end which lays the canoe up indefinitely. Do not be afraid to be very cautious at such a piece of bad water. Caution does not mean that one is a coward. Your seasoned trapper and woodsman never cares what the other fellow thinks when he is in doubt about such a journey. He always plays on the safe side. Sometimes such a portage means a wearisome hike of a mile or two carrying your duffle as well as the boat. It may cost you half a day or more but it is cheaper in the long run than to risk losing both the cargo and the craft, to say nothing of one's own life or limb.

When you see rough water in the distance, and the stream is unfamiliar to you, tie up and reconnoiter. Send one man ahead to report on the going for the next mile or so. If he finds everything all clear up to a certain point he can go out on a convenient part of the shore and give you a prearranged signal to go ahead. The man or men left in the canoe then bring the craft on up to the place where the scout is in sight. This can be repeated so long as squally water prevails. Where there are signs of the use of portaging, rest assured that others have decided to take the land route, and do not hesitate to follow them around the rapids or other obstructions.

The proper way to portage is all important. Of course, two husky men can take an end of the canoe under their arms and carry it down the trail, but this is an awkward way to manage the matter. It is better for one man to carry the empty canoe upside down, leaving all luggage for the other man. If too heavy for one trip, better make two lots of it and two trips.

The time-honored method by which the Hudson Bay trappers used to carry their canoes is to lash the paddles to the middle of the canoe and the forward thwart braces, the blades of the paddles resting on the middle thwart. If the canoe is turned over, these paddles form a brace for the canoe and rest with their flat side on the shoulders, allowing the head to go between the paddles and inside the canoe. By protecting the shoulders further with heavy coats or sweaters, which need not be worn but which can be bunched under the canoe paddles, one can carry the ordinary sixty-pound canoe for a long distance without undue fatigue, that is, if the going is moderately easy.

It is not wise if one anticipates rough water to carry a heavy outfit in the canoe. The portaging will be twice as wearisome and twice as difficult if there is a large amount of stuff to pack. Furthermore, a canoe heavily loaded becomes logy and unmanageable in a choppy sea, while a canoe moderately loaded will withstand a remarkable amount of rough going if handled by two alert resourceful paddlers.

CANOEING RACING

The canoe as a racing machine has not been developed to any high degree of efficiency. It is a popular feature in any aquatic carnival or other series of sports, which so often pertains to the close of the season at the summer resort or watering place. It is seldom regarded seriously, however, but more as a lark on the part of both participants and spectators. No great amount of practice is indulged in beforehand, but instead the participants trust to brawn and luck.

Nevertheless there are many fine points about the use of the paddle and team-work which, if properly developed, could bring the canoe forward as a serious contender among racing craft. For example, if it is a two-man race, the two paddlers can gain both power and direction by abandoning their stem and stern positions and kneeling down in the body of the canoe. The man in front puts his shoulders and back into an effort to propel the canoe forward without regard to direction. He leaves the latter point to his team mate, who has a somewhat heavier paddle as well as being a heavier man. The stern paddler is the one who trims the course of a vessel by the slight twist of the paddle at each end of the stroke. His ideal position is just forward of the rear cross brace. Here he keeps his paddle on the opposite side from that of his team mate and can keep the canoe headed in the given direction without having to shift.

If the wind or the current tries to sheer the craft away from its straight course, the helmsman can shift a bit further forward and alternate the angle of his paddle until he feels the balance of the canoe beneath him, which indicates that he has reached about the right position and stroke. The shift of the paddle should be accomplished with as little effort as possible, because too much of a twist to the paddle tends to retard the speed.

We have seen more than one race lost to the weaker team because of the fact that the steersman could not hold a straight course. A canoe by nature veers rapidly and unless its course is corrected at the end of each stroke it will within a dozen yards sometimes swing almost at right angles to its true course. The steersman should and must keep his eye on the goal itself and constantly endeavor to keep the prow headed in that direction without interfering with his partner's efforts unnecessarily.

CANOE SAILING

Most of us are so constituted that we do not like to work any more than necessary. Paddling a canoe is hard work as the man who finally rigs up a leg-o'-mutton sail finds out. For a canoeing cruise a light sail is a godsend. One sits comfortably in the stern of the vessel watching his craft skim along like a bird over the waters which before were painfully navigated.

However, canoe sailing is for the adept—the one who has already mastered the intricacies of canoe paddling. Your sailing canoe is like a high-spirited steed that is liable to take the bit between his teeth at any time and upset you, if you are not up to his tricks.

There are many types of sails, but we shall describe here only one or two of the simple types which can be adopted for use in any canoe. If you are going away on a camping trip by water, many miles of paddling may be saved if you will provide yourself with a leg-o'-mutton sail about 8 feet up the mast by 9 feet along the boom. Make this of good stout American drilling hemmed to prevent ripping and provided with grommets about eight or ten inches apart. The mast and boom can be carried along also, or can be cut from saplings in the woods if you are passing through wooded country, but it saves trouble to provide these light timbers and wrap the canvas around them so that no time is lost in stepping the sail. The mast is stepped with a cross brace which is set well forward in the craft and can be so screwed to the side ribs as to be taken off easily and without any injury to the craft itself. The foot step can be screwed in tightly below and in such a way as to give the mast a slightly rakish tilt backwards. There is, of course, no jib but only this single triangular sail, which sweeps well out from the side of the canoe and is managed by the man who sits in the stern and who can steer, if he so desires, with a light paddle or other improvised rudder. A sail rigged up in this fashion is very fast and even in a light breeze will carry a light craft over the water at an amazing rate, but for this very reason one has to watch his currents; a hatful of wind too much and over you go. Some owners try to counterbalance the heavy pull on one side of their canoe by rigging up a counter board which extends out and across the thwarts in the opposite direction, and upon which the venturesome canoeist will sometimes sprawl in an endeavor to keep the craft upright. This is really canoe gymnastics rather than true canoe sailing.

In order to make your canoe answer its helm and not merely drift across the water in front of every wind that blows, you should have lee-boards. For canoe voyaging, these can be made to fold up and thus take little space on board. If one has a work bench and handy tools, such lee-boards are easily constructed at home. Take two pieces of clear spruce and whittle out two blades about the size and shape of paddle blades with square stocks about 3x1 inches. Provide a pair of three-inch hinges, preferably of brass, as these do not rust, and get a length of spruce timber 3x1 inches and a foot longer than your canoe is wide. Mark on this piece the directions exactly where the shanks of the lee-boards will come on the outside and swing up against the gunwale. Then screw all the hinges facing inwards so that the two lee-boards will fold toward each other.

When dropped down over the outside edge of the boat the lee-board should not exceed 2 feet in length and should be tapered off to a thin edge somewhat like a racing paddle. When the boards are fastened by the hinges to the cross pieces they should stand upright a little away from right angles—that is away from the side of the canoe. Next set two heavy brass hooks into your cross rail, and in such a fashion that the eye of the hook when placed in the back of the paddle will hold the lee-board upright and firm. This keeps it from collapsing when in use.

The lee-board is used by being set straddle across the canoe with one board resting in the water on each side. The cross rail is locked so that it remains firm a little forward of midship and when thus set down into the water it acts much as a center-board would act in giving the craft leverage in the water. In other words, when you turn your rudder and bring your sail around against the wind, the sharp blades of the lee-board not only prevent the canoe from skimming across the surface of the water but also enable you to steer in any desired direction.

Some canoes are rigged up with two sails, one being stepped in the bow of the canoe and the other in the stern. The forward sail is usually much larger than the other—possibly three or four times as large. The small sail is used more to balance the craft and aid in steering. Where a great deal of sail is carried it has been found advisable to deck

Canoeing

the canoe. There are two methods of doing this, the most common being a wooden deck which is staunch and reliable. This kind of a canoe, however, is too heavy to paddle and boys do not find much sport in it. The other variety, the canvas-covered canoe, is much the lighter and when equipped with two sails, a main sail and jigger, they surely fly under favorable conditions.

Says one canoeist: "As to rigs for canoes, I have tried them all; leg-o'-mutton, bat wing, lateen and Canadian Club or battened leg-o'-mutton; and have settled on the latter for all my later canoes. Leg-o'-mutton is a slow sail, because of its bad leach, and its spars are so long as to be unstowable in a canoe with six-foot cockpit. Bat wing is too complicated a sail for most men to make, and easily gets out of gear. Lateen has not only too long spars, but is un-reefable, and is a dangerous sail before the wind in a heavy blow. For a twelve-foot canoe, a larger sail can be carried, but you will have to reef it most of the time. A single set of reef points in mizzen and mainsail gives you canvas for a heavy blow, while reefing her down to her battens will give you a rag that you can navigate a gale in."

Because of its weight, variety of uses and general adaptability, the canoe will always be popular. It is the ideal companion for the growing boy who is resourceful and knows how to swim. Whether for idling on a sunlit lake, or as a means of conveyance

81

Sports and Games

on a camping trip, or as a racing craft flying full sail across some friendly bay, your canoe seems a thing of life. Viewed from afar it is a thing of beauty, as much a part of nature as the white-winged sea-gull darting above it.

SAIL BOATS

AMONG the oldest of pastimes of which we have any record is that of sailing and boat handling—although it was probably first learned through necessity. Mankind began very early in the dawn of civilization to propel and guide his craft by means of sails and rudders across the rivers and seas. Even now among types of primitive savages still found in the South Sea Islands the first evidences of seamanship may be found along the lines of war and pleasure canoes.

For the outing to-day, where there is a sizable expanse of water, a sail-boat is almost indispensable. The ability to handle one—even if only a sailing canoe or skiff—trebles the joy of such an excursion.

THE SMALL OPEN SAILING BOAT

A small boat which can be sailed single-handed without difficulty, and which is easy to row—so that, if the wind fails, one can put out the oars and pull her along at a fair rate of speed—is the best sort of craft on which the novice can pass his early apprenticeship. That he can quickly lower his sail if he finds himself in a difficulty, and take to his oars,

83

considerably lessens the risk consequent on his in-experience.

We will first confine ourselves to the description of *open* boats only, of various sorts, for a boat so small that she can be easily rowed should not be decked in, nor be half-decked. A partly-decked boat—that is, one decked in the bow and stern, and having a narrow deck with coamings on either side—is safer than an open boat, as she can heel over to a much greater angle without shipping water than would be possible were she entirely open. But when a small boat is thus decked or half-decked, her owner is apt to imagine that he is in possession, not of a boat, but of a small yacht, and is likely to over-spar her, over-ballast her, and over-canvas her, and, consequently, to over-sail her. The decked boat is only to be rec-ommended when the craft is big enough to be used entirely under sail, with a cabin or cuddy under the decking forward. The above remarks, of course, do not apply to boats intended for racing. These, however small, must, as a rule, be heavily ballasted, and may be partly decked.

Wooden boats are generally constructed in three ways: (1) Clinker, or lap-streak; (2) carvel or smooth skin; and (3) diagonal. Small boats are generally clinker-built. In this type the planks over-lap each other, whereas a carvel-boat has very light frame-work to support the planking. The carvel-built boat is put together much in the same way as a big vessel—that is, she has a framework of solid timbers to which the planking is fastened.

The carvel-built boat has the following advantages over the clinker-built boat: She has a heavier frame, will last longer, and is more easily repaired; thus, if a portion of her planking has been damaged, it can be easily replaced, whereas it is difficult to patch the planking of a clinker-built boat.

On the other hand, the clinker-built is much cheaper than the carvel-built. She is also lighter—an important consideration when a boat is intended for rowing and for hauling up on a beach. For this reason the clinker-built boat is also more buoyant and lively in a seaway.

A diagonal built boat is much heavier in construction, and amateur boat builders would do well to avoid it. In this form of construction two layers of planking are used from keel to gunwale, the first running upward and forward at an angle of about forty-five degrees; and the second layer running in the opposite direction. A waterproof material may be laid between the planking, making an exceedingly durable boat. Sometimes the outer layer over the first diagonal planking is carvel-built.

The wood most in favor is oak for the frame, and cedar, cypress or white pine for the planking. Fir and spruce are sometimes used. For pleasure boats mahogany is a favorite wood.

The ballast of a small boat, more especially if she

has to be frequently drawn up on a beach, should be so arranged that it can be readily removed. Iron or lead blocks, of half a hundred-weight each, with handles to them, are a very convenient form of ballast for a small boat. Battens should be fastened to the bottom of the boat to keep the ballast in its place; otherwise, when the boat heels over in a squall, the ballast may fall to leeward, and so cause a capsize. As metal ballast is heavier than any other, it can be stowed low, more especially if it is molded to fit into the flooring; and consequently the boat ballasted with it will be stiffer under canvas. Such ballast also takes up much less room than a more bulky material, such as stones or sand, though sand bags weighing 40 or 50 pounds each are often used in small boats.

The risks of sailing are much reduced for the novice if his craft is unsinkable. If a boat will float though full of water, her owner, in the event of a capsize, can hold on to her side until someone comes to his rescue; and in most cases his craft also will be recovered undamaged, whereas a boat of higher specific gravity, sinking in deep water, will in all probability be lost. If lead or iron ballast be employed, the boat should be rendered unsinkable by making water-tight compartments, which convert her into a lifeboat. One compartment in the bows and another in the stern will suffice, and if made to fit closely they occupy little room.

Sail Boats

Center-board. The most effective method of preventing the lee-way of a small boat is to provide her with a center-board. This is generally constructed of iron, but if lightness is an important consideration, it might better be of wood. On the other hand, the iron center-board acts as ballast, and, being so deeply immersed, produces a far greater effect in stiffening the boat than would a greater weight of iron stowed inside of the hull. The center-board is generally of triangular shape. When hauled up it is contained in a water-tight trunk, or case, in the body of the boat. It works on a pivot at its fore end, and when lowered passes through the centre of the keel. If the boat strikes on a shoal, the center-board is forced up into the trunk, and warns the helmsman that it is time to go about or make for deeper water. If the center-board is not jammed, it rarely bends or breaks when the boat runs on shore; but this does occasionally occur. It is better to employ an iron handle than a chain for hauling up the center-board. The handle has a joint, so that it can be doubled back and laid snugly along the top of the trunk when the center-board is up. The advantage of the handle is that by forcing it down one can reelase the center-board if the latter be jammed, as not infrequently happens, by pebbles or bits of wood or weed that have found their way into the trunk.

The center-board trunk occupies a good deal of space in the boat, and is often found to be much in the way. To obviate this, a folding center-board has been invented for use on small boats, which requires little space. This consists of three or more plates of iron, working at one end on a pivot in the keel, and made so as to open out and close like a fan. The plates are hauled up or lowered by a rod working in a tube which passes through the keel into the boat. When hoisted, the plates fold up and lie snugly alongside each other in a chamber cut into the middle of the keel.

Lee-boards. The simplest method of supplying a boat having no deep keel or center-board with the means of offering lateral resistance to the water, and so checking leeway, is to fit her with lee-boards. These have several advantages over center-boards; they do not jam, break off, or strain the boat when one runs aground, but always come up at once on touching the bottom. Some shallow waters are in summer overgrown with weeds, through which a center-board craft could never force her way; on the other hand, a lee-board can always be pulled up without difficulty when it gets foul, and be quickly cleared of the weeds.

If expense is a consideration, the novice can not do better than fit his first small boat with lee-boards. We will suppose that he has purchased a second-hand craft for a comparatively few dollars. To fit a center-board into her would be a costly bit of work, only to be undertaken by a skilled boat-builder. But any boy who has even a very small experience in the use of carpenter's tools can construct a lee-board and fit it to his boat.

In the chapter on Canoeing, we have given definite instructions for constructing small lee-boards, which will serve for a craft as light as a canoe. Such lee-boards can, of course, be constructed a little bit heavier and to set deeper in the water for almost any size boat. Many skilled boatmen have a prejudice to their use, but it is undeniable that in an emergency the lee-board answers a definite purpose. Lee-boards can be made to hinge to cross pieces and open up at right angles well off the side of the boat. They can be so fastened by eye-screws as to be perfectly rigid while in the water, and folded into small space when not in use.

TYPES OF SAILING BOATS AND RIGGING

Fashions in sailing craft differ widely, and what is well-known in one section of the country may be practically unknown in another. There are a dozen different types of sailing vessels in use along the Atlantic coast from Maine to Florida, each of which has its own special devotees; for example, on Long Island Sound the small jib and mainsail boat or sloop is most popular. "Down in Maine," where there are deep land-locked bays, a type of yawl is in high favor. A little further south we find boats called "sneak boxes" which are lozenge-shape in hull.

Sports and Games

In and about Cape Cod waters, the great favorite is the cat boat which is described elsewhere. The cat boat is found in widely scattered waters and for an all-around vessel is hard to beat.

Of course, there are many types of small sailing craft which strictly speaking are not sail boats at all. Almost any ingenious boy can step a mast and rig a sail on a boat, provided the boat can be managed at all for such purposes. Center-boards are improvised or lee-boards are constructed, and even canoes are pressed into service for sailing. You will find sails attached to life boats, launches, jolly boats, whale boats, cutters, dories, gigs, punts, bateaux, skiffs, yawls, and many another. While these widely differing types of row-boats can be propelled by sails, the patterns of the sails themselves have a good deal to do with their sea-going qualities.

For pleasure boats the following are the best known types: cat rig, sprit-sail rig, sloop rig, schooner rig, yawl rig, leg-of-mutton rig, balance lug, sliding gunter, and lateen sails.

Cat Rig. This will be described later more in detail in connection with the cat boat itself. In this type the mast is stepped close-up in the bows of the boat and has only a head stay to hold it. The mast is often as tall as the boat is long and carries one large sail secured by mast hoops and held out at the top with a gaff and at the bottom with a boom. This sail lends itself to one-man control. He can sit at the tiller and trim the sail as well as steer the boat.

Sprit-sail Rig. A very handy type of rig for small boats which has certain advantages in the way of hoisting sail, but is not particularly easy in setting is the sprit-sail. The sprit itself is a sliding pole set diagonally to the mast and so placed as to take all the sag out of the sail. It is supported on the mast by means of a strap called a "becket" or "snotter." The "snotter" is a loop of short rope which is fastened around the mast and allows the free turning and sliding of the sprit itself. One advantage of the sprit-sail is that it can readily be rolled up on the sprit alongside of the mast.

Sloop Rig. One of the handsomest of all types of sailing vessels is the sloop, and this is probably used more often by school boys for making small models than any other type. In small boats, for actual sailing purposes there are two sails, the mainsail and the jib. The mast must therefore be stepped far enough back to allow for the play of the jib. From one-quarter to one-third of the distance back from the bows is about the proper distance. The jib is set from a jib-stay. It slides freely up and down the stay on rings or hanks. This jib-stay runs from the mast head to the bow and thence to a bowsprit which projects beyond the bow a few feet. The mainsail is very much of the same shape as that in use for the cat-boat, with a gaff at the top and a boom at the bottom. The addition of the jib makes this type of craft much more manageable and better balanced than the single-sail boat. The sloop rig, however, is not well adapted for handling alone, as the two sails require two sheets (as the rope by which they are trimmed is called) to be tended. We will discuss this popular boat later.

Schooner Rig. This type of rig is adapted to larger boats such as fishing and commercial craft and is seldom used on small boats. It requires two masts and a bowsprit for the jib. The mainsail is provided with a boom and gaff similar to the cat boat and is handled in the same way. The forward mast carries the foresail and the jib. The foresail has a gaff and boom, also, although occasionally the boom is dispensed with, making what is called a loose-fitted sail.

Leg-of-Mutton Rig. A simple type of sail which can be used to advantage with a boat with sloop or cat rig is the leg-of-mutton. This is triangular in shape with one point extending upward so that it can be raised and lowered on the mast by a single halyard. The lower edge is attached to the boom which is controlled by the sheet. It can be raised (or "set" as it is called) and lowered quickly.

Balance-Lug. A type of rig which is much more common in European than it is in American waters, is the balance lug. The sail comprising this rig is four-sided and is suspended from a yard which in turn is hung from the mast about one-third of the way from the forward end of the yard. This hangs obliquely and allows a small portion of the sail to extend in front of the mast. The boom is only slightly if any longer than the yard. Sometimes, in small boats, the boom is dispensed with altogether and the sheet is attached to the lower, after corner, which is called the clew, but this is not generally so satisfactory as having it stretched along a boom. In some types of the balance lug sail, there are two masts of equal height set far enough apart to allow for two standing lug sails. In the standing lug the sail does not have to be lowered, or dipped at each tack to pass the yard around the mast. This type of boat has not been as popular in American waters as elsewhere, as it is somewhat clumsy and hard to handle when coming about, and because it does not behave as well when setting a sail.

Sliding Gunter. Another rig employing the yard is the sliding gunter. In this type the sail is secured to the yard, as is the lug, which in turn slides up and down the mast by means of rings or hoops. A boat thus rigged usually carries two masts and sails of about the same size.

Lateen Sails. In foreign waters, chiefly in the Mediterranean, lateen sails are popular for medium-size boats. They can be best described by saying that they resemble the balance lug at the top in being suspended across the mast by means of a yard. The sail itself, however, is triangular instead of square, and the yard is extremely long and limber. It may or may not have a boom at the foot. Many racing canoes in our own waters are so rigged.

THE BEST RIGS FOR THE BEGINNER

The beginner would do well to start in with the simpler types of sail. The single-sail boat, rigged with a sprit-sail or a leg-of-mutton sail without a boom, is easily handled and is much safer than it looks. When the sheet is let go in a squall it blows out before the wind like a flag, and cannot capsize the boat. This is not the case with a sail stretched out on a boom, which always offers some resistance to the wind, even when the sheet is let go. With a sail on a boom, a jibe in a strong wind may be a risky proceeding. On the other hand, a boat cannot sail her best without a boom, as the sail does not set as well, and when running before the wind it forms a bag, and does not hold so much wind as it would if its foot were extended on a boom. It is only when the boat is on a wind that the boomless sail can be got to stand flat, and then only if the sheet is led aft and made fast to a place exactly in the line of the foot of the sail.

The simplest rig of all for a boat is the cat rig. The advantage of this rig is that there is only one sail to manage, but to the skipper who has had but little experience, when it breezes up, this simplicity is outweighed somewhat by the fact that such a sail makes a boat hard on her helm and it is sometimes hard to bring her about. A boat is much easier to manœuvre if she has a jib. The jib creates that nice balance which is the delight of every expert sailor's heart.

One of the fastest rigs is the jib and mainsail. The kind of sail which best suits any special type of boat can only be figured out to a nicety by experiment. Your flat, square-ended boat will probably do as well with a single sail as with anything else. As you approach the racing craft, however, the cat rig may not be satisfactory. The skipper demands speed and effectiveness which the single sail cannot effect. In American waters our skippers usually follow any one of half a dozen generally accepted types of rig.

One should always remember that the wind pressure is not so great right on the water's surface as it is a few feet above it. This is the reason why the small boat sail will often have her sail limp in a light breeze while the big boat alongside of it goes along with the sails well filled out. Some small boats try to obtain this advantage by excessively high rigging and long masts. This is not advised, however, for the beginner, where seas are uncertain and winds are apt to come in puffs or gusts.

The leg-of-mutton sail with small jib is in some respects the safest of all rigs for the small open boat, and it is very easy to handle. The weight of canvas is mostly in the body of the boat, and there is very little weight aloft. The sail is laced to the mast, which need be but a light spar, as it has no heavy gaff or yard to support, and small strain comes on any part of it. One halyard hoists the sail if it is not laced to the mast.

THE CAT-BOAT

The cat-boat has an almost flat floor. It has a great beam in proportion to its length, the former being in some boats more than half the latter. It is one of the handiest of boats, is good to windward in sheltered waters, but in rough seas a boat with deeper draft is much more comfortable and will not slide off to leeward as fast.

The cat-boat can be handled by one person very readily if he is skilled in sailing a boat of any sort. With one hand on the tiller and the other in reach of the rope controlling the boom (the main sheet, it is called) he is master of all he surveys. In ordinary weather one can thus sail for hours at a time in the laziest and most comfortable fashion. The forward end of the boat lends itself well for decking over, so that necessary supplies and even cooking equipment can be carried in a snug cabin there, if necessary. Then, too, the floor space is roomy. The deck plan bears some resemblance to a flat-iron.

The American cat-boat is generally provided with a wooden center-board; in England an iron center-board is preferred. The mast is stepped in the bow, and the one sail generally has a gaff and boom. The sail is held to the mast either by lacing or by mast hoops and is hoisted by two halyards, one leading from the after end of the gaff, called the peak, through a block on the mast and to the deck, where it is cleated, the other leading from the jaws of the gaff, called the throat, through another block aloft, and to the deck. In setting the sail, hoist both throat and peak together until it is nearly set, then hold the peak and hoist the throat of the sail well up. Then go back and set up the peak hard. The boom should always be provided with a topping lift, for unless the boom is topped up it will fall into the water when the sail is lowered, and the outer end will dip into it when the boat is running before the wind.

Though the cat-boat is usually flat-bodied, her excessive beam gives her great stability, and in the smaller sizes she can be sailed without any ballast; but, as has already been explained, boats of this class, though stiff up to a particular point, capsize as soon as they have heeled beyond a certain angle, and must be sailed with greater care than the deep-keel boats. Being so flat-floored she is uncomfortable in rough water, pounding heavily into the seas and straining herself. Moreover, the weight of the mast, situated as it is so far forward, tends to drive the bow into the seas and thus make a wet boat in the wind. The cat-boat also is liable to drive her nose under and go down by the head when running before a strong squall. The great sail and the length of the boom also make the boat roll when running before the wind; she is then apt to steer very wildly, and is more liable to broach to, than a boat provided with a jib.

A SAILING DORY

In New England, where people sail a good deal out on the open sea and the harbors themselves are subject to heavy swells or rough water, there has been developed a different type of boat from the cat-boat. What has been evolved is a sea-going boat of good rough water qualities which will ride the seas well and stand up in fairly heavy weather—the sailing dory.

This boat answers the demand for a craft which is not easily swamped because of her flaring bow and side constructions. It is used for fishing, and by the New England fisherman, for hauling fish trawls and for hand fishing. In the hands of those who know how to manage them they are the most sea-worthy small boats in existence. But they are quick in motion, heel easily unless the weight is kept amidship, and are all on top of the water, so they are hard to row in a head wind when they are light. In the smaller sizes, modified to meet the needs of a sailing craft, it is a good boat for the boy to learn to sail in, and to take short cruises along the shore.

Sail Boats

It will not sink and should it fill and capsize, it can be righted and bailed out easily.

THE KNOCKABOUT

Another type of small sailing boat which has become widely popular is the knockabout. It is evolved from the sloop-rigged yacht, which in earlier days always carried a long bowsprit projecting several feet beyond a long and sharp bow. Together they tended to make the craft cranky when running before the wind or where quick manœuvring was essential either in squally weather or a race. Noting this defect, some weather-wise tar argued, Why have a bowsprit at all? Why not make it a part of the hull itself? Hence came the knockabout, a sturdy but quick racing boat, with a jib set entirely inboard, and a mainsail of modern lines with gaff cocked well up, and the center of gravity kept low. These boats range in size from about 20 feet length by 7 feet beam, to the 30-footers or more. But the smaller sizes are preferred for amateur racing.

THE SAILING SKIFF

Another boat, which is somewhat similar to the cat-boat, is the sailing skiff which is rigged with jib and mainsail. An ordinary oyster skiff can be easily converted into such a craft with very little trouble. The average skiff measures about 20 feet by 6½ feet on beam. A sailing skiff should have a center-board and is commonly rigged with a large sprit sail and removable mast. The boat is decked fore and aft with light washboards. The rudder is hung on the stern and is operated by a tiller working underneath the main sheet traveler. The proper size of mainsail for a boat of this size is about 13 feet on hoist and 15 feet on boom, 9 feet 7 inches gaff, and 22 feet 4 inches leach. As previously mentioned, the boat is also supplied with a jib which should be about 14 feet 6 inches hoist, 12 feet on the luff, and 6 feet 6 inches foot. For racing purposes a spinnaker may also be provided with the pole measuring 10 feet 6 inches.

THE CANOE YAWL RIG

The main and mizzen is a favorite rig for canoes and small boats, and is also a very handy one. Sometimes the boomkin for the mizzen is fastened on to the rudder head and so moves with it. The result is that in tacking, when the helm is put down, the mizzen is forced to windward and helps the boat around. This plan, which is adopted on some sailing-barges, will certainly prevent a clumsy boat from missing stays; but the mizzen thus gets aback every time the boat goes about and must stop her way to some extent. Moreover, with the mizzen so arranged the helmsman dares not leave his tiller for a moment, for if he does, the wind pressing on the mizzen forces the rudder down, and the boat falls off before the wind instead of luffing up into it, as all open sailing-boats should do when left to themselves.

One type of main and mizzen rigged boat has wooden battens in her two lugs, after the fashion of a Chinese junk. With the assistance of battens a sail attains the maximum of flatness. The battens do not materially increase the weight of the sail, as they are made of light deal. They are passed through the reef bands of the sail. This rig is peculiarly adapted for single-handed sailing; for a very large sail can be carried with safety if it be provided with battens, as reefing becomes an exceedingly simple and almost instantaneous process. To take in a reef, the halyard is slacked off a sufficient length to allow a pull on a line, which is rove through thimbles fastened at both ends of the batten and boom; then draw the boom and lower batten close together, and the reef is down, for the reef points need not be tied. The other reefs can be taken down in the same way. In squally weather reefs can be taken in and shaken out very quickly if necessary. Of course, if one has time to do so, one will tie the reef-points, as the reef will then be snugger.

THE SLOOP

The sloop rig is well adapted for seawork, but is not handy for single-handed sailing if the sailor be a novice, for the tending of the jib-sheets when tacking gives the helmsman more work than he may care for on a windy day. The sloop is rigged much like an English cutter; its mainsail, like the cutter's, has a boom and gaff and is hoisted by two halyards, the throat and peak halyards; but whereas the cutter has a forestay fixed to the stem, carries two head-sails, a jib and staysail or foresail, and has a bow-sprit, the sloop has but one large jib and a fixed bow-sprit to the end of which the forestay is carried. If the sloop is a knockabout the stay is carried to the stem head. A topsail can be carried on a sloop as on a cutter; and a spinnaker can be used for running before the wind. The running and standing rig-ging of a sloop is practically the same as that of a cutter. In the United States the term, sloop rig, is used almost entirely for a single-masted vessel, whether she carries a single or double head rig.

If the mainsail of a small boat—whether she be cat-boat, or sloop—have a boom, it is usual to have the foot of the sail laced to the boom instead of hav-ing it secured at the two extremities only, as is often the case with the cutter's mainsail. A sail thus laced undoubtedly stands flatter, and as the lacing dis-tributes the strain along the boom, that spar need not be so stout and heavy as it would have to be with a sail that was not laced.

Many different types of open sailing boats are provided with jibs and mizzens, but for river and smooth water sailing the single-handed sailor had

Sail Boats

best confine himself to one sail; it is difficult to see what advantage he can gain by having more, except to get better balance. The boat with the single sail is not only the handiest, but it is the fastest, that is, given a certain area of canvas, that canvas is far more effective if it be all put into one sail than if it be divided into several sails, especially when a boat is on a wind. It is only because large sails are difficult to handle that seagoing vessels have so many sails—an objection that does not apply to small boats.

But when a boat is intended for cruising on rough waters it is inadvisable to fit her with one big sail, which also involves a tall mast. When tumbling about in a seaway in a strong breeze the less top hamper the better, so that a smaller mainsail and a jib constitute the best rig. When running or sailing with the wind abeam, a boat is easier to steer if she has a jib; a boat with one sail is apt to miss stays if the sea is rough, but with the assistance of a jib her head can always be paid off.

On some small craft, which, like the sloop, carry one head-sail only, the foot of the jib is laced to a small boom, which makes the sail stand much flatter.

SEAMANSHIP

After the amateur sailor has become familiar with the various types of sailing craft, he should learn how the principal manœuvres connected with the sailing of the boat are executed. Practice alone will enable the amateur sailor to decide promptly what course of action he should take in any set of conditions that may arise, and to perform the required operations smartly and without hesitation. For that "he who hesitates is lost" is an adage that has but too often been proved true at sea. He must get so that he knows what to do instinctively. The sailor must be able to put his hands upon any rope on board, in a moment, in the darkest night; and to reef, tie, or untie any knot, as well with his eyes shut as open. But the novice must not be discouraged if he makes mistakes at first.

Before explaining how the different manœuvres are performed on a yacht, we will describe how the sails are hoisted, lowered, and reefed.

The Mainsail, when stowed in harbor, is rolled up neatly, the middle of the leach having been first hauled forward and laid along the boom. When the sail is furled, its folds are tied together by short lengths of rope, or canvas strips, called *stops* or *gaskets.* The sail is then covered with painted or waterproofed canvas, which is laced underneath the boom; but this cover should never be put on unless the sail is thoroughly dry, else mildew will soon make its appearance. The boom, when the sail is furled, rests on a wooden crutch.

To *set* the mainsail. Remove the sail-cover; hook

on the peak halyards; slack off the main-sheet so as to allow the boom to be topped up a few feet with the topping-lift. Then get the main-sheet taut again, and belay it; cast off the stops. The sail is now ready for hoisting. To get it up, haul on both throat and peak halyards until the throat is as high as it will go and the luff of the sail is drawn taut; but while doing this do not let the peak of the sail get higher than the throat, for if the peak be hoisted too fast the throat will travel up the mast with difficulty, and cannot be got taut. Take care also that the gaff passes between the two topping-lifts, or on the right side, that is the windward side, or what will be the windward side of the single topping-lift, if there be but one topping-lift, as is usual on small cutters. The throat being well up, belay the throat halyards; then haul away on the peak halyards until the peak is well up—that is, until the sail begins to wrinkle at the throat.

If the clew of the sail has not been hauled out taut along the boom before the sail is hoisted, this should be done before the peak is right up.

When the sail is up, stow away in a locker, or other place set apart for the purpose, the boom-crutch, sail covers and rope-ends; for nothing is more unseamanlike than to leave lying about on deck gear which is not required for immediate use. "Where the dickens have those other two rope-ends got to?" "I don't know, Ted. They must have been washed overboard when we shipped that sea," is the sort of conversation over the stowing of a sail after a cruise, that betokens a slovenly crew.

Having belayed the halyards, coil them neatly from left to right, "with the sun," and then capsize them—that is, turn the coils over, so that the last coil is on the top, as the halyards, if let go in a hurry, are likely to twist around some of the coils and carry them up the mast, to jam the block and prevent the sail from lowering more than half-way down.

To *reef* a mainsail. One reef-pennant, or reef-earring, at least, should always be kept rove, in readiness for use. A reef-pennant is a rope which passes through a comb-cleat at the end of the boom, through the reef-cringle on the leach of the sail, and down through a comb-cleat on the opposite side of the boom. The comb-cleat has two or three reef-holes or more—one for each reef-pennant. At the end of the reef-pennant is a knot which prevents its slipping through the hole in the comb-cleat.

To take a reef down in the mainsail, top up the boom a bit, and haul it well inboard with the sheet; slack away the throat and peak halyards to allow the reef-cringle to be brought down to the boom. When the cringle has been got well down, haul out the sail with the reef pennant until the reef band lies flat along the boom, and secure the earring to the boom with a reef-pennant bend, the method of forming which is shown in the figure. Hook the tack on the reef-cringle at the luff of the sail, bowse it down and secure it. Roll up the foot of the sail tightly, and tie the reef-points as taut as possible, making sure that they are all tied on the same side, then haul on the halyards till the sail is once more properly set.

To set a *jib*. In the first place, if the jib is to be set flying and is not permanently fastened to the jib-stay, lay it on the deck forward, with its tack turned to the bows. Hook the tack of the sail on the shackle or hook on the bowsprit end and the halyards to the head-cringle of the sail, not without looking aloft first to see that there are no turns in the halyards. Pass the jib-sheets through the fairleaders or leading blocks, and tie an overhand knot at the end of each sheet, to prevent its running out through its fair-lead when the jib is flapping about. Fasten the jib-sheets on to the clew of the sail, and if clip-hooks are employed for this purpose mouse them with twine.

It is usual, when setting a big jib flying, first to hoist the head of the sail about half-way up with the halyards, then to haul the tack out on the bowsprit, and lastly to hoist the halyards till the sail is right up; but with a small sail it is better to haul the tack out and make fast before pulling on the halyards; for, unless it is blowing hard, it is easy so to handle the sail as to prevent its falling into the water. It is sometimes convenient to make up a jib with light stops,—short cotton yarns with which it is tied when rolled up. When the sail is hoisted, a pull on the sheets breaks the yarns and the sail falls out free.

If the jib is being hoisted when the vessel is under way, take the halyards to the lee-side of the foresail before hooking them on to the sail. On many yachts the jib is fastened to the stay with such hooks. These should be snapped on as the sail is hoisted.

To *take in* a jib, slack up the out-haul and pull the sail inboard (if it is set flying), "mussling" it—that is, gathering it with your arms as it comes in. Then let go the halyards and pull the sail down. If two hands can be spared for the work, one of them should commence to lower the halyards as the sail is coming in along the bowsprit. It requires an experienced hand to take in a jib smartly in a strong breeze when the boat is tumbling about; and the novice, when undertaking this task single-handed, must be careful not to let the jib blow out of his hands into the water, to tow under the keel. If the jib is fastened to the jib-stay with hooks or hanks, just let go the halyard and hawe it down to the bowsprit with the down-haul, when it can be secured with stops.

Topsails of any sort should be hoisted and lowered on the weather-side of the mainsail. If hoisted or lowered on the lee-side they are apt to blow away. Topsails are passed up between the mainsail and the

Sail Boats

topping-lift, and care must be taken when bending the sheets to lead them inside the topping-lift.

To *set the spinnaker,* the spinnaker boom is first laid on deck on the required side of the vessel (the side opposite to that on which the main boom is carried) the outboard end forward. The spinnaker halyards are then bent on to the cringle in the head of the sail, and the sail, which has previously been made up with light cotton stops, is hoisted. The tack is then hooked on to the end of the spinnaker boom with a snap hook, and the boom is shoved forward until the jaws of the boom rest on the mast some three or four feet above the deck. The fore and after guys are then led to the two extremities of the vessel and with these the boom is guided until it is trimmed at the proper angle. The guys are then belayed and a pull on the spinnaker sheet, which has been kept inboard, breaks the stops and the sail fills. Any subsequent trimming can be done by means of the sheet of guys. In a large vessel the spinnaker boom is handled by a lift, the lower end of the boom resting in a socket.

To take in a spinnaker, let go the after guy. The boom will then go forward against the headstay, spilling the wind. The halyards can then be let go slowly while the sail is gathered in as it comes down.

To get under way is not so simple a matter as might be supposed, and is often, indeed, a difficult and delicate business that taxes the skill even of the experienced sailor. A slight error of judgment when weighing anchor or slipping from one's moorings in a crowded anchorage may result in one's craft drifting across another vessel, before she can be got under control; and if there is a strong breeze, or the tide is running strong, considerable damage may be done.

Before proceeding to get under way, get whatever sails you intend to use ready for hoisting; cast off their stops, leaving, perhaps, one around the "bunt" or middle of the mainsail to keep it from blowing loose; bend on halyards and sheets, top the main boom, and see that the runners, etc., are belayed in their right places.

The usual method of getting under way with a sloop when she is riding head to wind and tide, the wind being moderate, is as follows: Heave short, that is, get up the chain until it is nearly straight up and down, and the yacht is almost over her anchor. Hoist the mainsail. Trip the anchor smartly, and just as it is leaving the ground hoist the jib; at the same time, cant the vessel over on the required tack by putting the helm to port or starboard. To cant the vessel the quicker, keep the jib to windward by hoisting it with its weather-sheet belayed and ease off the mainsheet. As soon as the vessel has paid off sufficiently and her mainsail is filling, let the head-sail draw. If you wish to sail close-hauled, do

Sail Boats

not flatten in your main-sheet until you have gathered good steerage way. If you wish to run before the wind, ease the mainsheet well off, and you may keep the peak lowered until the vessel's head is well round. If the vessel is of good size it may require two hands to get under way in the manner described above. But on a small sloop or cutter the operation can be performed single-handed. Hoist jib and mainsail before heaving upon the cable, leaving the jib-sheets flowing, but not so loosely that they can get entangled or get foul of the rigging. Heave on the cable; when it is straight up and down flatten in the weather jib-sheet and lash the tiller to leeward with a line. Run forward and get the anchor a-trip and on deck as quickly as you are able. Then let draw the jib-sheets, cast off the tiller line, and sail away.

If your vessel is riding to tide and wind, and it is blowing hard, hoist no canvas before heaving on the cable, for the pressure of the wind upon the sails would cause the anchor to drag. Just as the anchor is leaving the ground put the helm over to cant the vessel, and hoist the jib smartly. Hoist the mainsail when the vessel is under way.

If the tide and wind are in opposite directions, and the vessel is riding to the tide with the wind astern, set jib, or jib and staysail, just as the anchor is leaving the ground; you will then be running before the wind; and if you wish to luff quickly haul the mainsail up as smartly as you can.

If the wind and tide are in opposite directions, and the wind be so strong that it masters the tide, the vessel riding to the wind with the tide coming up astern, the effect of the rudder will be reversed, so that to cant the vessel's head to port, the helm must be put to port, instead of to starboard, as would be the case if the vessel had headway.

It sometimes happens, when one is anchored in a crowded narrow place with a strong tide running and but a slight breeze blowing, that one cannot get under way in the ordinary manner without running a great risk of drifting foul of vessels anchored close astern. The following method can then be employed with advantage, more especially if the bottom be of mud. The cable is hove short. One hand goes forward and keeps the vessel dragging slowly astern by taking chain in until the anchor is almost off the ground, while he stands by ready to give her back a little chain should she begin to drag too fast. The tide, running under the vessel at a faster rate than she is dragging, gives steerage way and enables the helmsman to steer his craft so as to avoid the anchored vessels, as he drifts downstream stern on. As soon as the vessel gets into more open water, the anchor is got up and the sails are hoisted.

A vessel moored to a buoy is easier to get under way than one lying at anchor, as one has only to slip the cable, and there is no dragging of the anchor to be feared as it is hove short. One can wait till she is canted in the right direction before slipping from the moorings; and by bringing the mooring-rope to one side or other of the vessel, one can ensure her casting off the required tack. Thus, if one wishes to cast off on the port tack, the mooring-rope is brought to the port side and is made fast close to the main rigging; this turns the vessel's head to starboard. The sails are then hoisted; it takes a second to slip the moorings, and away the vessel shoots with all her sails full.

Until the anchor is well out of the water do not get much way on the vessel, but heave to, if you have plenty of sea-room; for otherwise the anchor may be driven back by the pressure of the water, and get foul of the stem or bobstay.

Having got the vessel under way, we will now describe some of the principal manœuvres which have to be executed in the course of a sail. We will suppose that all plain canvas has been set, and that the vessel is sailing "full and bye"—that is, as near the wind as she can go, while yet keeping her sails full. Nothing is gained by jamming a boat too close to the wind, with her sails all on the shake; for though she may be pointing more directly toward her destination, her speed will be greatly diminished, especially if there is any sea on, and she will make more leeway.

To sail a vessel on a wind so as to get the most out of her is an art not to be acquired without much patient practice and observation. At first, the tyro will find it wearisome business to take his trick at the tiller when a vessel is close-hauled. He will ever be anxiously on the watch lest he bear away or luff up too much; and yet, despite all his care, he will be disgusted to find that at one moment all his sails are flapping and the vessel loses her way, and that at the next moment he has brought the wind almost abeam and is sailing away to leeward. He has a tendency to push his helm hard up and hard down alternately, thus correcting one error with such violence that he at once falls into the opposite error.

Steering becomes in time a second instinct, and cannot be taught from books; but the following hints may prove useful to the novice: When steering (except in light winds when you want your weight to leeward) stand or sit on the weather-side of the deck. The angle at which the fly or burgee at the masthead is blowing out will show you whether you are too much off the wind when sailing close-hauled. If you are sailing too near the wind the shaking of the sail will warn you. When you see the luff of the jib and mainsail just lifting slightly, you are sailing as near the wind as you should be. The novice therefore, when steering full and bye, should always have his eyes on the sails and the burgee. But when practice has made him an experienced helmsman the feel of the tiller will tell him whether he is steering rightly, and with a sensitive hand he will hold the helm at exactly the right angle to keep her on her course, moving it but very slightly—almost imperceptibly—now and again, instead of ever passing it backward and forward from hard up to hard down, as he used to do in the early days of his novitiate.

The best of all guides is the feel of the wind on one's face, which indicates whether one is steering full and bye or yawing about. It is astonishing with what nicety a sailor can distinguish the direction of even a very light wind in this way. On a dark night when he is steering full and bye, and not by compass, this is the only possible guide to the helmsman; so, too, if the vessel is running before the wind, he can feel by the chill on his neck or ear if he is sailing by the lee or luffing up.

When sailing full and bye it is important that the sails should be properly trimmed; they should not be sheeted so flat that the vessel becomes sluggish, and they must all be sheeted as nearly as possible at the correct angle, so that one sail will not lift long before the other when the vessel comes up into the wind. It is a common fault to flatten in the jib-sheet too much, by which the sail's effect is wasted, and it tends more to drive the vessel to leeward than to propel her. If the mainsail is seen to lift before the jib, slacken up the jib-sheet a bit.

Tacking. When the wind is so much ahead that one cannot steer directly for one's destination, even

Sports and Games

when close-hauled, the vessel has to be tacked. The theory of tacking has been dealt with previously; the practice will now be explained.

If two or more sailors are available for the operation, the following is the procedure:—The man at the helm selects his opportunity, and if it be heavy weather he awaits a "smooth," for a vessel is liable to miss stays if struck by a sea before she has come up into the wind; then, having decided to put the vessel about, he sings out "ready about," when the men will stand by ready to handle the sheet. If necessary, he should keep the vessel a point or so more off the wind for a short time before he gives the next order, so as to get plenty of way on her. The next order will be "helm's a-lee," and as he gives it he puts the tiller down to leeward gently, and only about half-way over, thus allowing the vessel to shoot well ahead while in stays. When she is in the wind's eye he gives her some more helm to help her pay off on the other tack.

In the meanwhile the men at the sheets have been doing their duty. As the vessel comes up into the wind they slack up the jib and fore-sheets; and when the vessel has passed the head-to-wind position, they haul the sheets in on the other side, which now becomes the lee-side; but they must not do this too soon, else the head sails will act as back sails, prevent the vessel from paying off, and cause her to miss stays. The jib-sheet, for example, on a double head

116

rigged vessel should not be hauled over until the jib has blown clear of the fore-stay; but it should then be got in and belayed very smartly, before the vessel is filling on the other tack, else the strain will be so great that it will be difficult to get it in at all. If the vessel is sluggish in stays, or if there be a lumpy sea, the stay-sail sheet should not be let go with the jib-sheet, but it should be left belayed until the vessel fills on the other tack. The stay-sail, thus taken aback, helps the vessel's head to pay off; but the vessel's way is of course stopped to some extent by this, and the foresail must not be kept to windward a moment longer than is necessary. In order to go about smartly it is well to flatten in the main-sheet until the vessel is in the wind's eye, and then to slack it off again as her head pays off on the other tack.

If one is sailing single-handed, the mainsail must be left to take care of itself during the process of tacking; the jib must be allowed to pass over and its sheet must be belayed on the new tack before the staysail sheets are touched.

If, in consequence of the helm having been put down too fast, or the headsheets having been hauled in too soon, the vessel misses stays, she is left "in irons," that is, she lies helplessly head to wind, refusing to fill on either tack, her sails all shaking, her headway lost, and she soon begins to gather stern-way. In order to get her under way again (say, on

Sports and Games

the port tack) haul the head-sheets to windward, that is, to the port-side, and slack off the main-sheet. This will cause her head to pay off to starboard, then the sails can be trimmed and she will go ahead again. So long as she has stern-way, remember that the action of the rudder is reversed, that is, the tiller must be put over to starboard in order to pay the vessel's head off to starboard.

To run before the wind. When a vessel is running before the wind all sheets are eased off, the main-sheet more so than the others, so that the main-sail is almost squared to the wind. The runners, preventer backstays, and boom topping-lifts are belayed on the weather-side and slacked off on the lee-side.

When running, do not steer a vessel so that she is "by the lee," unless it be necessary to do so in order to avoid collision with another vessel, or for some other such good reason. A vessel is by the lee when she bears away so much that the wind comes from the quarter over which the boom is squared. She is then very near the point which would bring the wind to the back of the sails and cause a jibe. A jibe thus brought about is always more or less dangerous, and may even capsize a vessel. Serious damage is likely to attend an accidental jibe if it is blowing hard; the boom swinging over with great violence from one quarter to the other will carry all before it on its way—runners, preventer backstays, and topmast; and it probably will be sprung by the sudden jerk with which it is brought up by the mainsheet. The headsails always give timely warning that one is sailing by the lee; for the wind gets behind them and bellies them out from the other side before the mainsail is in any danger of jibing.

Jibing. When it becomes necessary to jibe a vessel, proper precautions have to be taken. Before preparing for a jibe, steer so that the wind is not quite aft, but on the quarter opposite to that over which the boom is squared. Haul in on the mainsheet till the boom is half-way in. Then put the helm slowly up to bring the vessel round, and continue hauling on the main-sheet till the boom is amidships. Before the vessel is by the lee, slack off the weather-runners (and weather-preventer backstays, if these be standing) and set taut the lee-runners, which will become the weather-runners when the jibe has been effected. As the wind strikes the mainsail on the opposite side, slack off the main-sheet so as to break the jerk and allow the boom to pass over easily to the other quarter. A vessel is apt to run up into the wind as she jibes, so the helm must be put up to meet her. Then sheet the headsails on what has now become the lee side.

If the wind is strong it is well to lower the main peak before jibing.

When running before a heavy sea a vessel is apt to yaw about a good deal, and therefore exceptional care must be taken to avoid an accidental jibe. The prudent plan under these circumstances is not to steer dead before the wind, but to sail for some distance with the wind on one quarter, and then to jibe and sail with the wind on the other quarter.

A vessel is said to be *hove-to* when she is made to remain stationary, by getting some of her head sails aback. To heave a cutter to, luff her up till she is close-hauled, haul the stay sail-sheet to windward, and haul on the jib-sheet until the corner of the jib is over the forestay. If the main-sheet is now trimmed properly—experiment will quickly show how much it should be flattened in—the headsails and the mainsail will balance each other, the former causing the vessel's head to pay off, the latter driving her up into the wind, with the result that the vessel will remain floating head to wind, making no headway, and the tiller can be lashed amidships. In a vessel with a single headsail the jib, if trimmed to windward, will do the same thing.

When sailing single-handed, provided you have sufficient sea room, heave the vessel to before undertaking to reef, shift jibs, etc. You can then leave the tiller and do the work at your leisure, while the vessel takes care of herself.

When hove-to under snug canvas, even a small fore-and-after will often ride quite comfortably and safely through very heavy weather. To ride out a gale a cutter is generally hove-to under trysail and storm-jib, the foresail or staysail being stowed.

To get under way when hove-to, hoist the foresail if it is down, slack up the main-sheet, and when the vessel has paid well off trim the sheets.

When shifting sails and reefing, care must be taken to preserve the balance between the head and after sails, so that the vessel remains in good sailing trim, having a decided tendency to come up into the wind, while yet not carrying excessive weather helm. Thus if a large jib be changed for a small one, while the mainsail is left standing, the vessel will gripe and the tiller will have to be put hard up to keep her off the wind, the rudder being at such an angle as to seriously retard the vessel's speed. On the other hand, if the mainsail be reefed while the whole jib is left on her, the vessel will probably carry a lee helm, which, as has already been explained, no yacht should under any circumstances be allowed to do; among other reasons, because, when in that danger-ous trim, she will be pinned down and possibly be capsized by a squall instead of luffing up into it.

That a vessel should be in good trim is of especial importance when she is beating to windward against a heavy sea. It is essential then that her canvas should not only be well-balanced, but that it should be sufficiently reduced, so that she can be sailed ramping full, and be ever kept well under control; whereas if too much sail is carried she will have to be luffed up into every strong puff, when the seas will quickly deaden her way, and she will plunge and tumble about uneasily in the hollows between the waves, and probably get in irons. When an exceptionally big sea is seen rolling up, the vessel must be luffed up into it, so as to meet it end on, but as soon as it has passed one must bear away and fill the sails. Unless one has been sailing full and keeping good way on her, one cannot perform this manœuvre properly, and with an over-canvased craft that has to be luffed up to puffs of wind as well as to seas, one will progress but slowly, and will make very bad weather of it.

When running before a heavy sea, the vessel, especially if she be a short, beamy one, will exhibit a tendency to yaw about, and will require most careful steering. Now is the occasion for the helmsman to show his skill. With the novice at the helm the vessel will steer in the wildest fashion, now shooting up in the wind, now bearing right away till there is danger of a jibe, and the tiller will be kept ever hard at it travelling backward and forward from one quarter to the other. But the experienced man will keep his helm steady, and the vessel's yawing will be slight; for the art of steering does not consist of violently forcing the tiller up and down to correct a vessel's deviation from her course after it has occurred, but in anticipating her movements with a gentle pressure of the tiller before she begins to fall off or come up. The helmsman feels that he is between Scylla and Carybdis when running before a heavy sea, and he needs all his nerve. For on the one hand he has to avoid an accidental jibe, and on the other hand, whenever a dangerously big and steep sea rolls up, he must so steer that the vessel is dead before it; for if it strikes her on the weather quarter it may cause her to broach to, that is, fly up into the wind till she is broadside on to the sea, a most dangerous position, in which she is in great risk of being swamped or rolled over by the next big wave.

Always carry a jib when running before the wind, it will help to pay the vessel off if she attempts to broach to. One can carry more canvas when before the wind than when sailing close-hauled; but if too much sail is carried the vessel will roll heavily. Do not crack on canvas under the impression that it will enable you to run away from the following seas and so avoid the risk of being swamped. No vessel can run as fast as that.

To anchor. When anchoring, do not pay chain out too fast, as it will fall on the top of the anchor, and possibly take a turn round the fluke, in which case the anchor will draw out of the ground as soon as a strain is put upon it. Having let the chain which the anchor takes as it goes to bottom run out, wait till the vessel goes astern and the chain tautens before giving her more; then do so gradually until she has enough to hold her—about three times the depth of the water suffices as a rule; but more will be required if the holding ground is bad or it is blowing hard.

Having come to an anchor or picked up your moorings, lower the main-boom on its crutch and stow the sails neatly. Put their covers on the mainsail and jib, or take the latter off the stay if these sails are dry; if they are damp furl them loosely and hoist and dry them as soon as you have a chance. On no account put the sail coats on wet sails, as to do this will infallibly produce mildew. Slack off the clew of the mainsail before stowing it, for by keeping the clew constantly hauled out taut along the boom (a common fault), you will pull the foot of the sail all out of shape. Belay all halyards, sheets, backstays, etc., neatly, but not too taut if they are dry; remember that a shower of rain will cause all your hemp rope to shrink considerably, and then an over-taut preventer backstay, for example, may put such a strain upon the topmast as to break it.

If it be blowing hard, or the holding ground be bad, or if for some other reason it is uncertain whether your single anchor will hold the vessel, *moor* her, that is, ride to two anchors placed at some distance apart, so that the two cables form an angle. To moor, let go on one anchor and veer out twice as much cable as you intend to ride by. When the cable is taut let go the second anchor. Heave in on the first cable and veer out the second until the same length of cable is out on both anchors. It is sometimes more convenient to take the second anchor out in a boat to the place where it has to be let go.

To unmoor, veer out chain to one anchor while getting the other anchor up. Then weight the second anchor. When lying at anchor in windless weather, the vessel is apt to float right over her anchor at slack water, just before the turn of the tide. The cable is then likely to take a turn round the upper fluke of the anchor, so that, when a strain is put upon it, it will pull the other fluke out of the ground, and so cause the anchor to drag. To obviate this, it is well to heave the cable short at slack water and let it go again when the vessel swings to the tide.

If one is anchored on rocky ground the anchor is apt to get foul, and may have to be abandoned unless one has adopted one of the two following methods for insuring its recovery. Before letting go the anchor fasten the end of a small line to the crown of it, and buoy the other end. If the anchor has got hold of a rock and refuses to come up when the cable is hauled upon, it can be liberated by hauling on the tripping line.

If a small vessel be overtaken by such heavy weather, when she is on the open sea, that she is in danger, even when hove-to under her storm canvas, a *drogue* or *floating anchor* can be put out, a contrivance which has enabled even small open boats to ride out the heaviest gales with safety. A drogue generally consists of a framework of iron or wood, with strong canvas stretched across it, so as to offer great resistance to the water when dragged through it broadside on.

A vessel riding to her drogue with some forty fathoms of hawser out, as she drags astern is ever kept head to wind and sea, and cannot well pay off or get broadside on the waves as they roll by her.

If no drogue is carried on board, a very effective one can be extemporized by bending one side of a small jib or other sail to a spar and riding to that. The hawser must be attached to the middle of a rope about twice the length of the spar, the rope being made fast at either end to the extremities of the spar, thus forming a span, and keeping the spar broadside on to the seas. A bit of ballast should be attached to the lower corner of the sail in order to sink it and keep it in a vertical position, so that it may offer the greatest resistance to the water. The spar to some extent serves as a breakwater as well as a floating anchor, and prevents the seas from breaking near the vessel.

When riding to a drogue it will be well, unless the gale be very heavy, to have a reefed mizzen set if the vessel be a yawl, and a reefed trysail if she be a cutter; in either case the sail must be sheeted amidships.

IN CONCLUSION

Now a word of caution and advice in conclusion. Don't take chances on the water any more than on shore; in fact, be even more cautious on shipboard. As the old Southern darkey said when asked to state his preference as to whether he would rather be wrecked on a train or on a steamboat: "I don't take no chances on no boat. When yo is wrecked on land, thar yo is, but when yo is wrecked on water, whar is yo?"

No matter how strong a swimmer one may be, there are times when a heavy sea or a gale will try the most expert. Come aboard always prepared for emergencies. Have a life-belt handy and also a life-preserver attached to the end of a long length of stout rope. A single misstep in going around a boom may throw one into the water at a time when such a mishap is least expected. This is especially true of landlubber friends who come on board for a visit.

Don't manœuvre into a tight place or where there are other craft which may run foul of your anchor line. Give the other fellow plenty of leeway and exact the same precaution from him. Before going on any extended cruise alone, be sure you know every inch of your boat, every inch of your sails, and every inch of your ropes. Always coil up your ropes in

Sports and Games

neat and seamanship style not only for the looks but also to prevent knotting or fouling in an emergency. Don't see how much canvas you can crowd on to a boat in a swift breeze or how close you can sail to the wind. Always allow a margin for safety and for sudden squalls. Don't allow your experience and familiarity with the craft to make you careless. Eternal vigilance is the price of pleasurable and safe boating.

There is no other exercise which calls into play more faculties of the mind and the body than this of managing one's own boat. One must be mentally alert and physically keen in order to get the most out of it; and by way of reward the more one puts in of such attributes, the more sport will be received in return.

MOTOR BOATS

THE term, motor boat, has now come to include many types of craft big and little—from the converted row-boat of the small boy to the expensive launch costing thousands of dollars. We will not try to describe here the more expensive types, but will discuss the kind of boat which is most frequently met with and which, in the long run, gives more satisfaction dollar for dollar, than the higher priced craft.

One of the simplest forms of motor boat is the converted skiff. This may be purchased and used as a row-boat, but by the addition of a two-horse power motor, a substantial little craft may be evolved capable of carrying four or five persons and making a speed of eight or ten miles an hour. Such a boat, motor and all, will not cost much more than $150, and if either the boat or the motor is bought second-hand, it can be obtained much cheaper.

Of course, the simplest type of motor boat is the canoe with a single cylinder engine suspended over the stern. While this is not a true motor boat, and your sea-going mariner openly scoffs at it, it undoubtedly gives the beginner a useful working knowledge of the habits of a gasoline engine. These little canoes can get over the water at a surprising rate of speed, but care must be taken against over-loading them. Motor canoes are also obtainable, in which the motor is already installed inside. They are built light so that they may be portaged if necessary, and complete do not weigh much more than one hundred and fifty pounds. The chief objection to the motor canoe is that it is too light in frame for all sorts of weather, and if the owner is unlucky enough to strike a sharp rock the weight of the motor speedily drags the entire outfit to the bottom.

TYPES OF BOATS

Punt. The most serviceable types of motor boat for ordinary use are those in which the motor is set amidships in a substantial wooden hull; and the simplest type of all is the punt. This is a box shape craft with square ends, square sides, and a flat bottom. It can be decked over at both bow and stern with planking, which serves as seats for the passengers. Most punts are deeper in the middle than at either end. This diminishes the resistance of the water in front, while the flat bottom at the stern allows the punt to slide across the water like a sled. Thousands of such boats are in use by fishermen and others, and while crude-looking affairs, they "deliver the goods."

Almost any boy who can handle tools can construct a serviceable punt. The engine can be obtained from any marine supply house, and such houses usually have plans for several types of suitable boats, or can tell where such plans may be obtained. The motor should be of the simplest type and if installed in the body of the boat about one-third of the way from the stern, it can be easily managed by one person who also operates the tiller.

Skiff. The next type of boat is an evolution of the punt—the skiff. This can best be described by saying that it is a punt with the bow sharpened to a point, the stern retaining its blunt shape. The bottom is still flat. The sharp bow allows the craft to cut through the water at a better rate of speed than the punt. It also presents a more professional and sea-going appearance. While this boat is a little more trouble to construct than the square, box-like punt, it also can be made at home by anyone with a mechanical turn of mind. The raw materials do not cost much and plans can be obtained easily. The motor will be the principal item of expense, but all told such a boat should not cost more than $50, if home built, exclusive of the motor which can be purchased, new, anywhere from $70 up.

Dory. The dory is the next step in the evolution of boat building from the square flat-bottom type to the true round-bottom type of boat. While the dory's bottom is flat it is much smaller in surface due to the tapering sides. The bow is pointed and the lines of the boat swing around in graceful curves to a stern which is also partly rounded. The sides are built up much higher than in the skiff, which admits of a heavier and therefore faster engine, and also allows more room for stowage. Altogether, the dory is one of the most serviceable and popular types of small motor boat. For those who like to build at home, suchboats can be obtained in knock-down shape. The knock-down material comes all ready to assemble, and with full patterns and working specifications. Two boys working together during their spare time of evenings and Saturdays can build such a boat for about one-third the cost of the same boat if purchased ready-made.

Skipjack. Another simple type of boat which is well adapted for motors is the skipjack. This does not pound in the water as badly as the skiff or punt, because of the fact that it is built with a wedge-shape bow. The bottom, which is almost diamond-shaped, lends itself well to fast going over the water. In fact, some racing types of motor boat are constructed on this principle. A powerful motor is placed amidships and the whole front end of the boat is decked over in these racing types. The helmsman sits just back of the cockpit and controls and steers the boat very much as he would an automobile. The boat when at full speed lifts the bow entirely out of the water and skims along on the stern.

Round-Bottom Boats. The type of racing boat above mentioned could not attain its maximum speed with a round-bottom hull, as it would not lift out of water at high speed. For many other purposes, however, round-bottom boats are preferable. They do not slap the water so hard, they ride more smoothly and they are thus more comfortable for cruising or for long voyages. Round-bottom boats come in a wide variety of styles and types. They are sometimes lapstreak. Most of the expensive pleasure craft are of the round bottom type.

The majority of motor boats (except those used for cruising) whether flat-bottomed or round-bottomed, rarely exceed thirty feet in length. Boats under this length can be obtained in many different models, or can be constructed at home. The motor need not be costly unless speed is desired, and the whole outfit of such an average boat, under twenty-five feet, if purchased, would not cost more than from $400 to $800. If built at home the cost would not be more than one-half this amount. Where the length runs thirty feet or more, costs mount very rapidly. Larger engines must be installed, construction is more difficult and more accessories are required.

BUILDING ONE'S OWN BOAT

Any simple type of boat running up to twenty feet or thereabouts can be built at home. Many boys now get shop practice in connection with their school work which teaches them many things about boat building. It is never wise, however, to begin on a large boat, or without proper oversight from someone who knows how. The kind of material to use, the best form of construction, the weight of the planking, the shape of the stern or the bottom —all of these things, and many others, must be weighed carefully before one begins sawing and hammering.

But no boat, no matter how simple, should be undertaken without very careful plans and specifications, not only as to the shape of the boat itself but as to the choice of materials. Some firms will supply for a small sum a complete set of patterns and blue-prints by which a complete hull can be constructed. These plans, while they may cost as much as $10 or $12, are well worth the price and will easily save the boat-builder their cost several times over.

The boat-builder will quickly find that there is a lot of sawing to be done. If he can set up a small motor-driven buzz-saw, well and good, but otherwise after two or three days of continuous sawing, he may feel like chucking the entire job. The best way is to make a dicker with the mill from which you obtain the lumber, and have it sawed up to specification—that is, if you cannot install a small power-saw of your own.

The knock-down boat, after all, is the most practical type of craft to construct at home. Strictly speak-

MOTOR BOATING

This speedy boat provides a thrill for the man on the aquaplane behind.

© E. Galloway

ing this is not home built, but it will provide the builders with practically the same amount of building experience; and the results are much safer. The knock-down parts are cut at the factory and are sent to you ready to assemble. The experienced builder, however, will be careful to specify that such parts must come from a boat that has been already set up and afterwards knocked down. Otherwise, he will find that there is any amount of finishing, beveling, mortising and hole-boring necessary on his part. Some concerns which make and sell knock-down boats send rough sawn material, with the ribs steam-bent over moulds, and not true to specifications. The timber itself may be full of knot-holes or checks. If, however, your boat has been previously set up and then knocked down, it insures a true hull, with properly set main timbers, and timber without any bad spots.

Says W. H. Miller: "Most of the cost of a boat is in the time spent by expert carpenters in fine finishing all over it, and much of this is equally staunchly (if not so finely) done by amateurs whose time is charged in as recreation—for it *is* fun puttering around a motor boat, believe me! And this is at the bottom of the success of the business of selling knock-down frames and patterns—your boat is a sure success, and not a 'lemon' as she will most probably be if you attempt to design as well as build her yourself. When I was a boy we had no knock-down frames to start with, and some of the most fearful tubs ever conceived in the mind of man came right out of amateur shipyards in my home harbor town. They looked well to the eye; but as sailers they were nix!—any craft designed by a regular naval architect could sail circles around them."

Another big saving in the cost of a knock-down boat as against the cost of the completed boat, is the matter of freight from the factory to the water-front where the boat is to be launched. It goes without saying that a complete boat crated for shipment will cost three or four times as much to transport as the one which comes to you in compact knock-down shape.

Whether building a boat from knock-down material, or direct from the lumber, sawing as you go, there is one thing to keep constantly in mind. Building a boat is vastly different from building a table or any other article for use on land. A joint that will get by for land use may not do at all in the water. All seams and joints must be made as tight as possible, and then finished and caulked with cotton to present an absolutely smooth and watertight surface. Nearly right will not do. It is better to take three times as long on the job and do it right, than to have to go back over one's work, and even then have a leaky craft.

Motor Boats

CHOICE OF MOTOR

It is not the providence of this chapter to discuss particular types of gasoline engines by name. Almost any well-known make of engine will be found serviceable. Like the automobile engine, vast strides have been made in simplicity and efficiency during the past ten years, with the result that such engines are practically "fool-proof."

As a general rule, a boat under twenty or twenty-five feet would not require anything larger than a two-cycle marine motor. The horse-power ranges from one-half to twenty, in this type of engine, and the cost, of course, varies with the power. The owner is the best judge of the size motor that he wants, depending upon the uses to which he expects to put his boat. If he is not looking for speed but wants a serviceable engine that will run day in and day out on short trips, say on an inland lake, he would not want an engine that would develop more than five or ten horse-power. Such an engine would be more economical of gasoline and upkeep generally.

For larger and speedier boats a four-cycle motor would be necessary. These also can be obtained in varying sizes. If speed is desired—and by speed we mean anything over fifteen miles an hour—the cost of the motor mounts rapidly. For example, a boat capable of traveling twenty-five miles an hour might cost $2500; while one geared up to thirty miles would be more likely to cost $10,000.

After all, the reader of this article will probably be more interested in the everyday type of motor boat than in the luxurious type. And for him we can offer no better advice than to say, visit two or three good marine supply houses and look over types of motors for yourself. If you are not in reach of these houses, send for their catalogues. You can find such houses advertised in marine periodicals like *Yachting* and *Motor Boating*. Write a line to the editor of such a periodical, stating the size of your boat and what purpose you have in mind for it, and ask him the best type of motor to place in the hull. If there are other boats in commission around you, take an opportunity to visit them and talk to their owners about them. The school of experience is the best of all for the motor-boater, and if you can profit by the other fellow's experience, it will save you both dollars and nerve-wear.

You will find that there is a constant traffic in second-hand motors and motor-boats. The owner of one is like the automobilist in tiring of one particular type of car after a season or so, and being ready to trade for some other. He has the advantage over the automobile owner in being able to rip out his motor from the boat at short notice, and install some other motor.

The ease with which engines can be installed in

almost any kind of a hull has led to the practice of converting any hull that floats into a motor boat. Last year's row-boat may become this year's power-boat. The hull of a cat-boat may do duty for the same purpose. It is not uncommon to see a sailboat which also has a "kicker" installed, and which proves most useful on calm days. The very ease with which such motors can be installed in any sort of craft leads to some curious alliances. We have seem diminutive motors of one or two horse-power chugging away manfully to propel some ungainly tub of a boat that ought to have ten or twelve horse-power to get it anywhere. On the contrary, we have seen a small skiff carrying a motor large enough to sink it when a good-sized wave came along.

If you are starting in on motor-boats, go slow and carry a tongue in your head. Do not take the first boat or the first motor that is offered you, but shop around a bit. The market in second-hand motors is always brisk. For some reason, the owners are generally willing to trade after the first or second season. This may only mean that they want a change; or it may mean that the motor is either cranky or ill-adapted to their particular boat. Do not buy such a motor or motor-boat without testing it out on the water, and preferably alongside of a man who is disinterested and who is experienced in their handling.

Begin with a small boat the first season, and put

in as little money as possible into it. A good second-
hand open boat twenty-five feet long and simply finished ought not to cost more than $250 to $300.
Smaller ones can be found for much less money.
Of course this does not have reference to the fancy
boats with brass rails and furnished cabins. New
boats under twenty feet long and without cabins can
be obtained for about $300 or for about $20 per foot
of length. A twenty-five or thirty foot boat with
a small cabin and many conveniences can be obtained for about $1000. The cost of upkeep of one
of these smaller boats is much less than for a larger
boat, they are more easily sold, and their deprecia-
tion is not nearly so great. Even owners of larger
craft like to have small, knock-about boats. So it
is just as well to begin by learning how to operate
one of the latter type.

It is really remarkable how many uses can be obtained from a little boat. It will run for hours at
a time with very little attention except for oil and
fuel. And it is astonishing what power can be developed.

"One of the greatest pleasures to be obtained from
a small motor boat," says Harold W. Slauson, "is in
preparing it for and entering it in a race with other
craft of its class—a race in which the smooth and reliable operations of the motor and the efficient handling of the jockeying by the navigator count for more
than does the possession of excessively high power.

Motor Boats

The ideal race consists of a speed contest between boats of exactly the same design of hull and driven by the same kind and size of motor. This enables each contestant to start on even terms with all the others, and even though the maximum speed should not be more than ten or twelve miles an hour, a close and exciting finish may be expected and the winner will have deserved his success on his own merits."

BOWLING

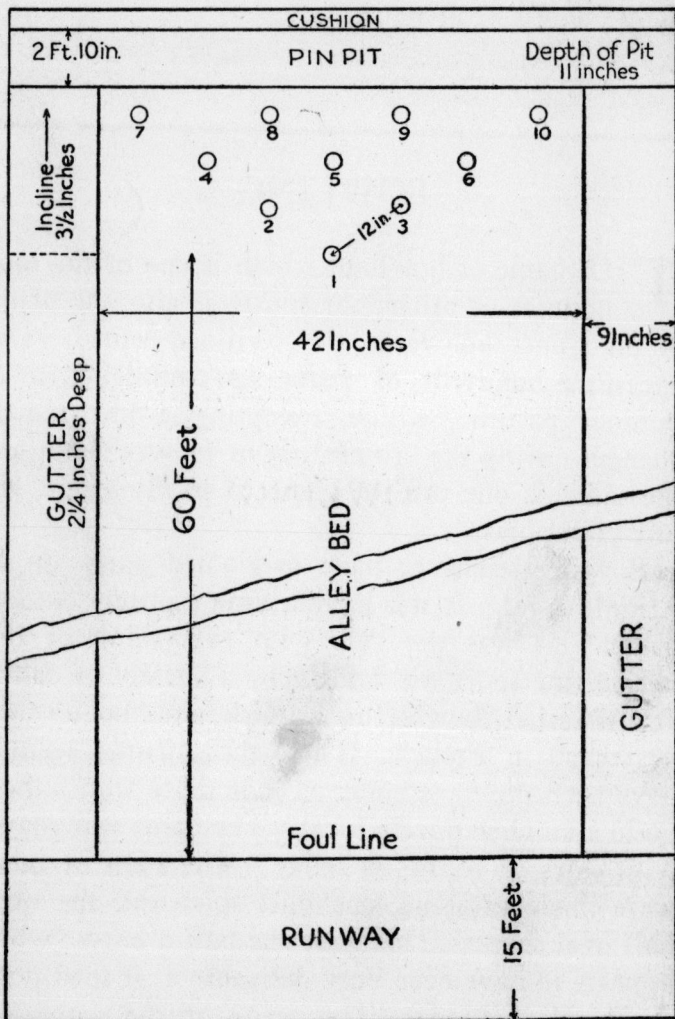

CUSHION

PIN PIT

2 Ft. 10 in.

Depth of Pit 11 inches

Incline 3½ Inches

7   8   9   10

4   5   6

2   12 in.   3

1

42 Inches

9 Inches

GUTTER 2¼ Inches Deep

60 Feet

ALLEY BED

GUTTER

Foul Line

RUNWAY

15 Feet

144

BOWLING

THE game of bowling, which is one of the most popular of all indoor sports, is also one of the oldest games known to the civilized world. Our ancestors hundreds of years ago indulged in an outdoor pastime, which, excepting a few radical changes during the last century or so, was materially the same as our present game of bowling and was just as popular.

Bowling seems to have originated early in the Middle Ages. It was at that time a purely outdoor game. As was the rule with everything of that period, the sport was known by a variety of names. It was called "bowles" in English, and "boules" and "carreau" in French. These three names seem to have been the most common, but there were others, quite a number purely local. The game was played with sides or teams, as today. The balls or bowls were made of stone, one half spherical, the other half oval shape. This gave the ball a curve, which appears to have been very desirable as it sped down the bowling green. The scene of the game was a plot of ground called a rink or bowling green. At each end was placed a cone, which was the mark for the bowlers. The cones were bowled from one end of the rink and then from the other. As in the game of quoits or "horse-shoes," the object of the game was for one side to place their ball nearer the cone than their adversaries. The side bowling last would, of course, try to knock the opponents' ball away from the cone, supplanting it with their own, the one nearest the cone scoring a point for his side. Skill was required to bowl in such a way as to curve around an opponent's bowl, so as to get nearer the cone without knocking the other ball closer. Later, the stone bowl was supplanted by one made of lignum-vitae. The latter was made perfectly spherical, and the outside of the tree being lighter than the heart naturally gave the bowl the desired bias, though often one side of the ball was loaded with lead to obtain the desired effect. The cones were finally done away with, and superseded by a stone or earthen ball about three and a half inches in diameter, and known as a "jack." Instead of having a stationary mark at which to bowl, the jack was knocked all over the green, while strategy and skill were required to play a good game. In this way was derived the game of Lawn Bowls, described elsewhere in this book (p. 291).

The bowling green of that period was one of the most cared-for spots about a village or an estate. A plot of ground as level as it was possible to find was picked out for it. Draining was the first process

Bowling

in the making. This was done in such a thorough manner that even the hardest rains would not soak the ground and put it in a muddy condition. After draining properly it was rolled, the grass kept cut to the proper length, and, by the most assiduous care, this spot would be made as hard and level as a table. The size of the plot was usually about 90 or 150 feet, surrounded by a ditch or gutter four or five inches deep. During the reign of Queen Anne and the first three Georges, a bowling green was as popular and necessary an adjunct to a gentleman's country seat as a billiard table is today. Usually this plot of ground was surrounded by evergreens, which kept the grass from being scorched by the burning rays of the sun, as well as protecting the spectators and players. In many places this formed one of the most picturesque spots about a well-kept park or garden, though very frequently it was situated in close proximity to the dining-room, from which it could be reached by a flight of stairs leading from a glass door or bay window. As an after-dinner sport of our burly British and Dutch ancestors, it was very popular, aiding in the digestion of their heavy meals of that time, consisting principally of beef and pudding, lubricated with heavy ale and potent punch.

The game was first introduced into America early in the eighteenth century, and possibly the latter part of the seventeenth. It seems to have been very popular in New York. An old map of that city, of the

Sports and Games

date 1728, shows a bowling green on the north side of the public garden situated near the King's farm, near the foot of Murray and Warren Streets. Also in 1732, the locality called Bowling Green, at the foot of Broadway and known by the same name at the present day, was leased from the city government and laid out as a public bowling green. From the time that the sport was introduced into America it has really never died out, though the outdoor game has long since given way to the indoor game in point of widespread popularity.

As an indoor sport the game originated from several games, cayles, French quilles, skittles, loggets, and sayles being the most popular. In cayles and loggets conical shaped pins made of bone were set up in rows of six or eight, and the players tried to knock them down by hurling clubs of "sheepe's joyntes" at them. Knocking the pins down by bowling a ball at them came at a later period. In the game of carreau, the players bowled at a fixed mark; while in skayles, closh, French quilles, clossynge, kittles, skittles, Dutch pins, four corners, half-bowl, rolly-polly, and ninepins, the marks bowled at were pins similar to those of the present day and bowled at with a ball. The games were immensely popular for a long time, until some laws were passed prohibiting ninepins and similar games. For a while this stopped the game, but it did not die out. The objectionable features were cut out, and instead of nine pins set up in a diamond frame, ten pins were set up in a triangular frame.

The first mention of a game being played indoors on a covered alley is found in William Fitz-Stephens' "Survey of London," about the twelfth century. The first record of a match game played indoors in America was a game played on the Knickerbocker alleys in New York City on January 1, 1840. Since that time the indoor game has continued to grow in popular favor until today it is one of the regular features of athletic and many other clubs.

Until 1875, when clubs became very numerous, there was much diversity as to the length of the alleys and the size of the pins and balls, as no standard had ever been adopted. Before that time the pins used were larger and heavier than the ones used now, and it was a much easier matter to knock all the pins down by hitting only one or two, making the score of 300 the limit. In 1875 a large number of bowlers, representing most of the cities of this country, held a meeting and adopted rules and regulations, which at that time answered the purpose. For the next ten or fifteen years, or up to 1890, bowling was a sort of "go as you please" game. In the East they played under the rules of the National Bowling League, while in the West, where a sudden boom started, any rule went. Under these conditions the boom west of the Alleghenies lived but a few years.

Sports and Games

In 1895, or with the birth of the American Bowling Congress, which at once wiped out the old rules and substituted new ones that brought the playing of the game down to a somewhat scientific order, things began to wake up again and the bowler from that day to this has been looked upon as an important factor not only in sporting circles but in social circles as well.

HOW TO BOWL

There are about as many opinions on this subject as there are grains of sand on the seashore, all of which are worthy of some commendation. The physical anatomy of bowlers makes it almost compulsory that each should adapt himself or herself to the style best fitted to them. It should, of course, be the first object to learn how to handle a ball. The balls vary in weight from one to fifteen pounds, and from the size of a baseball to a ball twenty-seven inches in circumference. It hardly appears necessary to warn the novice about the folly of beginning with the largest balls; it is an unwritten law of physical culture to begin with light weight first and gradually increase it; this every athlete will respect; but bowling is different, and, while the same rule applies with equal force, there seems to be an all-powerful inclination to begin with heavy balls. This has the effect of straining the tendons in the back, arms and legs, and gives the novice the feeling next morning

Bowling

that he must have run an endurance race during the night. He also finds after an hour's steady practice that the ball is very stubborn, and that he has made little progress.

Stick to the small ball until you acquire that familiarity with it which will assure you a certain amount of gracefulness as well as accuracy. In lifting a ball from the runway, turn it over until the holes are facing upward, insert the thumb and second finger and lift it from its position, letting the arm hang naturally by the side. Then walk to the position you desire behind the foul line. If you are inclined to roll a side or cross ball, naturally take up your place at the right-hand side of the alley; if you are a left-handed bowler, the left-hand side should be used. Step back about nine feet, holding the ball with both hands against the chest, or downward about opposite the knee; then draw an imaginary line by a glance of the eye from the head pin to the foul line; then start slowly until you have acquired the knack of getting the ball down toward the pins without its going into the gutter. This can be done with a little practice. To the player whose desire it is to begin bowling by rolling a center ball, the same will hold good, that is, draw an imaginary line from either side of the head pin to the foul line, as the one object should be not to hit the head pin full in the center, but a little to either side, so as to avoid making a hole or "split" through the middle.

Sports and Games

Whichever style a novice adopts, it should not be departed from, if an improvement is desired. Before stepping up the runway for a ball, the soles of the shoes, unless tennis or rubber-soled ones are worn, should be well chalked from the chalk-box at the head of the alleys; this will prevent any possibility of slipping while delivering the ball.

Don't take a ball from the runway while another ball is on its way down; this precaution will prevent the possibility of having your fingers smashed between two balls.

Don't try to learn all about bowling in one day.

Don't use too much speed at first.

Don't grip the ball too tight. It is not going to get away from you.

Don't lift or throw the ball; roll it.

Don't swing the ball too often before delivering it. This will cause you to lose all accuracy.

Don't start with a jump; walk one, and run two steps.

Don't deliver the ball with the right foot in front, if you are a right-handed bowler.

Don't step on or over the foul line.

Don't think you can change the course of the ball after it has left your hand.

Don't bend or twist your body, after the ball has been started. "Body English" will not change its course; it only causes amusement.

Don't expect a "strike" every time.

Bowling

Don't throw away a "spare" because you think you were entitled to a "strike."

Don't lose your temper.

The following hints given by a seasoned bowler, W. V. Thompson, are a good summary of style of delivery:

"Of course, any one can learn to bowl. Let all beginners step back from the foul line five steps. Stand erect, face the pins and let the weight of the ball rest on your left hand; take a firm grip with the right hand, swing the ball and see if the grip is all right. Now, don't run, just walk fast four steps, starting with your right foot, and deliver the ball with the left foot in front. Do not bend your arm or your back; keep your feet far apart and bend your knees. Form an imaginary line to the right side of the head pin and bowl on that line. Do not force the ball at first, you will have speed to burn in a week. Get the swing and delivery and you will get the pins."

RULES

The following rules of the game are abridged from the Official Rules as issued by the American Bowling Congress:

The alleys upon which the games are played must be not less than 41, nor more than 42 inches in width. The length from the center of No. 1 pin spot to the foul line is 60 feet. Back of the foul line there must be a clear run of not less than 15 feet. The pin spots must be clearly and distinctly described on or imbedded in the alleys and so placed 12 inches apart from center to center. They are $2\frac{1}{4}$ inches in diameter. The pin spots numbered 7, 8, 9, and 10 are placed 3 inches from the pit edge of the alleys measuring from the edge to the centers of such pin spots.

The pins are spotted on the pin spots placed upon the alleys according to the following diagram, and the pins and spots are known by the numbers as follows:

```
  7       8       9       10
  ●       ●       ●       ●
      4       5       6
      ●       ●       ●
          2       3
          ●       ●
              1
              ●
```

Gutters are placed on either side of the alley, which begin at the foul line and extend parallel to the alleys to the pit. The gutters are from 9 to $9\frac{1}{2}$ inches in width.

The foul line must be clearly and distinctly marked upon or imbedded in the alleys, in dark colored paint, or inlaid with dark colored wood or other material, and must be not more than one inch in width. The foul line, wherever possible, should be extended from the alley surface to and upon the walls of the alleys.

The pins are of the following design and measurements: Fifteen inches in height, $2\frac{1}{4}$ inches in diam-

Bowling

eter at their base, 15 inches in circumference at a point 4½ inches from their base, 11⅝ inches in circumference at a point 7¼ inches from their base, 5¼ inches in circumference at the neck, a point 10 inches from the base; 8 inches in circumference at the head, a point 13½ inches from the base. The taper from point to point shall be gradual so that all lines shall have a graceful curve.

The balls must not in any case exceed twenty-seven (27) inches in circumference, nor exceed sixteen (16) pounds in weight.

Two alleys immediately adjoining each other are used in all games. Each team starts all games on the alley on which it is scheduled. The contesting teams successively and in regular order roll one frame on one alley, and for the next frame alternate and use the other alley, so alternating each frame until the game is completed. Each player rolls two balls in each frame, except where he makes a strike, or when a second strike or spare is made in the tenth frame, or frames rolled thereafter caused by a tie score, when the player must complete each of such frames by rolling a third ball. In all such cases, the frame or frames from the tenth frame and thereafter are completed on the alley on which the first strike or spare is made in each frame, and play is so continued until at the close of even frames one of the teams shall have a greater number of pins than their opponents, which concludes the game.

In delivering the ball the player must not permit any part of his foot, while any portion thereof is in contact with the alleys, to rest or extend on or beyond the foul line, nor shall any part of his person be permitted to come in contact with any part of the alleys beyond the foul line at any time before the delivered ball shall have reached the pins. A ball delivered contrary to the provisions of this rule is a foul ball, and shall be so declared by the umpire immediately such ball so becomes foul.

No count can be made on a foul ball, and any pins which are knocked down or displaced thereby must at once be respotted. A foul ball counts as a ball rolled against the player.

Pins which are knocked down or displaced by a ball which leaves the alley before reaching the pins, or from a ball rebounding from the rear cushions, do not count, and they must be immediately respotted, and the removal or interference with pins by pin boy before they stop rolling shall be cause for umpire to order pins respotted.

Every ball delivered, unless it be declared a dead ball by the umpire, is counted against the player.

Pins which are knocked down by another pin rebounding in the play from the side partition or rear cushion, are counted as pins down, except where pins come in contact with the body, arms or legs of a pin boy and rebound.

Pins which are knocked down or displaced from

any cause, except by a fairly delivered ball, must in all cases be respotted.

Should a player by mistake roll on the wrong alley, or out of his turn, or be interfered with in his play by another bowler or spectator, or should any of the pins at which he is playing be displaced or knocked down in any manner before his delivered ball reaches the pins, or should his ball come in contact with any foreign obstacle on the alleys, then the ball so delivered by him must immediately be called a dead ball by the umpire, and such does not count, but must be immediately rerolled by the player after the cause for declaring such dead ball has been removed.

Pins which are knocked down by a fair ball, and which remain lying on the alley or in the gutters, are termed dead wood, and must be removed before the next ball is rolled. Should a standing pin fall by removing dead wood, such pin or pins must be at once respotted.

A strike is made when the player bowls down the tenpins with his first ball delivered in any frame, and is credited and designated in the score by an "X" in the upper right hand corner of the frame, and the count in such frame is left open until the player shall have rolled his next two balls, when all pins made, counting ten for a strike, are credited therein.

A spare is made when a player bowls down all the

pins with his second ball in any frame, and is credited and and designated with a wedge-shaped mark (') in the upper right hand corner of that frame. The count in such frame is left open until the player rolls his next ball in the succeeding frame, when the number of pins rolled down thereby shall be added to the ten represented by his spare, and the total credited therein.

A break is made in all cases where the player does not secure either a strike or a spare in a frame, and in such cases only the number of pins knocked down are credited in the frame where the break is made. The break must be scored as an error in all cases where the pins left standing after the first ball is rolled do not constitute a split.

HOW TO SCORE

The question which perplexes the beginner in bowling is how to keep the score. This can be easily explained by any experienced player who may be present; but for the benefit of those who are taking up the game for the first time and who have not the benefit of this expert advice, a sample diagram such as the following will be easily understood.

Players.	1	2	3	4	5	6	7	8	9	10

Bowling

The squares marked 1, 2, 3, 4, etc., are called the frames, and ten frames constitute the game. Two balls are allowed to each bowler in each frame and the highest score which can be made in any one frame is 30 points. This is the fact which seems puzzling to the beginner, but may be readily explained by saying that it is possible to score the same shot in three frames.

Should the first ball sent by the bowler knock down the entire ten pins, he is credited with a strike which may be indicated by the cross mark X placed in the upper right hand corner of that frame. He does not bowl his second ball in this frame, but the next time up, if again he makes a strike, another X is placed in the upper right hand corner of frame No. 2. If on the third time up he makes a strike, it is similarly marked in frame No. 3 and a score of 30 goes to his credit in the first frame, while remaining totals are carried forward.

If on the contrary, in any one frame he clears out the entire ten pins with two balls, he is credited with a spare which is marked with a wedge-shaped mark (') in the upper right hand corner of the frame. This means that the first shot in the next frame will count in both frames. Let us suppose that he gets seven on this shot; the total score in the first frame would be 17.

If the player should fail to remove the pins with two balls, it is known as a break and the bowler is

Sports and Games

credited with the actual number of pins knocked down. If he knocks down but seven this would be credited to him in the first frame and if he gets eight more in the two shots of the succeeding frame, the total would be 15, as totals are carried forward throughout the game.

Where two pins are left up in opposite corners of the alley on the first shot, or any equally impossible position, it is customary to mark them with a small figure 0, meaning "split shot," in the upper right hand corner. This does not affect the score, but simply indicates the nature of the play.

The highest score which can be made is 300, which can only be accomplished by making strikes in each of the ten separate frames and thus getting a credit of 30 to the frame. This score, however, is extremely rare, and anything over 200 is considered a high score in ordinary games.

VARIATIONS IN THE GAME OF BOWLING

There are several variations to the standard game of bowling, one of the most popular of which is known as Duck Pins. This is played with balls about the size of croquet balls, and with small pins. The regular height of the duck pins is 9 inches and the balls measure about 4½ inches in diameter. Each player rolls three balls to the frame instead of two. Beyond this all other rules in the standard game govern. The game is played practically the

Bowling

same as the standard game, but on account of the smaller pins and balls it is impossible to get a high score. Anything over 125 is considered a good game.

Another game known as Cocked Hat is played with the head pin and the right and left corner pins.

Still another is called Cocked Hat and Feather where four pins are used.

Another called the Head Pin game depends for its success up hitting the first or head pin at every shot.

Another variation of the game, called Candle-pin, is used with pins 14½ inches high, but very slender.

Each of these games has its own set of rules, which may usually be obtained from the dealers who supply the playing outfits.

CAMPING

CAMPING

CAMPING has come to be recognized as one of the most popular and healthful of outdoor recreations. It is by no means limited to the Boy Scout, or Girl Scout, or even to young people. Entire families now go camping, many of them aided by the useful automobile.

The simplest form of camping trip is the two or three day hike, where the trampers travel light.

HIKING TRIPS FOR BOYS

The following rules based on Boy Scout work will prove valuable to any group of boys or young men out on a hiking or camping trip of only a few days.

When on a hike watch the character of your country carefully and pick out your camping spot long before night. In choosing it, consider what it would be if the weather turned rainy or windy. Find the dryest and most sheltered spot that you can, and one not too far away from your water supply. Choose sloping ground, so that in the event of rainfall, the water will run away from you. And even though you may be pitching camp for only one night, it is well to dig a shallow trench around the uphill side of your camp.

For a two or three days' hike, one can carry a

165

"pup" tent, or one-half of it, since it divides into two parts for easy and light loads. These tents have been used by the Government, and are large enough to provide sleeping quarters for two men. They are not high enough to stand erect in, and are useful only for sleeping.

When no tent is carried, resourceful boys can build lean-to's, which are fairly weather proof, and serviceable for overnight resting. These are constructed by using long poles or timbers such as fence rails, which are stood on end at an angle of about forty-five degrees, and may be further covered with brush, leafy branches, or bark. The open side should be away from the wind, usually looking south, but depending of course upon the lay of the land.

For the lean-to support, select two trees about four or five feet apart, and lash a cross timber about six feet up. If two trees cannot be found conveniently located, drive two stakes into the ground, lash the cross piece across the top, and use this as the main support.

If well-leaved saplings can be found, the lower branches can be cut away from several, and the saplings drawn together. The bunched tops form an excellent shelter. This may be improved and made nearly water tight by leaning poles against the saplings, and thatching with leaves or grass.

For a hiking trip where each boy is carrying his own equipment, his pack should have careful atten-

Camping

tion. It is just as easy to overload as to underload, and where the pack is too heavy or not well balanced upon the shoulders, it can become as grievous a burden as the bundle upon poor Christian's shoulders, in "Pilgrim's Progress." Such a pack should not exceed forty pounds in weight, and if it can be held down to twenty-five pounds, so much the better. The boy should have:

Waterproof sheet, with cord or straps. One-half of a "pup" tent is often used as this outside case.

Wool blankets.

Knife, fork, spoon, skillet, bucket, cup, matches.

Scout knife, and small axe or hatchet.

One flannel or khaki shirt.

Two pairs socks or stockings.

Two handkerchiefs.

Comb, soap, towel, toothbrush.

Some boys carry canteens, but unless the hike is through dry country this is unnecessary.

Food supplies. Carry as little as possible, unless you are plunging at once into the woods or other wild country where small stores or friendly farms are not at hand where fresh supplies can be bought. Buy as you go along, if possible. Carry salt, sugar, pepper, and tea or coffee, perhaps a can or two of beans, some bread or bacon. But study the country you are going into, and if any supplies can be bought within a radius of two or three miles, depend upon your purchases as you go along.

Avoid overloading—that too-common fault of the inexperienced hiker.

Choose easy, comfortable clothing — khaki shirt and trousers for the summer-time, or flannel and corduroys for between-seasons, and stout walking shoes. Puttees are useful for going through rough country. Golf stockings are excellent. For either men or boys short trousers make a better walking rig than the long ones.

For hiking, light woolen underwear is preferable to cotton, as it does not stick to the skin, but permits the free circulation of air and moisture. That is, its loose texture absorbs perspiration, but does not retain it like cotton.

HOW TO PITCH A TENT

First of all, pick your site. It should be level or nearly so, but with the ground sloping away from it. Avoid a hollow or depression, unless you wish to wake up some morning to find your sleeping cot turned into a bath-tub. Do not pitch the tent directly under a large tree. Even though a storm may not come up, in which case the tree attracts lightning, a gust of wind may send some dead branch crashing down on the roof of the tent.

A small clearing with trees all around for shelter and privacy is better than an open field. An easterly or southerly exposure is the best for a camp. The prevailing or storm winds come from the west or north. Set the tent so that the sun will strike it fairly for at least a few hours each day, as this adds cheer and prevents dampness and mildew.

The most common form of tent is the A or wedge-shaped, with the single triangular opening when the flaps are pulled apart. If two trees are conveniently spaced, a rope may be stretched between them which will serve as the ridge poles of the tent. If the trees are not available, cut two stout poles a little higher than the tent, drive them into the ground, and stretch the ridge rope between them. Next peg down the two rear corners of the tent, at the same time drawing the bottom of the rear flap as taut as possible between these two pegs. Then peg down the two front corners, using the same care to draw everything tight. A loose, flapping wall is an abomination. With the four corners secure, the other pegs along the side may be driven in. If either of the poles sags after the weight of the canvas comes against it, it may and should be strengthened by a guy rope.

Next a drain should be dug, and the ground cleared carefully under and around the tent. The ditch should be dug outside and all around the tent, at least four inches deep and with a lead off on its lowest side.

A serviceable tent for two persons (and large enough for three) is the 7½ by 9 feet size, with an inside sod cloth nine inches wide. Some experienced campers substitute for the front supporting pole two cut poles locked together at their tops by crotches in which the ridge pole will rest, and spread at about the angle of the tent front. This leaves the door space entirely open, when the flaps are thrown back, and makes easier draping to keep out the mosquitoes, flies and other pests. In fact, your experienced camper is likely to leave behind all ready-made tent poles and pegs, unless the camping is to be done in a treeless country. A mosquito net for the opening is light, folds up into small space, and is an ever-present help in time of trouble.

"To my notion," says Horace Kephart, "the best all-round size of wall tent for two people, if weight and bulk and cost are of any consequence, is the so-called 9 x 9 or 9 x 12, built with 3½ foot walls, instead of three foot, and 8 foot center, instead of 7½ foot. For four persons a 12 x 14 is commonly used; but a 14 x 14 with four foot walls and a 9 foot center has double the head-room of the standard 12 x 14, and 2½ feet more space between the cots, if these are set lengthwise of the tent, two on a side."

No matter how thick a canvas may be, it will not be entirely rain-proof but will require an additional top or fly. It is a well-known prank of boys to rub the inside surface of the canvas shelter during a rain storm and watch the rain drops trickle through upon the luckless person underneath. Though this inside surface may not be rubbed intentionally, it is hard to avoid rubbing it at times; and wherever this contact occurs, the rain will seep through. An extra shelter or fly prevents this from happening and insures dryer and warmer quarters.

The best weight tent canvases are duck, which comes in standard grades, 8 ounces, 10 ounces, 12 ounces or heavier. The 10 ounce material is a good standard weight.

A word as to color. While a white tent looks very pretty at the outset, it will speedily become discolored and mud spattered. The most serviceable color of all is the olive drab or khaki color.

CAMP SLEEPING

Next comes the all-important question of sleeping accommodations. Let us say at the outset that light cots are preferable, if the camp supplies are hauled in, and not carried.

The U. S. Army used in the recent war a type of cot which folds up into a three-foot space and can be carried on the running-board of a car. Extended it forms a bed about 6½ feet long. This cot can be used in connection with the "pup" tent, for casual camping, or for "regular" camps. It pays to have a comfortable bed, and while on this subject, do not neglect, when making up a cot for the night, to place as much covering under as above you. Straw or leaf mattresses can be easily improvised, by carrying along empty bags; but if these are not available, use blankets beneath as well as above.

An improvised cot may be made by taking two logs heavy enough so they will not roll, set two or more feet apart, and tacking the two ends of a seven-foot strip of canvas tightly at top and bottom.

If no cot is available, here is the recipe for making a comfortable browse bed, from "The Way of the Woods," by Edward Breck:

"Now the truth about browse beds is that, if well made, they are good; nay, more, they are delicious. But a carelessly made one is hard and humpy, and most are of this description, for the reason that the right kind is not made in a few minutes, but in thirty at least. The best is the balsam fir, on account of its delicious and wholesome odor and the resiliency of its boughs. Hemlock and spruce come next in order of fitness. You lay a thick row of fans at the back of the tent, butts toward the door and convex sides up. Stick them in almost perpendicularly and bend them over; the idea is to get springiness. Lay the next row six inches below the first, i.e., thrusting in the butts that distance from those of the first layer. Proceed on this plan until the whole ground is covered with a thick, smooth, springy mattress, paying particular attention to the rows under the hips. Over this bed spread tarpaulins or rubber blankets or ponchos, and lay the blankets or sleeping-bags over all. The trouble with many browse beds is that the evergreen fans are merely strewn over the earth and not thrust into it; they therefore flatten

172

out hard at once. The browse bed will be hard in two or three nights, and must be remade, some of the fans being removed."

Out West a popular covering is the "tarp" or tarpaulin, or cowboy bed sheet, which is a strip of canvas duck about eight feet wide and fifteen feet long. It should be wide enough to tuck in well, and not draw open when lifted by the body. It should be long enough to extend entirely under one, and over, with plenty of room for the feet. And it should be heavy enough to shed water. It is used on the outside, with the blankets between it and the sleeper, who is then snug indeed. The tarp is simple and cheap, and can be easily procured. If a few eyelets are inserted along the edges or in the corners, a first-class sleeping bag can be improvised. Or it can be stretched for an outside flap or shelter tent.

Eastern boys generally prefer a waterproof strip or poncho which can be worn as a raincoat, or used as a carrying case for the pack, and also for the outer cover for the cot at night. In damp weather such a cover keeps the blankets from getting soggy. Wool blankets have a tendency to suck up moisture from the air, which this cover prevents.

Above all things one should avoid having insufficient covering when out on a camping expedition. In the mountains even in midsummer it is liable to turn chilly after dark and the boy who goes around comfortably in the lightest khaki suit or a sleeveless shirt during the day will long for a blanket before midnight has come. We readily recall a dismal experience in the month of July where sufficient bedding was unavailable. There were several light cots without mattresses provided, and we discovered long before night was over that the cold air had a fashion of coming up from underneath quite as readily as from above. Such a cot is only comfortable when provided with a light mattress or heavy blanket of some sort underneath the sleeper.

In chilly weather it has been found of advantage to build a fire against the side of some friendly rock. Build up a good fire and have it ready for a generous log or two by turning-in time. This will reflect back upon the sleeper a large amount of extremely grateful warmth; and while you are building, don't build a stingy fire. Start with small wood but work up to one or two good-sized chunks or small logs. They will hold the fire better and require very little replenishing during the night.

CAMPING EQUIPMENT

We have already mentioned the minimum amount of equipment which is necessary for campers who are going off for only two or three days perhaps afoot. The list given is by no means ideal. It is the smallest amount that can be carried comfortably. The idea is to lighten the camp pack as much as possible.

However, where there is a means of conveyance

Camping

by all means plan comfortably for your camping trip. Says one experienced camper: "The man who prefers to go into the woods with one blanket, the clothes he has on, and the provisions he can carry on his back, two cooking and eating utensils, a piece of fish-line, and his rifle and axe, in order to 'match himself against the forces of nature,' and win from her by his woodsmanship a comfortable existence, is justified in his undertaking and plays a fascinating though arduous game. But he will have little time for anything but the scratching for food, fire and shelter. Most campers are not out for this purpose, but to breathe the pure air, to hunt, to fish, to botanize, collect, photograph, to paddle, to walk, to see the country."

Stewart Edward White writes in the same vein in his "Camp and Trail" regarding the man who makes it a creed to do without as many things as possible while off on a camping trip. "We all know the type," says Mr. White. "He professes an inordinate scorn for comforts of all sorts. If you are out with him you soon discover that he has a vast pride in being able to sleep on cobblestones—and does so at the edge of yellow pines, with their long needles. He eats badly cooked food. He stands—or perhaps I should say poses—indifferent to the downpour when everyone else has sought shelter. In a cold climate he brings a single thin blanket. His slogan seems to be: 'This is good enough for me' with the unspoken conclusion, 'if it isn't good enough for you fellows, you're pretty soft.' "

And the queer part of it is, that such a man usually manages to bully the other campers into his point of view! They accept his uncomfortable camp because they are ashamed to admit that they are less tough than he is. Back in town they are embarrassed when with a superior laugh he tells the company how you brought with you a little pillow-case to fill with leaves. "Bootleg is good enough for me," he cries; and everyone marvels at his woodsmanship.

As a plain matter of fact, Mr. White points out, this man is the worse of two types of tenderfoot. The greenhorn does not know better; but this man should. He has utterly mistaken the problem of the wilderness. The wild life is not to test how much the human frame can endure, although that often enough happens, but to test how well the human wits, backed by an enduring body, can answer the question of comfort. "Comfort means minimum equipment; comfort means bodily ease. The task is to balance, to reconcile these apparently opposing ideas."

Above all things, choose your wearing apparel as a matter of care. Many experienced campers prefer light woolen underwear to any other for outdoor trips. They say that it can be washed more easily, and in general keeps the skin in healthier condition. The best way to prevent such garments from shrink-

CAMPING

A typical camp scene in the White Mountains.

Camping

ing is to soak them in lukewarm suds, squeeze out without wringing, rinse in cold water, squeeze out again, and hang up where the wind can strike the material. To be on the safe side it is well to buy such garments oversize.

Many persons, however, do not wear woolen underwear summer or winter. For them a light short-legged, "athletic" style is the safest, as it does not hamper the movements of the arms or legs.

CARE OF THE FEET

Many authorities, including military officers, urge the use of woolen socks for hiking. For forest travel, regardless of season, choose woolen socks, thick enough to cushion the feet and absorb moisture, and not too closely knit. In hot weather and on smoother trails cotton is better, because wool "draws" the feet at such times. On an all-day hike it pays to change to a fresh pair at noon. Be careful as to the fit. If too loose, your socks will wrinkle and chafe the feet; if too small, they speedily become unendurable. To prevent woolen socks from shrinking, every night, or every time you come in with wet feet, remove your socks, bathe the feet in cold water, put on fresh ones, and put the socks you have worn to soak in a running stream. Draw them through the hand (do not wring) to squeeze out water, and hang up to dry.

The Plattsburg Manual contains the following sound advice to hikers and campers:

"The feet are your means of transportation. If you care for them properly, you will be rewarded.

"1. Wash and dry the feet carefully and put on clean socks as soon as practicable after getting into camp.

"2. Wash out the socks you have been wearing and hang them out to dry.

"3. Do not wear socks with holes in them if you can possibly avoid it. Should a hole begin to cause rubbing, turn the sock inside out or change it to the other foot.

"4. Just as soon as you decide to go into camp, cut your toe nails square across the ends so they will not grow in.

"5. In case of any foot trouble that you cannot relieve, get treatment at once. Don't wait until you cannot hike before reporting.

"6. A treatment for blisters. Be careful not to tear off the skin covering the blister. Heat the point of a needle until it is red hot, and when it cools insert it under the live skin a little distance away from the blister. Push it through to the under side of the bruised skin or blister and then press out the water. To protect the blister, grease a small piece of chamois with vaseline and place it so that it covers the blister and extends over the solid skin surrounding it. Then place a piece of oxide adhesive tape over the chamois. This method allows the protective covering to be removed without rupturing the

Camping

skin over the blister, and protects the new tender and sensitive skin so that the weight can be rested upon the foot without causing severe pain. One man should be provided with a needle, adhesive tape, a bottle of vaseline, and a piece of chamois for the common use.

"7. Shoes. (a) Be sure they fit your feet. The regular shoe you wear at school won't do for hiking when, with the additional weight you carry, your foot spreads in breadth and extends in length; hence your hiking shoes should be longer and broader than your regular shoes. This is a very important item and should not be neglected. If your shoes are too large, blisters will result; if too small, your feet will be cramped, and every step will be painful.

"b. Break your shoes in prior to wearing on a hike.

"c. Keep your shoes well oiled, so they will be soft and pliable and keep out water.

"d. If your shoes get wet on the inside, heat some small pebbles (not so hot as to burn leather) and keep them inside the shoes until dry."

PERMANENT CAMP OUTFIT

Your tent supplies should include:
One tent, size indicated in preceding pages.
One fly for same.
One 10 x 12 awning to serve as a shelter for

kitchen or dining room. This will be valuable in wet weather.

Five yards mosquito netting.

One strong clothes line.

Ball of smaller twine.

Spool of packing thread.

Axe, hatchet, small saw, and spade.

Pound or two of assorted nails and screws.

Small mirror.

Waterproof match box.

Soap, pan, and towels.

Toilet paper.

Ready repair kit for sewing on buttons and patches.

Small medicine kit including camphor, peroxide of hydrogen, arnica, vaseline, ammonia, iodine, surgeon's plaster, binding tape, small pair of scissors, etc.

One or two good lanterns and an electric flashlight, also some candles are important. Don't depend on flashlights alone, as they are liable to burn out, although they are excellent for special use. A good lantern hung on a convenient nail in the tent is the best light of all for such purposes.

A small Dutch oven for use in baking is desirable. This can be mounted over a one or two burner stove, using either kerosene or gasoline vapor. Such a stove is invaluable in wet weather or where any in-

Camping

door cooking is desirable. If too bulky, use a collapsible "baker" before an open fire.

Your supplies for the kitchen should include:

Riveted coffee pot
Skillet
Saucepan
Kettle
Bucket (canvas)
Griddle
Small basket
Butcher's knife
Large spoons
Ladle
Small jars for grease, lard, butter, etc.
Salt and pepper casters
Dishpan and dish cloths

In addition to kitchen supplies, there should be an adequate number of plain but serviceable knives, forks, spoons, plates, cups and saucers. It is a mistake to rough it too much and deny one's self such ordinary conveniences. Such cutlery can be purchased at any ten-cent store and adds greatly to the enjoyment of one's meals.

Don't try to eat off the ground or some convenient stump or log. That may be all right for a meal or two, but is back-breaking and inconvenient both to the diner and the overworked cook. An ordinary folding card table or sewing table makes an excellent camper's table, if supplies are hauled in. It takes up very little room on the running-board of a car and can be folded up and set out of the way when not in use.

Where campers are going to stop at one place for some days or weeks, they can readily make a table by bringing with them or obtaining three or four smooth white planks which can be fastened by cleats to convenient trees. Boxes can easily be turned into comfortable seats, and if a degree of further comfort is agreeable, folding camp stools can easily be brought along. A package of paper napkins is also of value not only for use at the table but afterwards in wiping the plates, etc., after which the napkins may be burned.

CLEANLINESS IN CAMP

Don't allow trash or litter of any sort to remain lying around the camp; it is both unsightly and unsanitary. After each meal see that all of the dishes, cooking utensils, etc., are properly cleaned and put back in their proper places. This seems like a useless caution; and yet we have seen more than one camp come to grief for lack of these simple observances. A dish or a pan can be easily washed soon after being used, but having been allowed to stand for several hours with the grease or particles of food sticking on it, its cleaning may prove a very difficult matter.

Usually in a camp of this sort the duties of the

Camping

different members of the camp are well defined. For instance, one cooks the meal, another serves it, another cuts the fire-wood and brings the water, while a fourth washes up the pans and dishes afterwards. If they work in pairs it goes that much the easier, but at the outset if such duties are well understood and members shifted about from day to day, there are no hard feelings and the work gets properly done. No camper wishes to be a quitter or shirker. A quitter would not last long in any self-respecting camp, but often things get neglected because some fellow thinks it is not his job. The choice of a camp leader often avoids any such misunderstandings, but failing in some one definite leader, the camp duties should be carefully parceled out from day to day.

In the morning, for instance, there are many little camp duties to perform. The fire must be replenished, water brought, the table set for breakfast and the latter cooked and afterwards cleared away. Cots or beds should be made up and the camp in general tidied up before any of the other activities of the day are indulged in.

In washing dishes, first scrape off the grease or other food particles from dishes, knives and forks and have them as clean as possible before putting into the water. Have a kettle of boiling water and dissolve some soap in it. Some campers wash dishes by quickly dipping them into hot suds, then rinsing in another pan and handing to the man who is to wipe them. Such an operation proceeds very quickly as the suds cut off all the grease and the rinsing water cleans off the suds, leaving the dish ready to dry properly. Where very hot water is used sometimes such dishes are stacked up on end and allowed to dry for themselves. Knives, forks and spoons, however, should be wiped, as they are liable to rust if put away damp.

Any refuse from the table should either be burned or carried some distance away from the camp and buried. If a camp is to be pitched for some days a small pit can be dug into which such refuse can be thrown, but sand or dirt should be thrown into it from time to time to prevent odors and the breeding of insect pests.

WATER SUPPLY

The ideal spot for a camp is one near running water. To have plenty of water available for all purposes adds to the comfort and health of the camp. Not all running water from open streams, however, is desirable for drinking water. If you are not sure of the sources of your stream or its cleanliness it is best not to use such water except when boiled. Spring water is all right in its raw state but stream water is liable to contain in solution all sorts of impurities. A swiftly flowing stream is more liable to have such impurities than a slower current. If you can explore your stream for a mile or so above your camp and find it pure from that distance, you may safely trust it. Lake water is usually safe. A good way to strain such water is to dig a hole in the ground a few feet away from the rim of the lake. The water from the lake will then seep through and fill up the hole and such water will be filtered by passing through the soil in this manner.

If your water is roily or looks impure in other ways but is the only water available, you can boil it in a large vessel for some minutes over a hot fire, at the same time stirring in a bit of charcoal or other charred wood. The charcoal tends to remove any odor from the water. If any scum rises to the surface, this can be removed, the water drained and boiled again. Such an operation should make almost any water palatable.

FOOD

We have previously spoken about the needs of living comfortably while at camp. This remark applies especially to camp food. In an outdoor camp where one is constantly active and exposed to the elements an ordinary human being can eat about a third more than he can in town. Provide fully for such needs and at the same time plan a well-balanced ration. Says Mr. Kephart: "Variety is quite as welcome at the camp-board as anywhere else—in fact, more so, for it is harder to get. Variety need not mean adding to the load. It means substituting say three 5-lb. parcels for one 15-lb. parcel so as to have something different from day to day." We have all met old-time campers who affect to scorn such things. "We take nothing with us," they say, "but pork, flour, baking powder, salt, sugar and coffee—our guns and rods furnish us variety." This sounds experienced, but there is a good deal of humbug in it. A spell of bad weather may defeat the best of hunters and fishermen. Even granting that luck is good, your kill is likely to be of one kind at a time. With only the six articles named, nobody can serve game in a variety of ways, or provide much variety for the board.

Figure it out for yourself. How would you like to sit down to ham and eggs three times a day? Ham and eggs—and then more ham and eggs—and if you tire of that, try bacon and sop your bread in the grease. Now it is just the same with trout or bass as it is with pork; the same with pheasant or duck, rabbit or squirrel, venison or bear. Go, then, prepared to lend variety to your menu. Food that palls is bad food—worse in camp than anywhere else, for you've got to eat it, or go hungry.

There are two kinds of food which should be found in every camp list—staples and luxuries.

The *staples* will include flour, corn meal, baking powder, salt, sugar, pepper, lard, tea, coffee, butter, cocoa, and milk (the last named can be provided in cans or powdered form in a very suitable fashion).

Camping

Prepared pancake flour, which can readily be made up into toothsome breakfast dishes, may be added, as well as oatmeal, rice, beans, peas, eggs, vegetables, fresh or dried, bacon, and canned meats and soups. Many soups and vegetables are obtainable in powdered form.

Luxuries.—To the above list may be added fresh fruits, whenever obtainable, lemons, oranges, molasses, syrup, marmalade, preserves, canned fruits, cheese, raisins, and the like. It is usually easier to think of the luxuries for a camp than it is to include all of the necessities. Be very sure that your list of staples includes enough so that in any emergency a well-balanced meal can be provided. Some packages of assorted cookies also come in handy, and bread should be either provided or baked. It is easier, however, to buy bread, that is, if a farmhouse or store is within hailing distance, than it is to try to bake it. Whenever possible, lay in a supply of fresh vegetables, as they not only add to the enjoyment of the meal but to the health of all of the campers. Canned meats, such as sardines, tongue, tuna fish, salmon and beef are good in an emergency, but are not good as a steady diet. Fresh meat should be provided wherever and whenever possible.

MOTOR CAMPING

A species of outdoor trip that has become increasingly popular in the last few years is that of motor camping. Motorists now travel across the country in increasing numbers, stopping from place to place as fancy dictates, and superior to the blandishments of hotels, both small and large. Among the advantages of this mode of travel is that the motorist is not schedule bound, he does not have to engage rooms in advance, and his expenses are greatly reduced. Furthermore, this is a thoroughly healthful and pleasurable way of spending one's outing.

Some motorists, especially in the West, provide themselves with a trailer or cart which is pulled along behind the automobile. These carts are so arranged that they can very quickly be transformed into sleeping quarters for the night; likewise providing abundant space to carry camping supplies. They have not become widely popular, however, because they do not make for easy traveling. The cart lumbering along behind retards the speed and is very clumsy, but some motorists will put up with these inconveniences for the sake of having more room in their car and greater comfort out on the road. A form of tent for automobiles which has proven popular is a species of half tent which fastens directly to the side of the automobile and slopes away from it, thus providing a room about 7 x 9 feet for sleeping quarters. Such tents roll up into small compass and they have no poles or paraphernalia to add to the weight or bulk.

We know of one motorist who contrived such a

tent with many little conveniences. He rigged up a "trouble" light connected with his battery and suspended from the top of the tent in such a way as to illuminate the whole interior. Two folding military cots were also carried along. These cots, as previously described, fold into a space of about 3 feet but when extended form a substantial cot about 6½ feet long. All of the camp supplies were carried in two racks constructed upon the running-boards of the car. These were covered with black oil cloth when in place, so they did not present an unsightly appearance.

Sometimes cots are fastened to one end of the running-board of the car and extend outwardly at right angles to it. This method of rigging up cots requires but one set of legs, at the lower end.

Strange to say, the automobile manufacturers have not as yet awakened to the possibilities of so constructing the interior of a touring car that it can readily be transformed into a sleeping car. If the front seats were hinged in the back so they would drop, something like the seats in a railway sleeping car, such a bed could readily be constructed. In fact, the writer has seen such a touring car provided with space for two very comfortable beds through the ingenuity of the owner, who was himself a mechanic.

To carry a separate type of tent has some advantages, as tourists camping at a place for two or three days often wish to use their cars for short trips; and if the tent is attached to it, this requires extra work every time such a trip is made.

Towns and cities all over the country are realizing the fact that the automobile camper has come to stay. They are providing campers' accommodations and in other ways making it attractive for motorists to stop in their midst. Such camping spots are provided just outside the town itself. There are open cook stoves provided, also running water, fire-wood and sometimes shelter. Frequently, a small general supply store as well as garage adjoins the grounds, and the motorist can obtain all needed supplies right at his own door, so to speak. Such camping sites are not only convenient for the motorists; they have also proved profitable to the town. The community that gets a name for hospitality will be stopped off at longer and patronized more freely by the appreciative camper. The little group of motorists drawn thus from the ends of the country frequently strike up pleasant friendships and have a good time socially while stopping in the same locality. It is not an unusual thing for a man to spend the summer on the road with his family, and coast-to-coast trips are by no means unusual. As our roads become better and such camping accommodations more general, this species of camping should prove to be one of the most popular of all outdoor sports.

CRICKET

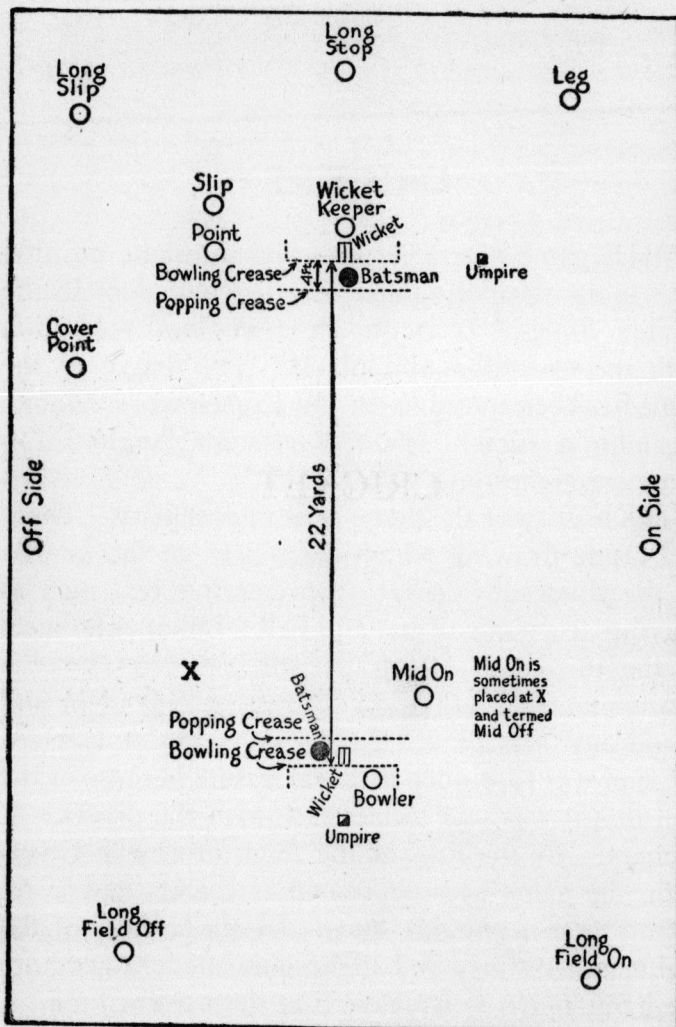

Long
Stop

Long
Slip

Leg

Slip

Wicket
Keeper

Point

Wicket

Bowling Crease ← 4ft ↑ ● Batsman   Umpire
Popping Crease ←

Cover
Point

Off Side

22 Yards

On Side

X   Batsman   Mid On   Mid On is
sometimes
placed at X
and termed
Mid Off

Popping Crease
Bowling Crease ← ● 🔲

Wicket   Bowler

Umpire

Long
Field Off

Long
Field On

192

CRICKET

THE game of cricket occupies the same position in sports in England that baseball does in the United States. It is the chief outdoor recreation with the exception of football. The origin of the name has been traced to the old French word *criquet,* meaning a stick. There is also an Anglo-Saxon name *crice,* meaning a staff.

The history of the game rests in obscurity. There is a crude drawing which dates back to the middle of the thirteenth century representing two men as playing at a game of bat and ball. Other references in the thirteenth and fourteenth centuries show a similar game. A pastime known as "Hand in and Hand out" was played during the reign of Edward IV, and was forbidden by royal statute because of the fact that it was said to interfere with the practice of archery. By the time of the reign of Queen Elizabeth, the game became known as cricket and is referred to as a popular sport. By the middle of the eighteenth century it had become modernized into the game much as we have it at the present time.

There are numerous cricket clubs scattered over England today, some of which date back for an uninterrupted history of upwards of a century. The London Club, in 1774, drew up laws regulating the game which are the oldest extant. While these have been amended somewhat during the succeeding years, the rules remain substantially the same.

While the game is played in a few scattered sections in this country, it is still a rarity or unknown to most American outdoorsmen.

IMPLEMENTS OF THE GAME

The cricketer requires, first of all, a bat preferably made of English willow. The length of the bat is now restricted to 38 inches (36 inches being the length most in favor) of which the handle is 14 inches and the blade the remainder. There is no law governing the weight of the bat but it varies between 2 and 4 pounds, the ideal weight being about 2½ pounds. It is usually made of willow, with a cane handle, and has a broad, flat surface, into which strips of rubber are inserted to give it driving power.

The cricket ball is made of cork and covered with leather, making an extremely light missile. It should measure not less than 9 inches nor more than 9¼ inches in circumference, and should weigh between 5½ and 5¾ ounces.

The wicket toward which the ball is driven comprises three upright pieces of wood of equal thickness and 27 inches high. On the top are placed two "bails" or short pieces of wood which fit into grooves

Cricket

made in the top of the uprights so as not to project more than one-half inch above them. These uprights, which are also called "stumps," form a wicket 8 inches wide. At the other end of the field 22 yards distant is placed another wicket.

Lines are marked at each wicket and at right angles to the line of play, which are known respectively as "popping creases" and "bowling creases." The batsmen stand between these creases when striking at the ball.

HOW TO PLAY THE GAME

A succinct description of cricket is given by the "English dictionary," which defines it as "an open-air game played with bats, ball and wickets by two sides of eleven players each; the batsman defends his wicket against the ball which is bowled by a player of the opposing side, the other players of this side being stationed about the field in order to catch or stop the ball."

The progress of the game is indicated by runs, as in our game of baseball, and the side which scores the greatest number of runs wins the match. Each team is allowed two innings taken alternately, except that the team which obtains a lead of 150 runs in a three days' match or a 100 runs in a two days' match, or 75 runs in a one day match, acquires the right to make the other side call a "follow their innings."

In playing, one side sends its men in regular order

to bat, while the other side is scattered in the field, as in baseball—but there the resemblance ends. There are playing positions, but no bases; and there are two batsmen up at once, one defending each wicket.

It is the object of the batsman either to stop the ball sent by the bowler and thus prevent it from striking the wicket, or to bat it out into the field. If he bats it, he may attempt to exchange wickets with the other batsman, while the ball is being fielded. If he does so successfully, he is credited with a run. He stays at bat until put out.

When 10 out of the 11 men constituting a side are put out, it completes an inning. The game usually continues two innings, and the side netting the most runs wins the victory.

The 11 positions in the field are as follows: bowler, wicket-keeper, long-stop, slip, point, cover-slip, cover-point, mid-off, long-leg, square-leg, and mid-on.

The wickets are placed opposite and parallel to each other, at a distance of 22 yards, as before stated. A "bowling crease" is marked with whitewash on the turf on a line with the uprights, and 8 feet, 8 inches in length. "Return creases" are marked on right angles at each end of these lines. A "popping crease" is placed four feet in advance of the wicket and parallel with it; this being a line of varying length.

Cricket

The game is begun by the captains of the opposing sides tossing up for choice of innings. The captain obtaining the winning toss generally sends his own team in to the wicket to bat first. He places one batsman at each wicket. When an "over" has been bowled, the batsman at the opposite wicket then attempts an over in his turn. At the end of every such over the fielders change position in order to intercept the batting from the other end. A "run" is made when the two batsmen at opposite wickets exchange places by running from their ends of the far wicket without being "run out" by one of the fielders. The aim of the side which is at bat is to make as many runs as possible, while the opposing side in the field endeavor to intercept their plays.

According to the official playing rules, there are nine ways in which the batsman can be put out. (1) The striker is "bowled" out if the bowler hits the wicket with the ball, when bowling, and dislodges the bail; (2) he is "caught" out if the ball after touching his bat or hand be held by any member of the fielding side before it touches the ground; (3) he is "stumped" out if the wicket-keeper dislodges the bail with the ball, or with his hand holding the ball, at a moment when the striker in playing at the ball has no part of his person or bat in contact with the ground behind the popping crease, i.e., when the batsman is "out of his ground"; (4) he is out "l. b. w." (leg before wicket) if he stops with any part of his person other than his hand, or arm below the elbow, a ball which in the umpire's judgment pitched straight between the wickets and would have bowled the striker's wicket; (5) if when the batsmen are attempting to make a run a wicket is put down (i.e., the bail dislodged) by the ball, or by the hand of any fieldsman holding the ball, at a moment when neither batsman has any part of his person or bat on the ground behind the popping crease, the nearer of the two batsmen to the wicket so put down is "run out." The remaining four ways in which a batsman may be dismissed are (6) hit wicket, (7) handling the ball, (8) hitting the ball more than once "with intent to score," and (9) obstructing the field.

HOW TO BOWL

The art of bowling is brought to perfection only by untiring practice. To become a successful bowler, one should commence when young, as it requires steady practice, patience, determination and strength. Of course a beginner must have a good eye and a love for the game, or he will never make a bowler. Some men become natural bowlers with little practice, while others must practice continually.

There are a few things that a learner should acquire, which are: First, hold the ball correctly with the finger tips on the seam, as a better grip can be obtained, which will assist greatly in giving a twist to the ball—not in the hollow of the hand. Take a short run of five or six yards before delivering the ball. Practice to deliver the ball on either side of the wicket. Do not bowl hurriedly (unnecessary haste destroys pitch and directness). All this is of importance to young bowlers, and should be remembered.

It is best for a young bowler to start in by bowling a slow or medium pace ball. The art of varying the speed and length of the pitch by dropping the ball shorter and shorter to a driving batsman, and pitching up closer and closer to a man who habitually plays back, has to be acquired, as is also the twist or bias which gives the ball such "life" after it touches the ground.

The young bowler must practice untiringly until he can pitch any length he desires, and gain command of the ball. (To do this I would suggest bowling at an undefended wicket until one has sufficient confidence and command to bowl at a batsman in front of the wicket.)

Wear spiked shoes in bowling, not rubber-soled tennis shoes; the spikes give a solid footing, and allow the bowler a better command of the ball.

It is useless to bowl so short that a ball falling from the pitch when it reaches the batsman can be cut or pulled at will, even if the ball is on the wicket, or so full that he can play into it and drive it away with ease. Lengths and changes of pace should be

well practiced. Study the style of play of the batsman to whom you are bowling, whether he is strong
or weak in his forward or back play, and bowl accordingly. If he is batting carefully and playing all
good length balls delivered him, bowl for catches, or
tempting balls for him to hit at, especially good
length "off" balls, which if touched are very apt to
give catches in the slips.

There are two deliveries, a high and a straight
arm. Both have their advantages, and it is well for
a bowler to practice to command both.

Good temper is more essential to a bowler than to
any other player in a game, for the best bowling
will be hit about, catches will be missed, and often
a sticking batsman will tire you out by blocking away
for an hour, contenting himself with making a half-
dozen runs. Let this not bother you, but when you
find you are losing "snap" or command of your bowling, make a change.

Position. When the batsman takes his place at
the bat he should be in an easy, natural position.
Suit yourself whether your heels are together or
three or four inches apart. Take guard from the
other side of the wicket from which the bowler delivers the ball. It is best to take middle, but if you
find you are likely to get your legs before the wicket
in the act of playing the ball, take the middle and
leg for guard. The safest place for your block hole
is three inches from the popping crease, and stand

Wide World Photos

CRICKET

A game at Bermuda, between a local team and one from Philadelphia.

with one foot just inside of the same crease and about four inches away from your block hole.

Play. As the bowler starts to bowl, rise slightly. Make your position easy, and do not allow yourself to be "tied-up" or stiff, but when you play or hit at the ball do so with freedom of arms and body. The best way to hold your bat is to have your hands half-way between the bat's shoulder and end of handle, with the hands two inches apart. Let the right foot act as a pivot in the forward play, forward cut, leg hit and leg poke. Always wear leg guards and gloves while batting.

Forward and Back Play. First learn to defend your wicket from the ball by steady and patient play. Your hitting powers will come afterward.

The Forward Play. It is only by patient practice that a batsman can master this play (and it is one of the most important). In playing forward, do so with the left elbow out from the body, as well as forward, getting over the ball. If this is not done you are very apt to play with a cross bat. Look out that the bowler doesn't draw you forward on a short pitch ball, which is very likely to result in a catch if it touches your bat; or cause you to be stumped if you should miss it, and have your foot outside the crease. See that you reach well on to the pitch of the ball, which will kill a shooter or block a ball that twists to the leg or off stump.

The Backward Play. In playing backward, judgment must be used in selecting the proper length ball to play. Do not allow the bowler to drive you back on a ball well pitched up that should be hit. If such a ball should shoot or hug the ground, the chances are it will bowl you. This play is generally made by moving the right foot backward twelve or eighteen inches from its stationary position, balancing well on that foot. In making the play, keep the left elbow well out from the body, and don't draw away from the ball. This will cause you to play with a cross bat.

The Cut. The cut is one of the most difficult hits to make, and can only be made when a ball rises a little wide of the off bail. Care must be taken to time the ball, and not hit too soon or too late, or the result will be a catch in the slips. When you see the ball about to rise, draw the right foot backward and across the wicket. In hitting at the ball make as late a stroke as possible, coming down on top of the ball from well over the shoulder. The hit is most successfully made by not trying to put all your power in the stroke, but by giving the ball a slight hit or touch, using freedom of the wrist (very much like snapping a whip).

The Forward Cut. The forward cut is made by placing the left foot forward and across the wicket, keeping the right foot stationary. The stroke is made from a short pitched ball, hit hard forward of point, and kept well on the ground.

Cricket

The Leg Hit. The leg hit is made by placing the left leg well forward in the direction from which the ball is coming, and hitting across at it hard with a swing of the bat from the shoulder. Be sure the ball is well off the leg wicket to prevent your being out leg before the wicket, should it hit your leg, and if not hit by the bat or does not touch the leg passing back of you and clear the wicket.

The Leg Poke. The leg poke is a very useful and effective hit against swift bowling. It is made off a ball that is bowled on the legs, and instead of being hit at, is gently touched with the bat and sent behind the batsman for one or two runs. In making the play the bat should be placed forward of the left leg.

Caught Out. If any fielder catches the ball direct from the striker's bat or hand before it touches the ground, he is caught out.

Run Out. If the batsman, in making a run, fails to reach his ground before the wicket to which he is running is put down with the ball by a fielder, he is run out.

Leg Before Wicket. If the batsman stops with his leg or other part of his body a bowled ball whose course, in the opinion of the umpire, is in a line with the wickets, and if not so stopped, would have taken the wicket, the play is called leg before wicket.

At every ball bowled, therefore, the batsman must guard against all these dangers, and avoiding leg before wicket, play the ball so that it will not strike the wicket and can not be caught. Having hit it away, he can make a run, or runs, if he can reach the goal before the ball is returned by the fielders and the wicket to which he is running is put down.

HOW TO FIELD

Fielding is a very important part of cricket, somewhat different from baseball in the handling of the ball, and good or bad fielding goes a great way toward losing or winning a match; although looked upon by a large number of cricketers as of little importance. They insist upon batting. How often one can save runs in the field when he is unfortunate in not making them off the bat. How discouraging it is to a bowler to have catches missed off his bowling. Bowlers should have the assistance of fielders to be successful. They can not be expected to bowl all the wickets down.

The fielding points shown us by English teams that recently visited this country should be a good lesson to cricketers on this side of the water. It was very noticeable how sure and well they stopped a ball, taking advantage of either hand, using one hand oftener than two; but this I would not encourage. They were generally sure catches, backed up the wicket keeper and bowler with judgment, and were very accurate on their returns or throws to the wicket.

Cricket

The most important positions on the cricket field are point, slips and mid-wickets. A fielder to fill these positions must be active, a sure catch, and always on the alert. The wicket-keeper's position should not be forgotten, as it is a very important one. There is one thing a fielder should always have in mind; that is, to expect every ball bowled to come to him when hit. He is then prepared to field it, but it is too often the case with cricket fielders that they are caught napping and have to be waked up by the captain or a ball hit their way. It is proper that every fielder should watch the game and notice his captain's or bowler's signs or word, and obey instantly, as he is the responsible one for placing you in the different positions on the field.

In catching a high-hit ball near the wicket get well under it as it is falling, holding your hands to receive it above the face, and let them give with the ball as it touches the hands. Hold it firmly, as balls so hit invariably descend with an awkward twist, and a "muffed fly" will be the consequence if at all careless.

A long-hit ball to the outfield which has seldom any twist imparted to it by the bat, is more easily held by the catcher. Considerable practice is required to judge the ball from the moment it leaves the bat, and it is this instinctive faculty that makes an outfielder valuable in proportion to his ability in this respect. Such a player can cover more ground

Sports and Games

in less time and with a greater certainty of holding the ball, than a player who is slower in judging, although a much faster runner.

To handle a low-hit or ground ball, get in front of it, and the moment before it reaches you, place your heels together, hold your hands apart about knee high, watch the ball closely, and with a quick movement bring your hands together in front of the ball. Should it shoot or pass under your hands it will be stopped by your feet; should it bound, your hands will meet it. Practice the above movements on a smooth piece of ground, at first slowly, improving the speed as you gain confidence. Don't rush in on a hard-hit ball, or wait for a slow hit to reach you.

To stop a ball with one hand while running sidewise to head it off, use care to place your foot behind your hand, so if you are late in getting your hand down, the ball will be stopped by your foot, as it is difficult to stop a ground ball with one hand when under full headway.

Throwing the Ball. Get the ball in proper position in your hand, between the thumb and two fingers, and throw with the hand well out from the shoulder and no higher than your head. Always aim to throw the ball so it can be handled breast high (at a short distance) and on the single bound to the top of the wicket from cover point, long slip or the outfield.

Cricket

Fielders should not forget to back up the bowler or wicket-keeper on a ball thrown in by a fielder, standing six to eight feet behind him. All fielders should have their shoes well spiked, as a slip of the foot is often the cause of a miss catch, a ground ball, or a poor return to the wicket, thereby losing the chance of a run out.

CROQUET

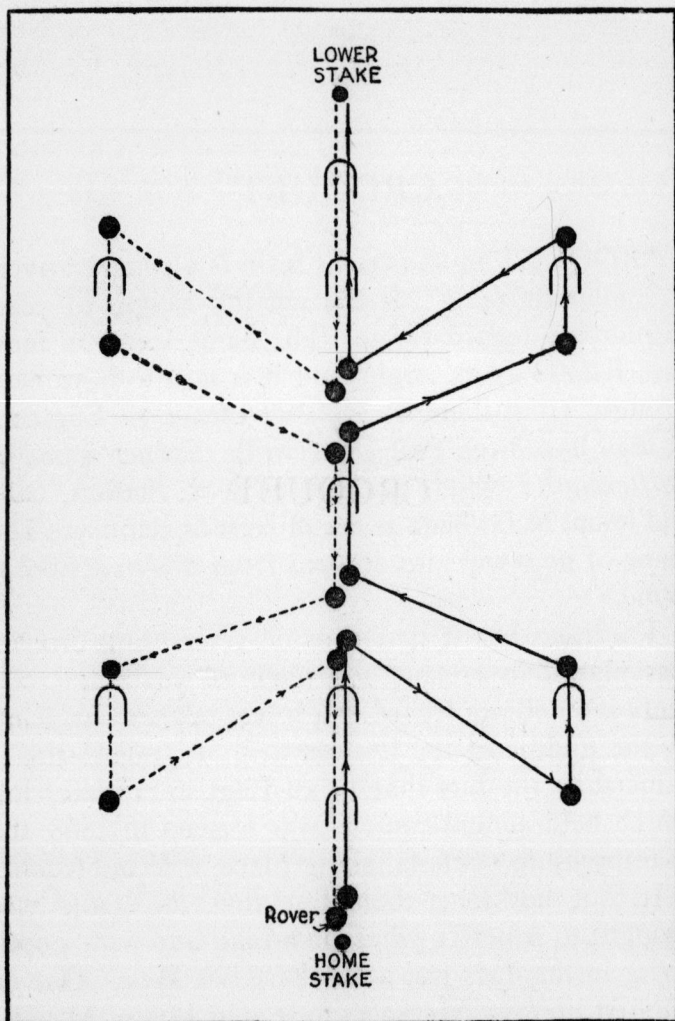

LOWER
STAKE

Rover

HOME
STAKE

CROQUET

CROQUET in its present form is a comparatively modern game. It has not the weight of years to increase regard for it. The name seems to indicate France as its origin, and it is said to have been brought from there to Ireland, thence to England. It may have been evolved from the French game of *paille-maille* which was played with mallets, balls and hoops as far back as the thirteenth century. The game of polo was also derived from this or a similar game.

Tradition has it that a game resembling croquet was played in Ireland one hundred years ago, and there is a definite record that it was taken to England by the middle of the last century. Its popularity is evinced by the fact that an all-English croquet club which held annual contests was formed in 1868, the championship contests taking place at Wimbledon.

It was not long thereafter that the game was brought to America where it sprang into wide popularity in the days just after the Civil War. One of the first literary references to it is in Louisa M. Allcott's *Little Women*. By the year 1890 it had attained wide vogue, and big public contests were held in Boston, Brooklyn and elsewhere. These were on carefully sanded grounds, and the game thus played differed in many essentials from the amateur sport which was a sort of go-as-you-please affair on any grassy plot or back lawn. With the coming of tennis and golf, croquet languished and is now played comparatively little.

One thing in its favor is that croquet needs no special dress. It can be played on the spur of the moment by persons of almost any age and of either sex and without any special preparation with regard to costume. The absence of excessive physical exertion is suited to those who would, if compelled to change suits, take no exercise at all, and they can return to business or any avocation after an hour of croquet with linen and clothes none the worse for their effort, and with an exhilaration that all outdoor exercises invariably secure. It is especially adapted to sedentary persons and those in mature life, to whom the vigorous roughness of baseball and the lively skirmishing of lawn tennis would be anything but a pleasure.

When played on a sanded surface or on a short firm sod, croquet is as scientific as billiards. There is a greater field (literally as well as otherwise) for strategy, the exercise of deliberate judgment, nerve, coolness and boldness of play in croquet than in billiards, much as some may question the truthfulness of the assertion. The eye and the hand become

Croquet

trained. Lawn tennis calls for muscular action in immediate response to counterplay. Judgment must be instantaneous and muscular movements rapid and fatiguing. Croquet stands in strong contrast with its deliberate strokes, its moderate exercise and non-fatiguing efforts even when prolonged. It is richly deserving of increased interest.

The high degree of skill made possible by the introduction of narrow arches, hard rubber balls, and heavy mallets, prevents the game from being regarded as fit only for children and elderly persons.

IMPLEMENTS USED IN THE GAME

Complete croquet sets can be purchased in any sporting goods shop and in many other general stores. It is not well, however, to purchase a cheap set, as the balls are of light-weight wood, easily chipped or cracked, and the mallets more like toys than real playing tools. A wide latitude is allowed in the choice of balls and mallets and in the width and distance of wickets.

First of all, one should have a level piece of ground either with sanded surface or with smooth, closely-cropped grass. It should be about 60 by 30 feet, although 50 feet by 25 will serve. The larger-size playing field with narrow wickets naturally conduces to a stiffer game.

Two stakes or posts are set up, one at each end, allowing 8 or 10 feet of playing space back of them.

Sports and Games

On larger fields the first wicket is placed 8 feet from the stake and the second in line with it and 7 feet distant. Two wickets at the other end of the ground are similarly placed. A center wicket or basket, in the middle of the ground, gives a total of five wickets down the field from stake to stake in a straight line. In the game of roque, a modification of croquet, the center arch is set up as a series of two arches a short distance apart and at right angles to the others. In both games, four other wickets are placed on the side lines, one at each corner opposite the second wicket from each stake. The wickets should be sunk into the ground 6 or 8 inches or set in blocks of wood buried under the surface to insure stability. In professional games the wickets are only a trifle wider than the balls; but in ordinary games they are twice as wide.

The best mallets are made of boxwood, with the heads 7 or 7½ inches long and 2½ inches in diameter, and the handles from 8 to 15 inches in length, as best suits the player. Individual taste has caused a great variety of mallets, those used by skilled players having long heavy heads and short handles.

The best balls are of hard rubber. They can be easily painted by using a preparation of shellac dissolved in alcohol, mixing with Chinese vermilion for red, Prussian blue, and zinc or flake white for white. Thus painted they will dry in a few minutes and wear for several weeks. Most balls for the ordinary game are made of hard wood and are painted with stripes of varying colors in order to prevent becoming confused in play. The standard size of the ball is $3\frac{1}{4}$ inches in diameter.

HOW TO PLAY THE GAME

The object of the game is to drive one's ball by successive strokes of the mallet through the various wickets by rotation until one has made a complete circuit of the ground and has arrived at and struck the home stake. While he is trying to accomplish this end, he is also trying to prevent his opponent from doing likewise. The players take turn about, and when one fails to pass through a wicket or to strike a ball or a stake, it becomes the next player's turn. The opponent's ball can be played upon and driven from position. The game can be played by any small number of persons but is really a better four-handed game, two to a side, as then there is a better chance for team work, generalship, and variety of play. A good game for two players, is where each player manages two balls. This brings out team work and generalship, as in the four-player game.

In this country a professional game known as roque was evolved from croquet and offers a skilled player an opportunity to play not only straight shots but also caroms from the side boundaries.

The chief points of excellence in croquet are:

First, accuracy in croqueting or making one ball

hit another from the blow of the mallet. Here the accurate eye and the trained hand are needed, for at a distance of twenty feet a ball three and one-fourth inches in diameter subtends a very small angle, and a very small divergence of the line of direction of the impinging mallet will cause the struck ball to go wide of its desired course.

Second, ability to take position in front of arches so as to pass through them successfully, for the arches being only three and one-half inches wide in professional games give little chance of passing through to a ball of three and one-fourth inches when in a "wild position."

Third, "wiring" or "staking" an adversary's ball so as to leave no ball "open" or "exposed." This is done sometimes from a distance of fifteen or twenty feet.

Fourth, and greatest of all, is good generalship, for without this all excellence attained in the three preceding points will be manifested in vain in a hard-fought game. Closely associated with the first is the ability to "drive" or "block" the ball at a certain angle to reach a position desired. This will be attempted only when the balls are near together, for at a long range croquet only is attempted.

It is possible that "jump shooting" ought to be added to these, for this, at first thought seemingly impossible method of play, is a special feature with some players, and not infrequently they are relieved from an otherwise inextricable position by a timely jump shot, by which a ball from a peculiar downward stroke of the mallet may be made to pass over one or more intervening arches and "capture" a ball supposed to be safe from all danger.

In this, as in every other game, there are certain general principles which should guide one in his play. Before referring to these we will notice first, mallets; and second, the position taken in the use of the mallet. The size and weight should be that which, after trial, the player likes the best. The mallets in the cheaper sets come with extra long handles and these do not lend themselves to any extremely accurate game.

As regards position in striking, different persons will stand in different positions, and there is no such rigid rule as in golf. However, the best stance is with the feet slightly apart and the stroke being made with an easy side-arm swing. To play with the mallet between the feet, or to make a shove shot, is distinctly bad form. Do not be too long in your aim; a quick stroke after getting your line between two balls is generally the most accurate; but there is one point that all must observe if the ball is to hit the mark: after getting your line of aim, and your mallet resting ready for the stroke, keep your eyes fixed on your own ball. Any deviation from this rule, either for short or long shots, will end in failure.

Sports and Games

And now as to a few general principles to be observed:

First. Keep your own balls together, and separate those of your adversary.

Second. Keep with you or your partner the "innocent" or last played ball of your adversary.

Third. Keep the "guilty" or next playing ball of your adversary wired as much as possible.

Fourth. When you can make no further run, give your partner the best set up you can.

Fifth. Do not play for the guilty ball when, if you miss, you give him a chance better than he had before.

Sixth. If you have but a poor chance to make a run, set up the balls for your partner.

Seventh. In making a run, provide as much as possible for points ahead. Do not leave balls behind you if you can avoid it.

TERMS USED IN CROQUET

To Roquet—To hit with one's own ball another ball for the first time.

To Croquet—To place player's ball against the roqueted ball and then striking his own ball, moving both.

Carom—A rebounding from an arch, a stake, or the border.

In Play—A ball is in play so long as points are made, or balls hit in accordance with the rules.

Croquet

Dead Ball—A ball on which the player has played since making a point. It is then "dead" to the player till he makes another point or has another turn.

Direct Shot—Roquet: this is a direct shot, whether the ball in passing to its destination does or does not carom from a wire, or a stake, or the border.

Drive or Block—English "rush": a roquet played so as to send the object ball to some desired spot.

Cut—To drive the object ball to a desired position, by causing player's ball to hit it on one side.

Run or Break—The making of a number of points in the same turn.

Set Up—To locate the balls so as to afford facility for making the next point or run.

Wiring—To leave the balls so that the next finds a wire between his ball and the object ball.

Object Ball—The ball at which the player aims.

Jump Shot—Striking the ball so as to make it jump over any obstacle between it and the object aimed at. To do this, the ball should be struck with considerable force on the top and just back of the center.

Guilty or Danger Ball—The next to be played on the adversary's side.

Innocent Ball—The last played ball of the adversary.

Rover—A ball that has made all the points except the last.

Sports and Games

Tight Croquet—Holding with the hand or foot the ball placed against another for the sake of croquet, thus allowing only the latter to be moved.

Loose Croquet—Striking a ball when it is in contact with another, where it has been placed for the purpose of croquet, thus moving both balls.

FOOTBALL

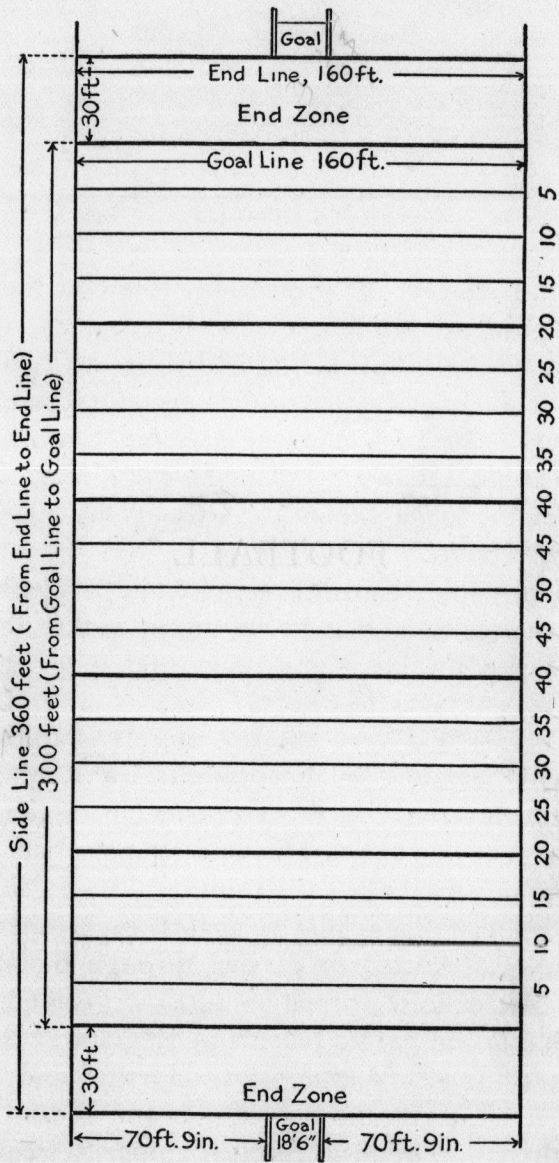

Goal

End Line, 160 ft.

End Zone

30 ft.

Goal Line 160 ft.

5
10
15
20
25
30
35
40
45
50
45
40
35
30
25
20
15
10
5

Side Line 360 feet (From End Line to End Line)

300 feet (From Goal Line to Goal Line)

30 ft.

End Zone

70 ft. 9 in.

Goal 18'6"

70 ft. 9 in.

222

FOOTBALL

FOOTBALL at the present day is one of the most popular of all sports. In this country its one rival is baseball, but in England it has no rival. It is particularly attractive to the spectators, and there are reports of an attendance at some English contests of over 150,000 people. In the United States some of the large games are attended by 80,000 or more spectators.

It is a game requiring activity, skill, pluck and endurance, although it by no means makes the demand upon the heart and lungs that long running races or boat races do.

Its origin was very ancient, and it is spoken of on many occasions in the literature of England of the twelfth century; and even further back than that it is evident that the Greeks and Romans had something which might be called similar. Later, in England, whole villages played against each other, and the ball was kicked or carried through the streets.

Its first definite formation as an organized sport was due to the public schools in England: Rugby, Charter House, Westminster, Harrow and Eton. Later it went into the universities and became popular there. Wherever English colonists went they

Sports and Games

carried the football game with them, and as it had become divided into the Association game, "soccer," which is more kicking, and the Rugby game, which is more a game for carrying the ball, so the countries which took their sport from England took sometimes one and sometimes the other. In America a kind of mongrel game was played more nearly resembling perhaps the Association game, but in the early '70's Harvard visited Canada, and there had some matches under Rugby rules which proved so satisfactory that, through the instrumentality of Harvard, Yale adopted them, and they then became common to all the American colleges. At the same time the rules were altered more or less and extended to meet the American needs.

American intercollegiate football is played on a field 360 feet long and 160 feet wide, including an end zone of 30 feet behind each goal. The goals are set 300 feet apart. The two sets of goal posts are set up 30 feet behind each goal line, and must not exceed 20 feet in height. They are placed 18 feet, 6 inches apart, and have a horizontal crossbar 10 feet from the ground. White border lines mark out this enclosure; and transverse lines every five yards are marked to aid in determining how far the ball is carried. Beginning with each goal line, these are numbered toward the center of the field, 5 to 50. (See diagram.) The ball is an oval rubber bladder, inclosed in a pigskin casing and inflated

224

Football

with air. The circumference, long axis, is from 28 inches to 28½ inches. Its short axis, from 22½ to 23 inches; weight from 14 to 15 ounces. The object of the game is for each opposing side to carry the ball across its opponent's goal line or kick it over the goal-bar, at the same time preventing their rivals from accomplishing this against them.

The game is played by two teams of eleven men each. For convenience in locating these players the following diagram shows them in a position of offense.

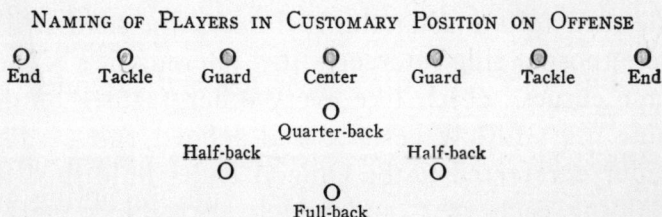

NAMING OF PLAYERS IN CUSTOMARY POSITION ON OFFENSE

O   O   O   O   O   O   O
End   Tackle   Guard   Center   Guard   Tackle   End

O
Quarter-back

Half-back   Half-back
O   O

O
Full-back

The general arrangement of players is in two groups, the "rush line players" or "forwards," at least seven of whom must be on a line with and parallel to their end of the football at the commencement of each scrimmage; and the "backs" who are usually located behind the scrimmage line. Various offensive and defensive combinations are resorted to in the endeavor to outwit the enemy.

HOW THE GAME IS PLAYED

The match is begun by the choice of sides. The referee tosses up a coin before the game in the presence of the captains of the opposing teams, first designating which captain shall call. The winner of the toss has the choice of goal or kick-off, which choice shall not be revokable. If the winner of the toss selects the goal, the loser has the choice of kicking off or receiving the kick-off. These privileges as to choice are reversed at the beginning of the third period.

The side having the kick-off, kicks the ball from the center of its own 40-yard line, and in the direction of the enemy's goal. The players on the kicker's side then follow after the ball down the field while the opposing side intercepts it. Thereupon a scrimmage ensues, which like every other feature of the game must follow certain well-defined rules. The reader is referred to the Official Rules published by Spalding each year, and which are subject to frequent revision.

In general, a scrimmage consists of a concerted effort on the part of either side to retain possession of the ball, after which they seek to advance it by a series of "downs," kicks, runs, forward passes, or other strategy, through the enemy's country to the coveted goal post or goal line.

A scrimmage ensues when a runner with the ball is stopped by one of his opponents. The ball is then placed on the ground, with the two teams lined up and alert to tackle each other. On a given signal the ball is snapped back by the center, either to the quarter-back or to some other player chosen to carry, throw, kick, or otherwise advance the ball. The side having the ball must make at least ten yards in four attempts, or else surrender the ball to the opposing side. The fourth attempt, however, is seldom made as—if sufficient gains have not been made in three trials—the side advancing the ball usually elects to kick it as far down field in the enemy's country as possible.

When the ball is put in play by a scrimmage, at least seven players of the side holding the ball must be on the line of scrimmage.

A player is considered to be on the line of scrimmage if he has both hands or both feet up to or within one foot of this line, or if he has one foot and the opposite hand up to or within one foot of it. He must also stand with both feet outside the outside foot of the player next to him, unless he is one of the two men standing on either side of and next to the center (commonly known as guards), in which case he may lock legs with the center.

If a captain desires to shift the center, guard or tackle into the back-field, he may do so after notifying the referee; but the player so shifted must not again return to one of the middle line positions. Any one of these men may, however, be taken five yards back without consulting the referee, and may later return again to his position.

There are other rules and penalties connected with

the scrimmage which we have not space to include
here, but to which the reader and player are referred in the Official Rules governing this important
element of the game.

The game itself is decided by the final score at
the end of four periods of play. The following is
the value of the plays in scoring:

Touchdown ....6 points
Successful "try for point" after
   touchdown ....1 point
Goal from the field............3 points
Safety by opponents ....2 points

The score of a forfeited game shall be 1 to 0 in
favor of the offended side.

The length of the game is four periods of fifteen minutes each exclusive of time taken out, with
fifteen minutes intermission between the second and
third periods, and an intermission of one minute
each between the first and second, and the third
and fourth periods. The time of these periods may
be shortened on account of local conditions by mutual consent.

The game progresses in a series of downs, followed by passes, runs, or kicks, as the case may be,
the only limitation being that of a rule designed to
prevent one side continually keeping possession of
the ball without any material advance or retreat,

Football

which would be manifestly unfair to the opponents. This rule provides that four "downs" or attempts to advance the ball, a side not having made ten yards toward their opponents' goal must surrender possession of the ball. As a matter of fact, it is seldom that a team actually surrenders the ball in this way, because, after two or three attempts, if the prospects of completing the ten-yard gain appear small, it is so manifestly politic to attempt a forward pass, or to kick the ball as far as possible down the field, that such a method is more likely to be adopted than to make a last attempt by a run and give the enemy possession almost on the spot. In such an exigency, if a kick be made, the rules provide that it must be such a kick as to give the opponents fair and equal chance to gain possession of the ball and must go beyond the line of scrimmage unless stopped by an opponent.

There is one other element entering into this phase of the game, and that is the fair catch. This can be made from a kick by the opponents, provided the catcher takes the ball on the fly, and, no other of his own side touching it, plants his heel in the ground at the spot where the catch is made. This entitles him to a free kick; that is, his opponents can not come within ten yards of his mark, made by heeling the catch, while he (and his side) may retire such distance toward his own goal as he sees fit, and then make a punt or drop, or give the ball to some one of his own side to place the ball for a place to kick.

He may, if he prefers, put the ball down for an ordinary scrimmage. His own men must be behind the ball when he kicks it, or be adjudged off-side.

We will suppose that the ball, by a succession of plays, runs, kicks, downs, fair catches, etc., has advanced toward one or the other of the goals, until it is within kicking distance of the goal posts. The question will now arise in the mind of the captain of the attacking sides as to whether his best plan of operations will be to try a drop kick at the goal, to attempt a forward pass, or to continue the running attempts, in the hope of carrying the ball across the goal line, for this latter play will count his side a touchdown, and entitle them to a try for one point more. On the other hand, if he try a drop kick and fail to score, the ball can be brought out to the twenty-yard line by his opponents for a kick-out. In deciding, therefore, whether to try a drop kick, or continue the running attempts, he should reflect upon this and also upon the value of the scores. The touchdown itself will count six points, even if he afterwards fails to secure the additional possible point, while, if he succeeds in securing it, the touchdown and point together count seven points. A drop kick, if successful, counts three points, but is, of course, even if attempted, by no means sure of resulting successfully. He must, therefore, carefully consider all the issues at this point, and it is the handling of these problems that shows his quality as a

FOOTBALL

Tense moment in a big game between Yale and Harvard.

captain. If he elects to continue his running attempts, and eventually carries the ball across the line, he secures a touchdown, and any player of his side may then bring it out for a scrimmage not nearer than the five-yard line, from which his side may add an additional point if in a single play they make a field goal or secure a touchdown.

There is one other issue to be considered at this point, and that is, if the ball be in possession of the defenders of the goal, or if it falls into their hands when thus close to their own goal. Of course, they will naturally endeavor, by running or kicking, to free themselves from the unpleasant situation that menaces them. Sometimes, however, this becomes impossible, and there is a provision in the rules which gives them an opportunity of relief, at a sacrifice, it is true, but with the score less against them than if their opponents should regain possession of the ball and make a touchdown or a goal. A defensive player may at any such time kick, pass or carry the ball across his own goal line, and there touch it down for safety. This, while it scores two points for his opponents, gives his side the privilege of bringing the ball out to the thirty-yard line, and then taking a kickout, placing it for a scrimmage.

DEFINITIONS

Place-kick—Made by kicking the ball from its position while it is resting upon the ground. It is

Sports and Games

allowable to scrape up the earth, but no artificial tees shall be permitted.

Kick-off—A term used to designate the opening play of the first and third periods and consists of a place-kick from the 40-yard line of the team entitled to kick.

Punt—Made by dropping the ball from the hand or hands and kicking it before it touches the ground.

Drop-kick—Made by dropping the ball from the hand or hands and kicking it the instant it rises from the ground.

Free Kick—Any kick when the opponents are restrained by rule from advancing beyond a certain point before the ball is put in play, and includes kick-off and kick from a fair catch.

Snapping the Ball—Putting it back from its position on the ground with one quick and continuous motion of the hand or hands, the ball actually leaving the hands on this motion.

Scrimmage—A scrimmage takes place when the holder of the ball places it flat upon the ground, with its long axis at right angles to the line of scrimmage, and puts it in play by snapping it back. The scrimmage does not end until the ball is dead.

Off-side—A player is off-side when the ball has last been touched by one of his own side behind him.

On-side—Any men who are off-side are put on-side as soon as the ball is touched by an opponent.

Football

Time of Game—The game continues during four 15-minute periods, with a 15-minute intermission between the second and third periods.

Officials—The officials of a game consist of an umpire who judges fouls, and a referee who rules upon the progress of the ball; also, in important matches, a timekeeper and linesmen are necessary.

Fair Catch—Made by catching the ball after it has been kicked by one of the opponents and before it touches the ground, provided the player, prior to an attempt to catch the ball, signals his intention of making a fair catch by raising his hand clearly above his head and does not take more than two steps after making the catch.

Try-for-Point—A privilege granted the side which has made a touchdown to add one additional point to its score by successfully executing a single play from scrimmage.

Goal from the Field—Made by kicking the ball from the field of play either by a drop-kick or a place-kick over the cross-bar of the opponents' goal. A goal cannot be scored by a kick-off. If after the ball passes directly over one of the goal posts, or if, after being kicked, it strikes an opponent and then passes over the cross-bar or one of the goal posts, it shall count a goal. In no case shall it count a goal if the ball, after leaving the kicker's foot, touches the ground before passing over the cross-bar or goal posts.

Sports and Games

Out of Bounds—The ball is out of bounds when it crosses the side line, or any portion of the player carrying it touches the side line; and it is brought back to that spot and put in play.

Tripping—Obstructing a player below the knee with the hand or with that part of the obstructing player's leg that is below the knee. Mere diving under the play is not tripping.

Down—A down occurs when the referee blows his whistle or declares the ball dead.

Touchdown—Made when the ball, lawfully in possession of a player, is declared dead by the referee, any part of it being on, above, or behind the opponents' goal line. The referee shall immediately blow his whistle and declare that a touchdown has been made as soon as the ball has been carried on, above or across the goal line, or upon the legal completion of a forward pass in the end zone.

Touchback—Made when the ball, in possession of a player guarding his own goal is declared dead by the referee, any part of it being on, above, or behind the goal line, provided the impetus which sent it to or across the line was given by an opponent. Other touchbacks are defined in the Rules.

Safety—Made when the ball in possession of a player guarding his own goal is declared dead by the referee, any part of it being on, above or behind the goal line, provided the impetus which caused it to pass from outside the goal line to or behind the goal line was given by the side defending the goal.

Crawling—Crawling is an attempt by the runner to advance the ball after it has been declared dead.

Forward Pass—An attempt by the side having possession of the ball to advance it into the enemy's territory by means of passing it from player to player or throwing it through the air. A player on the side which has put the ball in play from a scrimmage may pass or throw the ball any distance toward the opponents' goal under the following restrictions:

(a) The pass must be made from a point at least five yards back of the scrimmage line.

(b) Only one forward pass may be made in each scrimmage.

Hurdling—Jumping feet first over any opposing player who is not prostrate on the ground.

GOLF

GOLF

THE origin of golf is shrouded in antiquity. Long before Columbus discovered that the world was round, other folks had discovered the roundness of the small golf ball. The name may have been derived from the German, *kolbe,* meaning club. The Dutch once played a game called *kolf,* but this does not bear much resemblance to our modern golf. There were also early games in Belgium, France, and Italy, which suggest the modern game. One of these early games was called *jeu de mail* which in English became *pell mell.* In this game a smooth boxwood ball was hit with a long mallet, something like a croquet mallet. The later game of polo on horseback was also derived from this early game. The Scotch are credited with being among the earliest players of the game of golf, but whether they invented it as it is now known or adapted it from the Dutch is a matter of conjecture.

Golf was a popular game in England as early as the year 1457. We know of its vogue by that date for the reason that the stern members of Parliament had begun to take notice of it. For some reason it had come under their official displeasure, and we find

Parliament passing an ordinance to the effect that golf be "utterly cryit dune, and nocht usit." Some thirty-five years later another law was passed to the same effect, and "fut ball" was included in the ban. It may have been that there was too much gambling with these early games; or that the games caused people to neglect their work; or possibly that the "golf widows" of those early days petitioned Parliament to keep their husbands at home for them. But whatever it was, the law was passed and like many another law, good or bad, only served to stimulate the popularity of the sport.

Golf was a popular game, as we have said; this is proved by frequent denunciations of golf-playing on Sunday. In 1592 and 1593 the Town Council of Edinburgh contributed to the pious gloom of their country by forbidding this harmless and healthy amusement on Sundays. John Henrie and Pat Rogie, early masters of the club, were prosecuted for "playing of the Gowff on the Links of Leith every Sabbath the time of the sermonses." At Perth, Robert Robertson suffered in the same cause, and sat in the seat of repentance in 1604. There is a seat of repentance in the town kirk of St. Andrews, the City of Martyrs. Many a long driver, many a "fell" putter must have consecrated by his weight this inestimable relic. The old Church, the Catholic Church, never persecuted anybody for playing golf. The early Stuarts, on the English throne, wanted their Scotch subjects to play after church, but, of course, that was enough to prevent a true Scot from playing.

Golf was a royal as well as a popular game, and was played by the gentry. In 1503, in the Royal Accounts, we find £21, 2s., "for the King to play at the golf with the Earl of Bothwell." Only nine shillings were paid for the Royal club and balls; probably he had a bet on with Bothwell. Clubs cost a shilling each, and balls were four shillings the dozen. Needless to say, that these balls were of leather, stuffed with feathers. In 1603, Louis VI. of France appointed William Mayne to be royal clubmaker, and in 1618 he gave James Melvill a monopoly of ballmaking at four shillings each ball. Balls from Holland were pretty heavily taxed, for this was before the delightful discovery that it is sometimes good for a country to be undersold by foreign cheap labor. From a Harleian MS. we learn that the ill-fated Prince Henry, bemoaned by Chapman and other poets, was a golfer, and that the play was "not unlike to pale maille."

Among illustrious golfers we find the great Montrose, who played on St. Andrews, as well as Leith Links. These were the metropolitan links of Scotland, being "within a mile of Edinburgh Town." That a good many clubs were used then as now appears from Montrose's purchasing a set of six, besides having some "auld anes" mended. The anecdote of Charles I. breaking off a match at Leith because news came of the Irish Rebellion is very well known, but is said by Woodrow, no friendly critic of Charles, to be incorrect. His Majesty played his game out.

In the time of his son, James II. (then Duke of York), we hear of the "forecadie" who ran in front, to mark the ball down. Professionals were then apparently unknown, for when James wanted a Scotch partner to make out a foursome with two Englishmen, he was induced to choose a shoemaker by the name of John Patterson. The cobbler won his match, and the grateful king gave him a coat of arms with the device of a hand, dexter, grasping a club, with the motto, "Far and Sure."

Golf in America is in its infancy compared to these records of other countries; but it is an exceedingly lusty infant. At the beginning of the present century it was played only in a comparatively few chosen spots. Says Harry Vardon, the former British champion: "I made a long golfing tour through the United States in 1900, when Englishmen for the most part regarded the game there with as much seriousness as they would have bestowed upon golf in Timbuctoo. At that time it seemed to be taking a firm grip on our cousins, and I saw enough to convince me that America was coming on quickly, and that before long the old country would have reason to fear her. Everything that has happened since then has strengthened my belief, and the eyes of the British were at last fairly opened when the championship was played in 1904, resulting to the chagrin of our own leading amateurs, in a victory for an American. Mr. Walter J. Travis became the victor, and took back with him across the Atlantic the Amateur Championship Cup."

Since then there have been several upsets for British golfers at the hands of Americans; notably, when Francis Ouimet, a Boston amateur only twenty years old at the time, defeated the great Vardon and Ray from England and the best of other golfers from that country, France and America; and in 1921 when Jock Hutchison of the United States won the British Open Championship.

Nowadays, no town of any considerable size considers itself "in it," without at least one golf course. The town of Montclair, in New Jersey, boasting about thirty thousand inhabitants, maintains three clubs in the nearby suburbs and patronizes about five others within a radius of five miles; and each club at last accounts had a waiting list.

HOW THE GAME IS PLAYED

The underlying idea of golf is simple enough; in fact, to the innocent bystander it looks childish. The object is to drive the small ball by means of clubs across country a given distance and sink it in the cup. Where two or more players are engaged, the player who drops the ball into the cup in the fewest number of strokes wins the hole.

This may sound simple enough, but oh, what a wealth of anathema is conjured up in the words to any veteran golfer!

To be more exact in our description of the game, the players start from a given place called the tee. From this tee, which is a small raised platform usually of turf, they drive a carefully placed ball, which is usually elevated on a little pat of sand in order to facilitate a clean stroke. After leaving the tee the ball, if properly directed, goes along a fairway in the direction of the putting green. The fairway is a smooth sward of turf which, however, may present a number of hazards or obstacles. There may be water to cross, or ditches, or artificially constructed bunkers, of which more later. At each side of the fairway rough spots may be designedly left to catch the inaccurate driver.

As stated before, the object is to drive the ball from the tee to the cup. The latter is a small depression in what is known as the putting green, a very smooth, short-turfed area perhaps thirty feet or more in width which surrounds the cup. In the West and South sand putting greens are often used instead of grass.

The distance from the tee to the cup varies in different courses from the short "hole," as it is termed, of less than a hundred yards, to the longest ones of over five hundred yards. The average length is about three hundred yards. Nine such holes constitute one-half or round of the course, and eighteen holes a game. Some small clubs which have only a nine-hole course play it twice around in order to fill out the game.

The game itself is scored in two different ways—either for medal or match ball. In the *medal* ball the game is decided by the number of strokes actually used. In the *match* ball the number of holes won is the deciding factor.

CLUBS USED IN THE GAME

As the strokes in the game vary from the "long drive" off the tee of many yards to the put on the green of a few inches, and as various kinds of terrain must be played over, it naturally follows that several different kinds of clubs are required. For a long time golfers used only wooden clubs—drivers, spoons, brassies, and putters. Then came the "iron age," which has resulted in the following clubs in the average bag: two wooden clubs—the driver and the brassy, and five or six iron clubs—such as cleek, mid-iron, mashie, lofter, niblick, and putter.

The first club that the golfer will be called upon to use is the *driver*. This is a long-handled club with a heavy wooden head. Its face or playing surface next to the ball is almost perpendicular. It is intended to propel the ball for a long distance in a straight line and without raising it in the air very much. Beginners watching a game often exclaim at some driven ball that rises in the air like an insane sky rocket. A ball such as this looks pretty but does not get very far, and also has a tendency to drop "dead." Your old-time golfer tries to effect a ball that will arch itself in the air only enough to gain sufficient carry to go a long distance through the air and have a top spin to carry it along still further after it reaches the ground. The drive may be as much as 250 yards, but is likely to be nearer 150 yards, unless the man wielding the club is exceptionally long on his shots.

If the ball lands in the fairgreen and rests in such a position as to make the next shot also a clean one, the *brassy* is the next weapon that will be chosen. This club is protected on its lower surface with brass, hence its name. It is planned for rougher usage than the driver which it greatly resembles, having the same long wooden shaft and heavy head. The playing surface of this club is usually set at a little more of an angle than the driver, in order to get under the ball and lift it off of the flat playing surface. Quite as long distances can be made with the brassy as with the driver. In fact, if the distance of the hole from the tee is 300 yards, it is not wise to follow a good drive with a brassy shot, as the player is liable to overplay his hole.

A third wooden club which is springing into popu-

Golf

larity is the *spoon*. This is shafted and built along the same lines as the brassy, but has the driving face of the head scooped out, so as to loft the ball. It is useful in uncertain lies where the player wants to be assured of getting his ball well up into the air, and also desires distance.

Where the distance does not admit of the brassy or spoon, any one of two or three iron clubs may be used, depending upon the distance to go and the lay of the land. The three most popular iron clubs for mid-field work are the *cleek,* the *mid-iron,* and the *mashie*.

The *cleek* proper is a club of medium length and weight, with thin iron blade or face. It is used in preference to the wooden clubs when the lie is not good, its sharp edge and tilting face being then useful. It is also used for short strokes when approaching the green.

The *mid-iron* is somewhat heavier than the cleek, and is used for distance work, especially over rough or uneven courses. Properly used, this can become one of the most serviceable of clubs, combining distance with lift, in every variety of lie.

The *mashie* may be said to be a hybrid growth. But a few years back it was almost unknown. Now its use is universal. Some few golfers, when they formerly wished to pitch the ball unusually dead, were in the habit of using the *niblick*. But since the small surface of the blade of the niblick-head demanded almost greater accuracy of striking than the human hand and eye could master, it occurred to some bold spirit to invent a modification—a compromise between niblick and mid-iron—which, while allowing a little more scope for human error, should yet preserve the faculty of pitching the ball "dead." Thus was the mashie evolved—an intermediate type called into being by conditions which specially favored its existence.

Many golfers now carry a mashie to the entire exclusion of the niblick; yet, though it is doubtful whether in the multitude of golf clubs there be wisdom, it is questionable if it is wise to discard the niblick altogether. Your mashie, for approaching purposes, should be essentially a weapon of balance, while your niblick, for digging purposes, should be essentially a weapon of weight. Your niblick should be heavy, to dig through obstacles; your mashie should be comparatively light, to pitch the ball "dead."

The *lofter,* like the niblick, is used in cases of extreme peril, where bunkers and hazards of other nature confront the unwary player. The face of the lofter is set back at a more extreme angle than the foregoing clubs and it is built especially for lofting a ball out of a hole or over an obstacle. It is also used in approaching a green, as its ball has a tendency to fall dead, or without rolling. The lofter is still more tilted in angle, besides being short and

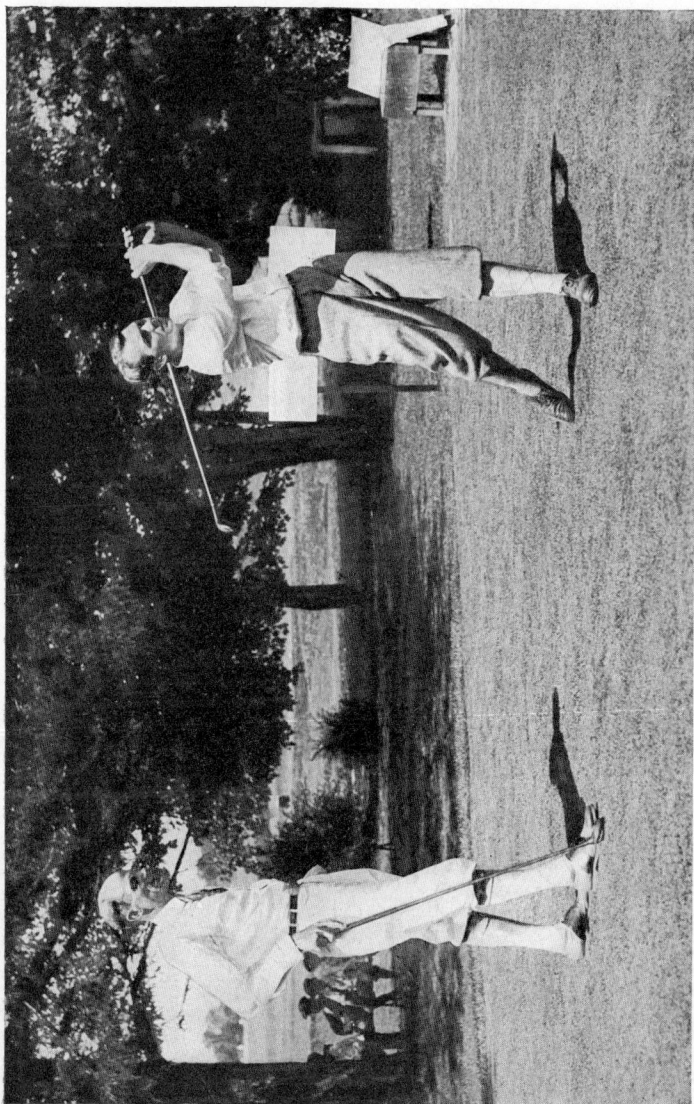

GOLF

In a "Father and Son" tournament, at Sleepy Hollow, N. Y.

rounded. It is the court of last resort in extreme difficulties.

Finally, the last club to be used is the *putter*—maker and breaker of many a hard-fought field. This is the shortest of all clubs, as the player is supposed to be standing directly over the ball, and is used much like a croquet mallet. Its field of usefulness is restricted to the green immediately around the hole, a sward free from obstructions where close accuracy rather than distance is desired.

SUGGESTIONS TO PLAYERS

As in every other game there is a right and a wrong way of doing things. Probably there are more wrong ways of playing golf than in all other games altogether—because of the variety of the clubs and the different playing conditions. No two courses are alike and no two lies alike. Therefore, what would be the correct way to play one shot might be totally wrong for the next one. The player, however, can learn certain definite things, which go to make up what is known as golf "form," without which he is liable to remain a hopeless duffer.

On the drive or opening stroke for each hole the idea is to gain both distance and direction. A full free swing is required with a definite carry through behind it. First, the driver should see to his stance. This is a golf term alluding to the position of the feet and the whole posture of the body. Here are

Sports and Games

some concise hints for the use of both the driver and the brassy:

Stance. Stand far enough from the ball so that the face of the club rests against the ball, while the other end of the shaft touches the left knee. Toes are turned outward.

Upward Swing. Club head is raised slowly, but not too straight, and its speed is gradually increased. Elbows are kept well in, the left wrist turning inward. The body must be held firm, the head still, and the eye fixed upon the ball. Weight goes over to the right leg, the left heel being raised.

End of Stroke. Do not jerk. Arms must be kept well down, and head remains quiet. Weight of body is thrown from right leg to left, until the right heel is raised and the left leg stiffens. After the stroke the arms follow the direction of the ball and the body swings forward.

Slicing is caused by standing too near, or by drawing in the arms.

Pulling is caused by loosening the grip of the left hand, or by allowing the head of the club to turn partly over.

To give oneself the best possible chance of hitting the ball surely and swiftly, to combine the far and the sure, the clubhead wants to be traveling, when it meets the ball, in the direction in which it is intended the ball should go; and it is exceedingly obvious that the longer the clubhead is so traveling, the longer

250

will be the space—the longer the segment of that rough circle which it describes—in which it is possible for it to meet the ball correctly. And this requires to be combined with sufficient speed. It may, therefore, be stated that the aim of the ideal golf swing is a combination of the utmost possible speed in conjunction with the utmost possible length of movement of the clubhead in the desired line of flight of the ball.

Certain points may be noted about the grip, but it is a mistake, in striving after a prescribed fashion, to work the hands into a position of discomfort. In the first place, a few inches of the shaft should be allowed to project above the left hand, for thus a greater command over the club is acquired. Secondly, since the club has to turn in the right hand at a certain point in the swing, it should be held firmly in the fingers, rather than in the palm, with that hand. In the left hand it should be held firmly, as this hand is to communicate the chief power of the swing. The right is more for guidance and control. The two hands should be as close together as conveniently possible.

While the player is getting set and giving his club two or three preliminary "waggles" he must not forget one cardinal rule, "Keep your eye on the ball." The golfer will have this constantly dinned into his ears from the time he misses his first drive through his entire golfing career, and he will probably forget it quite as consistently. To take the eye away for the fraction of a second means the risk of topping the stroke or missing the ball altogether. Not until the club has come back on its downward swing, collided with the ball, and the latter swung off into space with that clean "smack" which is dear to every golfer's heart, can the driver afford to take his glance away for the fraction of a second.

Some golfers are so anxious to see where their ball is going that they look up and away before the club has actually struck the ball. Leave it to your caddie or your partner to watch the ball on its flight, if necessary. Even after you have struck the ball there will be plenty of time to glance up and see where it is heading, but do not let this phase of the matter interest you, so long as the ball and the club have not actually met.

Once out in the field any number of trick lies may greet you. These require iron clubs or different faces and types, consequently different styles of shots. No amount of book rules can guide you under such conditions, and the soundest advice is to follow first behind experienced players watching their handling of difficult situations, and later playing around for yourself with some friend who is familiar with both the game and the course.

For example, if the ball has come to rest in a slight hollow in the ground, you would perhaps want to use the lofter, that is, the iron club with the lofted

Golf

face, to get it out. The same club may be necessary in a sand lie, such as in traps or behind bunkers, which are often encountered in golf courses. This club gets you out of trouble, but gives little distance.

The following is a summary of the bad lies you will encounter, with a general hint as to how to play them.

1. When the ball is in a depression, swing evenly downwards so as to nip in between edge of cup and ball. Do not think about the "jerk."

2. With obstruction in front, play to slice or lift the ball.

3. With slope in front, swing, with spooned club, over the surface of the ground, as if it were level.

4. Ball lying above, facing you, swing freely, with right hand gripping lightly.

5. Ball lying below, away from you, swing quietly.

The advice that we have given applies equally to wooden clubs and to full shots with cleeks and irons, and should your natural tendency be to "jerk" the ball with the iron clubs, it will make no matter.

APPROACHING SHOTS

As the player approaches the putting green, a different style of play is needed from the long full swing of the drive or brassy shot; likewise, a different class of shot from that which is simply an iron shot to get him out of difficulties. Let us suppose that a player has approached to within 150 yards or less of the green. His object now is to play his ball in one shot on to the green, but not to overrun it. In other words, he wishes to lift his ball in the air and drop it in such a way that it will lie "dead" on the green or without rolling more than a few feet. The favorite club for this purpose is the mashie, and we give below a summary of the improved style in playing the mashie approach shot:

Stance. The feet are placed nearer each other and nearer the ball than in the wooden-club strokes. The right foot is somewhat advanced, and the left heel is directly opposite the ball.

Upward Swing. Body is more relaxed than formerly, the elbows bend more, and the knees relax. Weight of body is on right leg, but even that knee is slightly bent. Head remains quiet, and eye is fixed on a point just behind the ball.

End of Stroke. Play is made more delicately and more accurately than the drive. Weight is transferred from one leg to the other, each heel in turn being raised. Finish with arms and body to the front.

To loft the ball extremely, it is necessary to strike just behind the ball so as to cut the turf slightly. This has a tendency to make the ball alight "dead"— or nearly so.

The approach shot when properly made has both distance and carry, and also has either a cut or back spin, which will prevent the ball from continuing to

Golf

roll after it has struck the ground. Some players do not handle their approach shots in this manner, but prefer to run up, that is, to allow every ball to strike the ground a few yards away from the green and trickle up to it. The best players, however, do not rely on these chance trickles. They strive to lift their ball cleanly through the air and deposit it at or near the pin, which means the cup. Oftentimes, also, sand pits may guard the green.

PUTTING

After the ball has reached the putting-green, the concluding stroke or strokes for the hole is in order. Let us suppose that your ball has come to rest twenty feet away from the cup. It is your object then to "sink" the ball in the cup at the next stroke, if possible; and failing to leave it so close that a second shot will make it certain. This sounds simple enough, and yet how many games of golf are played with third shots being constantly required upon the putting-green! More golf matches, little and big, have been settled on the putting-green than anywhere else. A golfer who may drive like a fiend on the long distances and extricate himself from many a tight corner, often lacks the delicate precision of the three-foot puts which will win a hole. As a matter of fact, a short put of three feet or less counts just as much on the score card as a drive of 200 yards.

Since the putter itself is the shortest of clubs, the player must stand well over it. The favorite method is to play from the right leg. The shaft is held firmly with an equal grip in both hands, perhaps a slightly stronger pressure being used on the right, the left hand being used more to steady the stroke. The shoulders are kept quiet and the arms equally so, the stroke being very largely with the wrists. One of the great secrets of the putting stroke is to do it quietly and cleanly and without jerking. The club may rest for a moment directly behind the ball without touching it, while the eye of the player measures the distance and direction. Even a foot distance requires care, as it is frequently missed.

The player keeps his head down, his body quiet, his eye absolutely set upon the ball and the distance between it and the cup. Then he swings the club back very quietly and brings it into contact with the ball smoothly and evenly, with a slight carry through touch. It is this delicacy of touch in putting which makes it the most difficult stroke for many otherwise good golfers. The inability to judge the force of the stroke is another crying sin. Most putters play too timidly, they stop two or three feet short of the cup on the long put. They forget the important adage, "Never up, never in." It is better to overrun the cup once in a while, than to suffer constantly from this tendency of stopping short. Many a ball which has the correct direction has failed to win the hole simply because it lacked an ounce or two of propelling force.

DEFINITIONS

The United States Golf Association has adopted the following definitions of golf terms:

(1) A "side" consists either of one player or two players. If one player plays against another the match is called a "single." If two play against two, each side playing one ball, the match is called a "foursome." If one play against two playing one ball between them, the match is called a "three-some."

(2) "Advice" is any counsel or suggestion which could influence a player in determining the line of play, in the choice of a club, or in the line of making a stroke.

A player may ask anyone to indicate the line to the hole before the shot is played. A player may ask any one for advice on the rules of golf.

(3) The "course" is the whole area within which play is permitted; more particularly it is the ground between the holes which is especially prepared for play.

(4) The "teeing-ground" is the starting place for a hole. The front of each teeing-ground shall be indicated by two marks placed in a line as nearly as possible at right angles to the line of play, and the teeing-ground shall include a rectangular space of

the depth of two club lengths directly behind the line indicated by the two marks.

(5) "Through the green" is all ground on which play is permitted, except hazards and the putting-green of the hole that is being played.

(6) A "hazard" is any bunker, water (except casual water), ditch (unless excepted by local rule), bush, sand, path, or road. Sand blown on to the grass, or sprinkled on the course for its preservation, bare patches, sheep tracks, snow, and ice are not hazards.

(7) "Casual water" is any temporary accumulation of water (whether caused by rainfall, flooding, or otherwise) which is not one of the ordinary and recognized hazards of the course.

(8) "Out of bounds" is all ground on which play is prohibited.

(9) A ball is "out of bounds" when the greater part of it lies within a prohibited area.

(10) The "putting green" is all ground, except hazards, within twenty yards of the hole.

(11) The hole shall be 4¼ inches in diameter, and at least 4 inches deep. If a metal lining be used, it shall be sunk below the lip of the hole, and its outer diameter shall not exceed 4¼ inches.

(12) The term "loose impediments" denotes any obstruction not fixed or growing, and includes dung, wormcasts, molehills, snow and ice.

(13) A "stroke" is the forward movement of the

club made with the intention of striking the ball, or any contact between the head of the club and the ball, resulting in movement of the ball, except in case of a ball accidentally knocked off a tee.

(14) A "penalty stroke" is a stroke added to the score of a side under certain rules, and does not affect the rotation of play.

(15) The side which plays off first from a teeing ground is said to have the "honor."

(16) In "teeing," the ball may be placed on the ground, or on sand or other substance, in order to raise it off the ground.

(17) A player has "addressed the ball" when he has taken his stance and grounded his club, or, if in a hazard when he has taken his stance preparatory to striking at the ball.

(18) A ball is "in play" as soon as the player has made a stroke at a teeing ground, and it remains in play until holed out, except when lifted in accordance with the rules.

(19) A ball is deemed to "move" if it leaves its original position in the least degree; but it is not considered to "move" if it merely oscillate and come to rest in its original position.

(20) A ball is "lost" if it be not found within five minutes after the search for it has begun.

(21) The reckoning of strokes is kept by the terms —"the odd," "two more," "three more," etc., and "one off three," "one off two," "the like." The reck-

oning of holes is kept by the terms—so many "holes up," or "all even," and so many "to play."

A side is said to be "dormie" when it is as many holes up as there are holes remaining to be played.

(22) An "umpire" decides questions of fact; a "referee" decides questions of golfing law.

RULES OF GOLF

The U. S. G. A. has issued a booklet of rules which are too long to quote in full in the present article. They may be obtained at any club or by application to the U. S. G. A. Spalding's "Official Golf Guide" includes the booklet in separate form, which can be readily detached and put in the pocket. These rules are based upon the Royal and Ancient Golf Club of St. Andrews, and have been revised up to the present year for players in America.

ETIQUETTE OF GOLF

No less important than the actual rules of the game is what is known as Golf Etiquette. This applies not only to the players but to the onlookers and its force is recognized wherever golf is played. The following hints on etiquette have been promulgated by the U. S. G. A.:

No one should stand close to or directly behind the ball, move, or talk, when a player is making a stroke.

Golf

On the putting-green no one should stand beyond the hole in the line of a player's stroke.

The player who has the honor should be allowed to play before his opponent tees his ball.

No player should play from the tee until the party in front have played their second strokes and are out of range, nor play up to the putting-green till the party in front have holed out and moved away.

Players who have holed out should not try their puts over again when other players are following.

Players looking for a lost ball should allow other matches coming up to pass them; they should signal to the players following them to pass, and having given such a signal, they should not continue their play until these players have passed and are out of reach.

Turf cut or displaced by a player should be at once replaced and pressed down with the foot.

A player should carefully fill up all holes made by himself in a bunker.

Players should see that their caddies do not injure the holes by standing close to them when the ground is soft.

A player who has incurred a penalty stroke should intimate the fact to his opponent as soon as possible.

Players who do not continue in the match play rounds of tournament should be considered to have forfeited any prize they may have won in the qualifying round.

ICE HOCKEY

Goalkeeper

Right Defense   Left Defense

Right Wing   Left Wing

Centre

Centre

Left Wing   Right Wing

Left Defense   Right Defense

Goalkeeper

ICE HOCKEY

THE origin of the game of hockey is obscure. The war-like Romans enjoyed a peculiar game that was most likely the percursor of hockey. Other modern variants are "hurley" in Ireland and "shinty" in Scotland, which, in point of fact, are now one and the same. A leather ball stuffed with feathers and a bat or a club were the essential requisites of the game, and the object was to knock the ball to a certain boundary line and thereby score a point.

The original Scotch "shinty" resembled it more closely than did "hurley" or English hockey, but savored a trifle more of Canada's winter sport, although, in the mildest of sarcasm, it is not probable that the votaries of the former sport would find anything of excitement in ice hockey as now played. The Scotch game was played on the hard, sandy sea-beach, with two or three hundred on each side, and their materials, or rather weapons, consisted of roots of trees, with a hard wood knob for a ball. History does not relate the number of casualties that occurred in these matches, of which the most important took place on New Year's Day, but if our imagination be given scope the effect is anything but pleasant.

Only a few years ago the present form of hockey

was an unknown sport. Shinny was played on lakes, rivers, and canals, but only a discerning eye could discover in this crude, but infatuating amusement, the possibilities that a refined game could offer. Without restrictions as to the proportions of the stick, the nature or quality of the puck, the size of the playing space on the ice, or the number of the players, the sport could not develop into a scientific game until such time as it would be discussed and regulated by those who sought its advancement.

To the McGill College and Victoria hockey teams of Montreal the game of hockey owes its present state on this side of the Atlantic. These two were the first regularly organized hockey clubs in the world, the former preceding the latter by a very short time. Previous to the formation of the above organizations about 1881, teams existed in Montreal and Quebec, but the only rule that was well defined was the one which demanded that every man should "shinny on his own side." Do what you might, play on what you liked or with what you liked—and as long as you shinnied on your own side you were within the law.

All kinds of sticks were used, long knotted roots, broom handles, clubs, and all kinds of skates were employed, from long, dangerous reachers to short, wooden rockers. On each particular occasion the captains agreed, before the game, upon the rules, so that the rules that governed one match might be

Ice Hockey

null and void for another. The puck was a square
block of wood, about two cubic inches in size, on
which a later improvement was the bung of a barrel,
tightly tied round with cord.

The game was soon after introduced in the United
States, and made rapid strides. Colleges and schools
took an interest in it, and organized teams, schedules
were drawn up, the public flocked to the rinks to see
the games, with the result that today it is a most
popular winter sport.

Artificial rinks are now found in the principal
cities of the country, and afford to players a great
advantage, as there is never a scarcity of ice. They
are opened in the autumn and remain open for
skating until spring. Besides, being comparatively
warm, spectators are not kept away from them, however inclement the weather may be. A short time
ago almost any Canadian team could defeat, with
comparative ease, the best seven that could be found
in the United States. But now a different complex-
ion colors the comparison between the clubs, because team work has arrived at such a high degree
of science that our leading clubs are eligible to compete with the best.

EQUIPMENT FOR HOCKEY

For many reasons the quality and species of the
skate is a most important consideration to a hockey
player.

Sports and Games

The hockey skate should be just high enough to prevent the plate of the sole of the boot from touching the ice when turning or cutting corners, because a low skate is not so straining on the ankle as a high one. The blade should be long enough and sufficiently flat on the ice to admit of great speed, but should not project at the toe or heel so much as to trip the skater on any occasion, and should be curved slightly in front and behind in order to allow of quick turning. Although it should be so pointed as to enable a player to begin a rush by running on the toes, these should not have a distinct, projecting point, but should be so shaped that they will admit of this start, because a sharp projection is often the cause of a nasty fall and also of a dangerous cut to the wearer of the skates or to one of his opponents.

A good hockey skate should be a combination of great strength and lightness of weight. It should be strong, because the thousand twistings and turnings of a player strain every inch of the blade, each plate and every rivet; it should be light because the lightness of the skate adds to the swiftness of the skater, and because a heavy skate is tiring. To refer again to the length of the skate, the blade should project about an inch in front of the toe of the boot and an inch or a little more behind the heel, and the width of the bottom of the blade should retain the same thickness from toe to heel, or rather on that part of blade that touches the ice when a skater

268

maintains a standing position. The two ends back and front should taper slightly in width, becoming thinner toward the points.

A player's clothes should be light enough to be of no perceptible weight, and warm enough to insure him against catching cold. A woolen jersey, short pants likewise of wool, a suit of light underwear and heavy stockings, are the necessary articles of clothing for a hockey player.

Hats are not needed if the hair is allowed to grow moderately long. Many players prefer, for outdoors, a close-fitting knitted cap.

Gloves, thin enough to permit the player to retain a firm, sure grasp of his stick, are used to prevent the hands from being cut on the rough ice after a fall. It is advisable to wear shin guards and any other appliances that afford protection. Unless a player's ankles are weak, straps should not be used, because they are of no other value than to strengthen the ankles, which, with plenty of practice and well-fitting shoes, do not, or should not, need support.

The hockey stick is the requisite next in importance. It should be strong, light and not too flexible, having a long blade and handle, which will increase the player's reach. It should be made of second-growth ash, which is the most serviceable wood, because it combines strength with lightness, and does not, like most other woods, absorb the water which frequently appears on the ice. When a player gets a stick that suits him, he should carefully note its particular points, so that when that one breaks, he may secure others of the same shape. A player should use the stick that he himself prefers, and should not be guided by the choice of others, although, of course, he should always look for an improvement of his own.

It is difficult to lay down rules regulating the manipulation of the stick. What there are of them are few and undefined. The stick should be held in both hands. The right hand should hold it firmly at the end of the handle and the left lower down, according to the reach of the player, because, even if most plays are made with both hands on the stick, there are times when it is necessary to use only one, in which case, holding the stick as above, the right hand is already in place without any change.

The stick should be held in both hands, because in that position a man is always ready to shoot for the goals, or to pass the puck. Besides, he can check better, dodge better, resist a heavy check more easily and sustain his position on his skates more securely when he has the stick thus held upon the ice.

Stick-handling, like confidence, coolness, strength and speed, is acquired by practice, and by practice alone.

The more you play the sooner you will become an adept in the art, and the better you can handle your stick the more effective a player you will be,

ICE HOCKEY

Match game played between Oxford and Cambridge teams, at St. Moritz, Switzerland.

because stick-handling is one of the essentials of the game.

The diagram printed herewith shows the plan of a hockey rink and also the playing positions of the two competing teams.

Each team has six players: centre, right wing, left wing, right defense, left defense, and goalkeeper. Six extra players are allowed as substitutes.

The rink must be at least 170 feet long by 58 feet wide. A goal is placed at each end of this rink. The goal posts are 6 feet apart and 4 feet high, and are further provided with goal nets.

The puck is a piece of solid rubber, circular in shape, 1 inch thick and 3 inches in diameter.

The game is played for three periods of fifteen minutes each, with intermissions of ten minutes.

The game is begun by placing the puck in the center of the rink between the sticks of the two left centers. At the call to "play!" on the part of the referee, both centers endeavor to drive the puck down toward the opponents' goal. Whichever side thereupon secures control, tries by successive passing and dribbling to shoot the puck between the enemy's goal-posts. Such goals count for points in the game.

While in play the puck may be stopped by any part of a player's person, or his skates, but, it can only be propelled toward its destination by means of the hockey stick. The stick must not be raised higher than level with the shoulder, except when actually striking the puck.

A puck which has gone off the ice behind the goal line is brought back to that line in a plane at right angles with it from the point where it went out, but no nearer than five yards to either goal post. When it goes out at the side, it is brought in three yards. Play resumes in the same manner as at the beginning.

The objective point throughout is to send the puck through the opposite goal and at the same time prevent a similar play on the part of the antagonist. A team, and each individual member of a team, should concentrate every idea, every thought on this one desire, and each play, each move should point to it, as the rays of the sun are converged through a glass to the focus.

That play is vain which does not tend to bring a team, or a member of a team, to a position from which the desired point can be gained—a useless move affects the position of a team, and throws the players out of poise.

The fancy play, the grandstand play, is a waste of energy, childish, worthless. The play that counts, the play that shows the science of the man who makes it, is the immediate execution, in the simplest manner, of the plan that a player conceives when he considers the object of his playing. In other (geo-metrical) words, the shortest distance between two points is a straight line, and applied to the science of hockey, it means that a player should take the shortest and quickest way of obtaining the desired effect, which, by analysis, is oftentimes the most scientific.

When it is said that every player of a team should strain nerve and muscle to score a goal, the meaning is not that each individual member should strive to do the act himself, but that he should use every effort to assist him to score who is in the most advantageous position to do so. The selfish desire on the part of even one man to make the point oftentimes entails the loss of a match.

Although by nearing his opponents' defence with the puck a player naturally approaches the position from which to shoot, he will invariably confuse his adversaries more successfully, and often secure for himself or his partner a much more desirable vantage ground, by passing the puck to the latter before reaching the defense. Indeed, if the question of praise be mentioned, there is often more due to the player who assists by a clever bit of combination work than to the man who scores the game.

The secret of a team's success is combination play, in other words, unselfishness. It means the giving of the puck to a player of one's own side who is in a better position to use it than the man who first secures the rubber. It is the science of mutual help. As in basketball and football, it is a *"sine qua non."* The team that indulges most in this scientific play has the less hard work to do and is necessarily the freshest when the trying end of the match comes round, because combination play minimizes the work in this arduous game.

As soon as a player secures the puck he should first look for an opening and then size up, at a glance, the position of his confreres. It is, indeed, a question whether it be not more scientific, more successful to look first for a good opportunity to pass the puck to a partner; and then, if none such presents itself, to force a clearing.

It happens that a fast forward can, by his own personal efforts, score one, two, or perhaps three goals, but toward the close of the game he is no longer able to do effective work, because his selfish exertions have played him out, and when necessity demands that because of poor assistance from his partners, a good man should indulge in individual work, such may be permissible, but the team thus handicapped cannot expect to win from a well-balanced aggregation.

Combination in hockey is the scientific means to the end at which the players aim, viz., the placing of men of the team that makes the play in the best obtainable position to shoot a goal, and should be carried on only until that position is attained.

Ice Hockey

It is possible to indulge even too much in combination work, necessary as it is on most occasions, and thus the virtue may be turned into a vice. It should not be played too freely by men in front of their own goals, and as it is merely a means to an end, an over-indulgence in it is a loss of time, of which hockey is too fast a game to allow.

In close quarters the puck should be passed to a man's stick, and not in a line with his skates. A scientific player, rushing down the ice with a partner, will give the puck to the latter, not in a direct line with him, unless they are very close together, but to a point somewhat in advance, so that he will have to skate up to get it. The advantage in this style of passing is that the man who is to receive the rubber will not have to wait for it, but may skate on at the same rate of speed at which he was going before the puck was crossed and proceed in his course without loss of time.

The puck should be passed in such a manner that it will slide along the ice and not "lift," because it is difficult to stop and secure the rubber when it comes flying through the air. There are times, of course, when a "lifted" pass is necessary, for instance, when the line on the ice between the passer and the receiver is obstructed, but otherwise the "sliding" pass is advisable.

When two "wing" men play combination together in an attack, the puck should scarcely ever be passed directly to each other, but should be aimed at the cushioned side of the rink, some distance in advance of the man, so that he may secure it on the rebound. The rink is so wide that it is difficult to pass the puck accurately from one side to the other, especially during a rush, so the above means is recommended.

When three or four forwards are making a rush, the puck should be held by one of the centre players until the cover-point is reached, because in such a play the latter does not know to which man the rubber is to be passed, for it may be given to the right or the left wing or even to the other center player, but when, in an attack, a wing man has the puck, the defense man knows that he must necessarily cross it out to the center and is prepared for the play.

Each player should be careful to remain in his own position, and in order to acquire the habit of so doing, every man should make it a point in each practice, however unimportant, to cling to the particular position on the team which he is intended to fill. It is a grievous mistake for a wing man to leave his position and play in the centre of the ice or on the side to which he does not belong, or for a center player or rover to wander to the wings, because as each man has a cover, a check, on whom, in turn he should bestow his attention, he gives his opponent, when he leaves his place, an opening that the latter should not and would not have if he were properly watched. The forwards and the defence men of an experienced team should know where their assistants are at all times. When a man strays from his own territory, a brilliant combination play may easily be lost through his absence from his proper place.

Each player of a team should occupy his position so unfailingly in practice, and the team should indulge in combination work to such an extent, that, in a match, a forward ought, at times, to be able to slide the puck to an assistant without even having to look to know where the latter is located. If perfection be aimed at, and it should be, the point of following up should be so regular, so systematic, that this play may be successfully indulged in, because, with every man working in his position, like so many movements in a clock, a forward with the puck, in advance, should know without looking, where each of his partners follows.

POINTS OF A GOOD PLAYER

Coolness, in hockey parlance, is the power and practice of taking time to think out a move. A player must be cool-headed to a degree that verges on slowness, because, so fast a game is hockey, that an expert player, an experienced team, should take advantage of every opportunity that the changing plays present, and this to do, even in the quickest rushes, the swiftest combinations, the fiercest "mix-ups," it is necessary that one should remain as cool as the proverbial cucumber.

As a hockey axiom, it might be said that "it is better to think more and rush less, than to rush more and think less."

The cool, collected, calculating player is worth more to a team than two or three of the class whose main object seems to be the possession of the puck for a "big" rush down the ice.

If any man among your opponents is to be feared, let it be the one who thinks out each move, who makes no useless plays, who shoots for the goals only when there is an opening, because "such men are dangerous." Many a game is lost, many a chance is missed by the man who will not, or cannot take time enough to think out a play.

Another requisite is confidence, both in your assistants and in yourself. Just as that regiment whose soldiers rely upon one another is a better one than another in which the members have no confidence in their comrades, so, in a hockey game it is absolutely necessary that each player should be able to depend upon his confreres.

A team should feel that it can defeat any seven that opposes it, and each individual man of a team ought to believe that, if necessary, he can pass any one of his adversaries. A team that goes on the ice thinking that defeat is probable is already beaten. A player who fears that he can not elude certain of his opponents is a factor for success for the opposing team. Care should be taken, however, that confidence may not be exaggerated. Over-confidence is a greater fault than confidence is a virtue. While each team should feel that it can probably defeat its opponents, it should also bear in mind that until the game is ended its own goals are in danger, and act accordingly.

Pluck is essential to a man who aspires to perfection in the game, and is as indispensable to him as it is to a football player or a soldier. The calculating player often saves himself by avoiding unnecessary dangers, but occasion demands, at times, a fast rush through a "bunch" of fighting players, through swinging, smashing sticks that, in noise and movements, resemble a threshing machine—a desperate jump, or a block of the puck, at the expense of a sore punishment, to score or save a single goal, and the risk must be run.

The cringer, the man who waits outside of a scrimmage until by chance the puck slides to him, the man who fears an opponent, is not a hockey player. It is, of course, scientific play on certain occasions to wait until the puck is shoved out of a crowd, or from the side, but reference is made above to the time when a "dive" is needed. Even if a man knows that an opponent is mean, unfair, this should be but a poor excuse to fear him, because the referee is on the ice for the protection of all the players.

A hockey player must necessarily be strong physically and constitutionally. If his muscles are well-developed, but his constitution is weak, so violent a game as this will do him an irreparable injury. Hockey is so fast, so trying on a forward player, who is rushing continually from the opening to the closing of a match, that, in order to play without hurting himself, he must be in perfect condition. This condition means both the state of his health and the condition of his mind and muscles.

Training for the game of hockey is the simplest, perhaps, of any, and consists for the most part in careful practice.

Nothing prepares a player for the opening of a hockey season so well as a thorough course in gymnastics. This to do properly, it is necessary to make use of every appliance that the gymnasium affords (except the heavy weights), because the game of hockey calls into play every muscle that a complete gymnasium develops, which is attested to by the stiffness in every muscle after a good, hard game. Exercises that aid in enlarging and hardening the muscles in the arms, back, chest and stomach are specially recommended. The legs are quickly brought into condition by skating and walking.

The three fundamentals of a good hockey player, as summed up by S. Trafford Hicks, are as follows:

"Ability to skate on ice is the most necessary qualification. Nobody can play hockey unless they can move about rapidly on the runners with some stability. To play hockey does not require finesse

Ice Hockey

on skates or a wide knowledge of the art of skating; but a hockey player must be able to start, stop and turn in a flash, with sureness of balance.

"Next in importance to the skating comes speed. Hockey is a fast and furious game, where speed counts for everything. A player may know the game thoroughly, and yet, if he is not as speedy as a less experienced opponent, his experience will count for little towards scoring a goal.

"Thirdly, the knack of handling a puck with the hockey is almost, if not quite, as important as the first two fundamentals. All three of these points are learned simultaneously and unconsciously by a young schoolboy as he strives to imitate the older fellows in a game of 'shinny.' Of course, a player is better off at hockey for an earlier start, just as in any game. Many good players have developed, however, who never played hockey until their college days."

FIELD HOCKEY

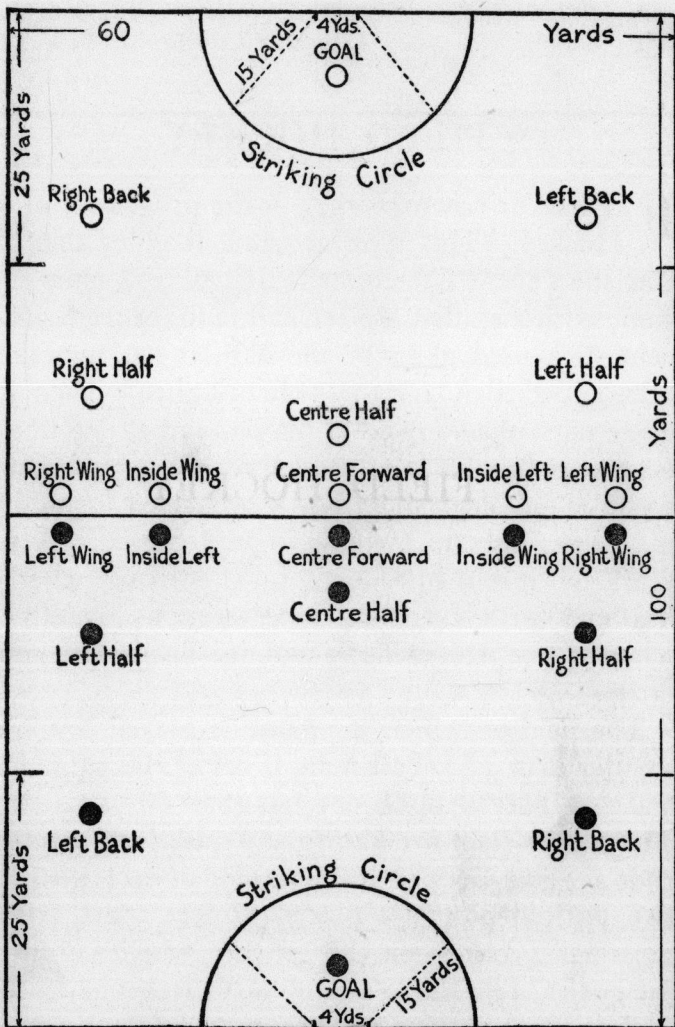

60   4 Yds.   Yards
              15 Yards   GOAL
                  Striking   Circle

25 Yards   Right Back   Left Back

           Right Half   Left Half
                        Centre Half
Right Wing Inside Wing Centre Forward Inside Left Left Wing

Left Wing   Inside Left Centre Forward Inside Wing Right Wing
                        Centre Half
           Left Half   Right Half

           Left Back   Right Back
25 Yards
                  Striking   Circle
                        GOAL
                        4 Yds.   15 Yards

284

FIELD HOCKEY

FIELD, or Lawn Hockey, is the progenitor of Ice Hockey. This type of game is older than the Christian era. The Romans first played some such game with a stuffed leather ball, and, because of the bent stick used to strike the ball, it has sometimes been called Bandy Ball. The English played this game more than any other nation, and at one time it became such a popular sport that it was regarded as a public nuisance, and a law was enacted forbidding the game, but the law was soon repealed. A few years ago it was introduced into America, where it has met with favor in some sections, chiefly in schools; but it does not equal ice hockey in popularity.

The field on which the game is played is a little smaller than a football field, it being 100 yards long and not more than 60 nor less than 50 yards wide. The longer sides are known as "side lines," and the ends as "goal lines." In the center of each goal line two upright posts are placed 12 feet apart, with a cross-bar 7 feet from the ground, which constitute the goals. The ball is an ordinary cricket ball. The stick is curved at one end and must be small enough to pass through a ring two inches in diameter.

There should be eleven players on each side, but it may be played by six, seven or nine. The accompanying diagram shows playing positions for eleven men, who are known collectively as forwards, rushes, backs, guards, and a goal tend.

At the beginning of the game and after each goal, the ball is put in play at the center of the field, by what is known as the "bully," to be played as follows: one of each side shall stand facing the side line and shall strike the ground on his own side of the ball, and the stick of his opponent over the ball alternately three times; after which either player may strike the ball, and the moment the ball is touched it is in play. During this bully the players on either side shall be "on side," i.e., between the ball and his own goal line.

When the ball is put in play the "forwards" rush down the field on their opponents' territory, and the "rushes," by a system of diagonal passing, advance the ball past the rush line of their opponents, and endeavor to get the ball into the hands of the "forwards," who should be inside or near the "striking circle." The "striking circle" is made by drawing a line twelve feet long in front of each goal, parallel to the goal line, and fifteen yards from it. The ends of the line are curved round to the goal lines, using each post as the centre of the arc. This circle is the only place from which a goal may be scored.

The forwards now having possession of the ball,

Field Hockey

all the rushes assist to pass the ball through the goal, if possible, which, if accomplished, counts one point for them. The advance guards should fall back a few paces behind the line of scrimmage to return the ball, if the opponents get it past the other rushes. The guard lies well back, and, as his name indicates, his principal duty is to check any assault made on his goal. He should never advance past the center of the field, and always hold the same relative position. He must be a sure hit, and never allow the ball to pass him. He should also be able to make accurate long hits.

It must be remembered that no definite place can be assigned each player at all times of the game, as the position will vary with the strength of the opposing team, or the individual members, the speed of the men, etc.; but each man on the team should hold, as far as possible, his own relative position, which will enable the other members of his team to pass the ball to him without taking time, which is valuable, to locate him. This will simplify matters, and teamwork thus be made stronger and the play more effective.

The goal tend stands firm, never neglecting the space allotted to him between the goal posts, and when the ball is forced to him, he kicks the ball (he being the only person on the team allowed to kick the ball), or strikes it, placing it to one side so as to prevent the ball from passing the goal. In no case when the ball is in the striking circle should it be allowed to remain in front of the goal; the defenders must use their skill and agility and put it off to one side.

No player is allowed to raise his stick above his shoulders at any time when striking at the ball, and the stroke must always be from right to left. The ball may be stopped by any part of the person, but advanced by the stick only (except in case of goal tend). Hooking sticks is allowable when within striking distance of the ball. Great skill may be developed in hooking sticks, e.g., when an opponent has the advantage and is about to have a strong hit, one is often able to hook his stick and allow another of his own side to take the ball.

Play with the back of the stick is not allowable. If during any part of the game, the ball passes the side line, it must be rolled, not thrown back, from the spot where it crossed the line, by one of the opposite side to that of the player who last touched the ball. It may be rolled any way except forward.

A "free hit" shall be given to opposite side when any player shall transgress any of the following rules:

1. Raise stick above shoulders during stroke.
2. Kicking ball (except goal tend).
3. Off-side play, i.e., when a player hits the ball and another player of the same side is nearer his opponent's goal line than three of his opponents.

Photo by Underwood & Underwood

FIELD HOCKEY

Spirited match between two school girl teams, at Philadelphia.

4. Playing with back of stick.

5. Striking ball other than from right to left.

6. Pushing, tripping, collaring, kicking, charging, or any unnecessary rough play.

7. Fouling, i.e., crossing a man from left to right when he is about to strike the ball.

On a free hit no player of the offending side shall be within five yards of spot where the hit is made, and the striker must not touch the ball again until it has been touched by another player.

When the defending side transgresses any of the above rules (except Nos. 1 and 5), *inside* of the striking circle, a "penalty bully" shall be given, at which time all players, except the offender and one from the other side, shall be outside of striking circle, and the two shall bully as at the centre, only no other player may interfere until a goal has been scored or the ball passes outside of striking circle. In the event of the latter, the ball is again in play for all the players.

Breaking rules Nos. 1 and 5 by defendants inside of striking circle, a "bully" only may be given.

When the ball passes the goal line outside of goal, by the stroke or kick of defendants, a "free hit" shall be given from the corner where the side and goal lines meet; and, during this hit, all of the defending side shall be back of goal line, and the attacking side outside of striking circle. If the attacking side puts the ball over the goal line outside of goal, it shall be a "bully" at the twenty-five-yard line, to be played the same as the bully at the center.

The time of the game is two thirty-five minute halves, with ten minutes' intermission, subject to change if both sides are agreed.

LAWN BOWLS

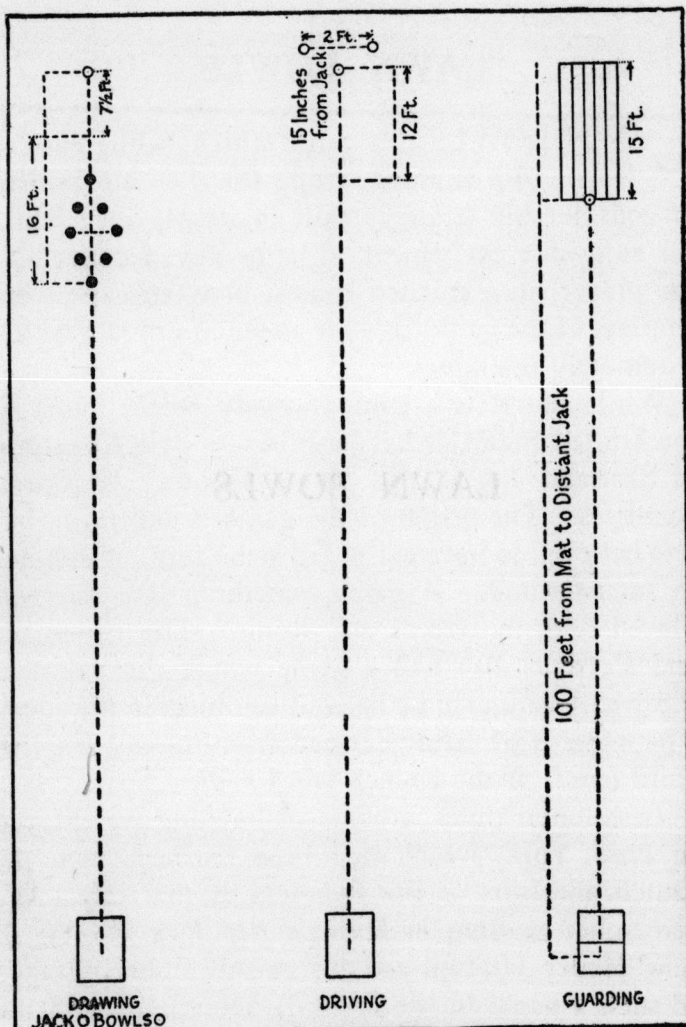

DRAWING
JACK O BOWLS O

DRIVING

GUARDING

7½ Ft.

16 Ft.

15 Inches O
from Jack

2 Ft.
O

12 Ft.

15 Ft.

100 Feet from Mat to Distant Jack

LAWN BOWLS

L AWN BOWLS is a game which, while easy to learn, affords ample scope for the employment of considerable strategic skill in its playing; while for enjoyable excitement, alike to the spectator and the player, in a spirited contest between expert exemplars of the game, it is far ahead of croquet which it remotely resembles.

While bowls is a comparatively recent game in the United States, it has long been a prime favorite in Scotland and is also played in other European countries. The origin of the game is uncertain, but it is believed to have existed in some form or another in ancient times. A game something like this was played both in Greece and Rome. The Egyptians and Persians also had a game where the ball was thrown or delivered by hand at an object in the court. The name is probably derived from the old English word *bowle* or the French word *boule*.

In colonial times, a game of bowling was played in New York, which had been learned from the Dutch ancestors of the founders of that city. We remember reading in Irving's *Rip Van Winkle* of how Henry Hudson and his ghostly crew indulged in such a game in the Catskill Mountains, and the peals of thunder were said to be the noise made by the balls rolling and striking the pins. The New Yorkers themselves used to play at "bowling on the green" down on a green sward near the Battery; and the name "Bowling Green" is perpetuated to this day for that locality. This early game of bowling was the origin of ten-pins which soon after became an indoor sport. (See Bowling.)

Lawn bowls, which as its name implies, is played only on the turf or ground, does not involve the use of pins as marks or objects, but is played only with balls. It is similar in principle to the old Scotch game of curling, also to shuffleboard and to quoits. In bowls, the "jack" is the center of attraction for the bowler, as the "tee" is to the curler, or the "pin" to the quoiter. The player aims to bowl his ball as near to the jack as it can safely lie, while the curler slides his curling stone as near as possible to the tee or center of the circle; and the quoit player strives to ring the pin with his quoit. It requires great muscular strength to engage in curling or quoiting, but in bowls strategic skill rather than mere strength comes in play.

HOW THE GAME IS PLAYED

The directions for playing the game are as follows: A small ball, perfectly round, and called the "jack," is placed on the ground. The bowlers—each using two balls which are numbered to distinguish them from each other—take up their positions at a

Lawn Bowls

certain distance from the jack, and each in turn bowls toward it, he whose ball comes nearest counting one. When there are more than two players, sides are formed, the balls being played alternately, and the side that lands a ball nearest the jack counts one point. The number of points necessary to win the game varies, but is generally fixed at twenty. When only two play they may stand side by side to deliver their balls; when there are several on a side the usual plan is to bowl from opposite ends of the green, the jack being placed in the middle.

Where there are four players, the first one is called the Lead; the second, Second; the third, Third; and fourth Skip or Driver. The playing green should be not less than forty yards square, and should have a smooth level surface. The ground is bounded by a ditch 6 inches deep and 18 inches in width. The playing space is sub-divided into spaces called rinks, each not less than 19 nor more than 21 feet in width.

The balls which are used are of lignum vitae and are not exactly round, but are made with a bias.

The object ball at which the playing balls are hurled is called a "jack" or "kitty." This is a small white ball about 2½ inches in diameter.

RULES OF THE GAME

The following are abridged from the official rules adopted by the Scottish Bowling Association, which are generally recognized among bowlers in this country:

Rinks or Divisions of the Green

The green shall be divided into spaces called rinks, not less than 19 nor more than 21 feet in width, numbered consecutively, the center of each rink being marked on the bank at each end by a pin or other device, and the four corners of the rink by pins driven into the ditch. The side boundary of the rink shall stretch from bank to bank.

Bowls and Jack

No bowl shall exceed 16½ inches in circumference, nor 3½ pounds in weight, nor have a less bias than the standard bowl.

Markers. In single-handed tournaments one marker only shall act in each game. The marker may answer queries as to position of bowls and their distance from the jack, but shall not give directions to, nor consult with, either player as to the play. Markers shall be appointed by the directors of the tournament, local secretaries, or umpires, whom failing, by the competitors themselves.

The jack shall be about 2½ inches in diameter.

Conditions of a Game

1. A game may consist of any number of shots or heads, or may be played for any length of time, as previously agreed upon.

Lawn Bowls

2. When a match consists of more than one risk on each side, the total scores of the respective parties shall decide the contest.

3. When a game consists of a stated number of heads, and there is only one rink on each side, should it be found when the given number of heads has been played that the scores are equal, one extra head shall be played so as to decide the contest, and should the extra head result again in a tie, one more shall be played.

Rink or Team of Players

1. A rink or team shall consist of four players, each playing two balls, and called respectively, according to the order in which they play, leader or lead, second player, third player, and skip or driver. Unless otherwise mutually agreed upon, it shall be determined by tossing or by playing a trial head, which party is to play first, the winner of the toss or the head to have the choice. In all subsequent heads the party which won the previous head play shall play first. The leaders play their two bowls alternately, and so on, each pair of players in succession to the end. The order of playing shall not be changed after the first head has been played. No one shall play until his opponent's bowl has ceased to run; a bowl so played may be stopped, and sent back to be played over again.

2. A bowl played by mistake shall be replaced by the player's own bowl.

3. When a player has played before his turn, the opponents may stop the bowl in its course, or allow it to remain when it comes to rest, or cause it to be played over again in its proper order. If it has moved either jack or bowls, the opponents shall have the power to cause the end to be begun anew.

4. No player shall change his bowls during the game, except with the consent of the opposing party.

5. If less than three players appear on either side, the game, so far as that rink is concerned, shall not proceed, and the rink with which this occurs shall be held as having *failed to appear,* and shall forfeit the game. Should such forfeiture take place where more rinks than one from each club are concerned, and where the aggregate or average scores are to decide the contest, the scores of the remaining rinks only shall be counted, but such average shall, as a penalty in the case of the defaulting club, be arrived at by dividing the aggregate score by the number of rinks which should have played, and not, as in the case of the other club, by a number actually engaged in the game.

Skips or Drivers

1. The skips shall have sole charge of their respective rinks, and their instructions must be obeyed by the other players.

2. The skip shall have the control of the play, but

he may delegate this duty at any time to a substitute, who is usually the third player.

3. As soon as a bowl is greened, the director must retire behind the jack.

4. The players not engaged must stand *jack-high,* or behind the mat-line.

5. The last player should remove the mat to the bank.

6. The two skips shall be judges of all disputed points, and when they agree, their decision shall be final; if they cannot agree, the point shall be decided by the umpire previously appointed, whom failing, by a neutral person mutually chosen.

The Cloth or Mat

1. Each player, when playing, shall stand with at least one foot on the mat.

2. The mat shall, at the first head, be placed by the leader of the party which is to play first, and in every subsequent head by the leader of the party which lost the previous head; but it shall be in the option of the winner of any head to have the mat laid at the place where the jack lay, or between it and any point backward not less than one yard from the ditch, the mat in any case being placed in the center of the rink. In starting play, or when the jack at the finish of a head lies in the ditch, or less than one yard from it, the mat shall be placed forward to about that distance. The mat shall not be

moved till the head is finished, but if moved by accident or inadvertently, it shall be replaced as near its original position as possible. It is recommended that the size of the mat be 22 by 14 inches or thereabouts.

Throwing the Jack

1. The leader of the party which is to play first shall throw the jack.

2. If the jack run into the ditch at the first throw in a game, it shall be placed 2 yards from it. If it be thrown into the ditch at any subsequent head, the opposing party shall throw it anew, but shall not play first. When thrown less than 2 yards from the ditch, the jack should be moved out to that distance.

3. The jack shall be thrown not less than 25 yards from the mat, and if it run to one side it shall be moved straight across and placed in the line of the pins numbering the rinks. If it be thrown less than 25 yards, it shall be treated according to the rule applicable to a jack thrown into the ditch after the first head.

4. If none of the foregoing rules have been transgressed, the jack shall be played to wherever it has been thrown; or, if moved, it must be by mutual consent of parties.

5. After having been played to, it shall not be touched or interfered with in any manner otherwise

than by the effects of the play, until the result of the head has been determined.

Movement of the Jack and the Bowls

If the jack be driven into the ditch, within the limits of the rink, its place shall be accurately marked, but it shall not be removed from its place either on to the green or elsewhere except by a toucher. Should it be driven beyond the limits of the rink, that is to say, over the bank, or past the side boundary of the rink by a bowl in play, *it shall be counted dead;* but if moved by a bowl *out of play,* it shall be restored to its place.

Should the jack run against the bank or a bowl in the ditch and rebound on to the green, or after being played into the ditch it be so operated upon by a toucher as to find its way again to the green, it shall be played to in the same manner as if it had never been moved. But a bowl similarly rebounding shall, *unless it be a toucher,* be counted dead, and any bowl or jack moved thereby shall be put back to its former position.

The term "burned" is applied to a jack or bowl which has been interfered with or displaced, otherwise than by a bowl in play. (See Rules.)

Touchers

1. A bowl which touches the jack during its original course on the green, although previously it may

have also touched one or more bowls, is called a *toucher,* and counts in the game wherever it rests if on the rink, but should a bowl, after it has ceased running, fall over and touch the jack, *after another bowl has been delivered,* it is not to be accounted a toucher. No bowl can in any circumstances become a toucher when the jack is in the ditch.

2. If a toucher run into the ditch when played, or be driven into the ditch during the course of the subsequent play, the place where it rests shall be marked, but its position shall not be altered except by the action of another toucher or the jack.

3. A toucher must be distinguished by a chalk or other distinct mark. Unless it be marked before the second succeeding bowl is delivered, it is not to be accounted a toucher. If the mark be not removed from the bowl before it is played in the succeeding head, it may be regarded as a *burned* bowl, and be removed to the bank.

4. If a bowl be moved *outwards* from the jack while being marked, it must remain as it is; but if moved *towards* the jack it must be restored to its original position.

5. Touchers may act on the jack or touchers in the ditch.

Ditchers

1. A bowl which does not touch the jack in its original course on the green, and runs against the

bank or into the ditch, or is driven into the ditch by the effects of the play, is called a *ditcher,* and must be immediately removed to the bank.

2. Should a ditcher under any circumstances return to the green, it must be placed on the bank.

Possession of the Rink

1. As soon as each bowl stops running, the possession of the rink is transferred to the other party, time being allowed for marking a toucher.

2. The party in possession of the rink for the time being must not be disturbed or annoyed by their opponents.

DEFINITION OF TERMS USED IN THE GAME

Rink. A term applicable not only to the space marked out on the field of play as the green, but also to the quartet of contesting players on each side.

Jack. The object ball in the game. It consists of a round ball, not less than $2\frac{1}{2}$ inches in diameter. It is made of potter's clay, hardened and enamelled.

Cloth. The base from which the player delivers the ball to the field, and on which the player must have one foot when the ball leaves his hand.

Bowls. The balls used in play: they number eight in a full rink, exclusive of the jack used on each side; the total number of balls on each side used in a full game being eight, making a total of sixteen balls and two jacks.

Skip or Driver. The captain of the team who plays last in order.

Leader. The first player in the game; followed by the "second" and "third" players and the "skip."

Bias. A term applicable to the formation of balls which are made not strictly round, but more or less oval; the bias given the ball by its peculiar form being intended to curve it in its direction to the right or left.

Jack Burned. A technical term applied to a ball which has been interfered with or displaced by anything except by a ball in play.

Throwing the Jack. No ball in lawn bowls is, strictly speaking, "thrown," but only bowled or rolled along the green.

Green. A term used to describe the field of play, on which either one or more rinks are laid out.

Ditch. The gutter or ditch which marks the boundary of the green.

Ditcher. A ball which rolls off the field of play into the surrounding ditch.

Toucher. A bowled ball which touches the jack. If the bowled ball drives a resting ball so that it touches the jack, such ball also becomes a toucher.

Rest. Said of a bowled ball when it stops rolling.

End or Head. The innings of a game; that is, after the quartet of players finish playing on each side.

Fore and Back Hand. For all right-handed play-

Lawn Bowls

ers the "fore" hand is on the right of the player, and the "back" hand is on the left.

Footer. An old term used to indicate the square of cloth or mat on which each player places his pivot foot in delivering the ball to the jack.

Guarding. After the jack has been thrown by the leader, and the second player has rolled his ball to the jack, it is the point of play to guard the rested ball near the jack by rolling his own ball in front of it as a protection from its being driven out of its favorable position by the ball from an adversary.

Draw. To roll a ball to the mark where the skip desires it to lie.

Block a Ball. To roll the ball so that it may lie as an obstacle to the played ball of his succeeding opponent.

Rub and Set. Terms applicable to a ball which caroms off a played ball, and rests nearer the jack after caroming.

Point or Shot. To be credited to each player whose ball rests nearer the jack than any of the balls of the opposite side.

Overman. The title of a referee called in to settle a disputed point in which the umpires fail to agree.

Greened Ball. A ball that has been rolled to a resting place.

Jack High. A position which outsiders at a match must occupy; that is, they must stand back of the line of the mat, cloth, or standpoint of the player who delivers the ball.

Mat. The cloth on which the player places his foot when he first plays the ball. It is another term used to designate the "cloth" or "footer." Its size is 22 by 14 inches.

Dead Ball. A ball is regarded as *dead* the moment it ceases to roll on the field. Also if it be rolled beyond the limit of the rinks.

Innings. The playing of two balls — after the jacks have been played—by each of the contestants of each side. The term "head" is used in place of the word *inning* by old players.

Running Ball. A rolling ball.

Shot. The point made by the ball which lies nearest the jack at the close of the head or innings.

POLO

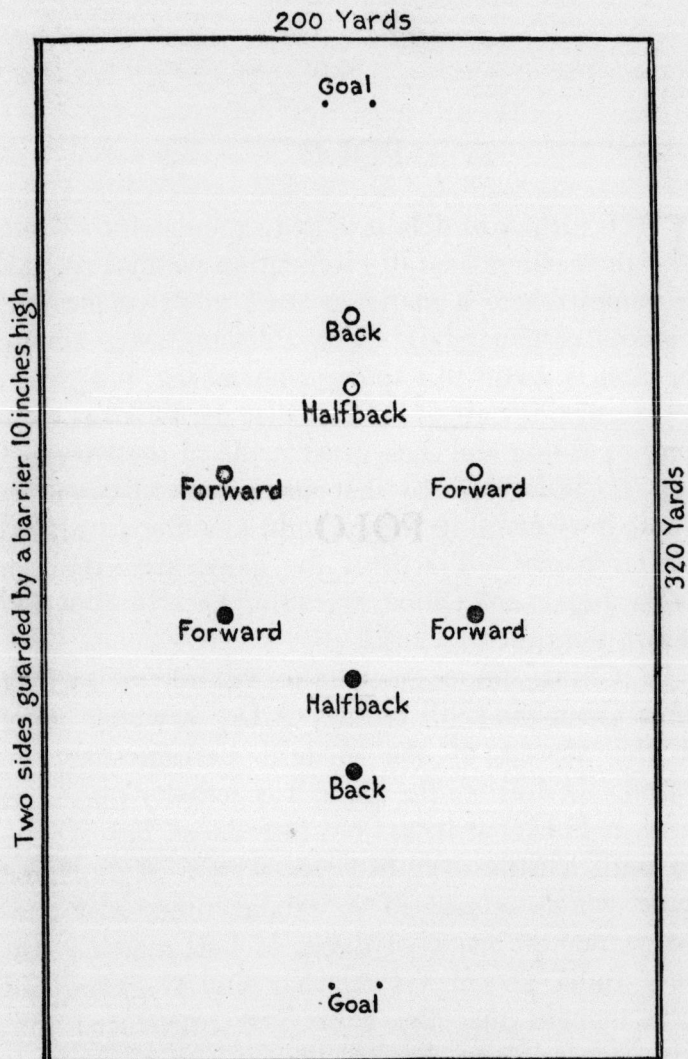

200 Yards

Goal

Back

Halfback

Forward   Forward

Forward   Forward

Halfback

Back

Goal

Two sides guarded by a barrier 10 inches high

320 Yards

308

POLO

THE history of polo is veiled in obscurity. From the earliest days of civilization we find records of games where a mallet is used to drive the ball towards certain goals. The Persians were among the first to adapt this sport to horseback, but this is not strange in view of the fact that the Persians were fond of riding and took great pride in their trained horses. It is believed that other Eastern countries where horsemanship was brought to a fine art played similar games. Traces of the game are extant in India, Japan, and China, extending back for a period before the time of Christ.

In China, there is definite record of such a game about the sixth century A.D., in which many of the aspects of the modern pastime may be traced. In Europe the game was actually played as early as 1143, but it was not introduced into America until a little over fifty years ago. A Japanese game which originated in feudal times still persists under the name of dakiu or ball match. Ancient India played a somewhat similar game, and it is thought that the game was introduced into this country from Persia, thence passing on still further east. The East Indians played the game with very little modification for several centuries, and it is still found in that country among the better class and the military.

When India came under English rule, the English army officers soon adopted this outdoor sport. They took it back to England with them where it speedily found favor among horsemen. It was played by the 10th Regiment of Hussars in 1869. Several clubs were established and by the year 1877 definite rules were formulated and a championship cup established. These rules divided the game into periods of ten minutes of play with intervals of two minutes allowed at the end of each period for changing ponies and five minutes at the half. The height of the ponies was fixed at 14.2 hands and all ponies were officially measured and registered before being allowed upon the ground. Penalties for off-side play, fouls, etc., were also fixed.

In America, the game was of slow growth, because of the fact that an expensive equipment was needed and we did not have an extensive military establishment to support it. It was considered a "gentleman's game," as it could be played only by men of means who could maintain the stables that it required. Later on, it was introduced into academies and colleges, especially where a feature was made of riding. Today it still occupies pretty much this position in American sports. It is not generally played by the masses, but is in favor with certain private clubs and may be found at various large colleges where a string of horses is kept.

The game, while exciting, does not arouse the wide applause of the masses, such as may be found at baseball or football, or even in our larger tennis matches. It is a sport for the quiet appreciation of those who can really discern the fine points of the game and recognize both good horsemanship and good generalship.

Added interest has been given to polo by the international matches which have been played between big teams of the United States and those of other countries. These matches began back in 1886, when a team from the Hurlingham Club, England, visited this country and easily captured our national cup. In 1900 and at intervals thereafter, America sent teams to England which were defeated, until the year 1909, when the team under Mr. Harry Payne Whitney's leadership regained the trophy, which was held by us until 1914, when England won again. There was a lapse in the sport due to the World War. Contests were resumed in 1921, when America regained the cup.

In the match of 1927 America captured the trophy by victories in both contests.

Sports and Games

IMPLEMENTS OF THE GAME

The first requisite of the polo player is, of course, his mount. The ponies are a special breed, the best ones having an Arabian strain. They are wiry, tough, active and intelligent beasts who speedily learn to follow their master's slightest motion; in fact, the best of them seem to know the playing points of the game itself. They are limited by law to a height of 14.2 hands.

The player is equipped with a long mallet, the handle of which permits him to strike an object on the ground without leaning very far out of his saddle. The mallet head is 7½ to 8¼ inches long. It may be either of uniform diameter or cigar shape. English players generally prefer the former while American players incline to the latter type of head. The stick may be of any length, but is usually 4 or 4½ feet long. The grip is wound with tape or leather, and a light strap attaches it to the wrist.

The ball is made of willow root, is 3⅛ inches in diameter, and its weight must not exceed 5 ounces.

The goal-posts, which are set eight yards apart, are made of some light material which will avoid injury to the player in a collision. They are usually made of light wood or papier maché. The two goals are not less than 250 yards apart.

The dimensions of a polo ground vary in different clubs, depending upon the tract of land at their disposal and the contour of the country. Where possible, it should be 320 yards in length and from 160 to 200 yards in width. It is guarded on the sides but not on the ends by a white board 10 inches high.

Any number of players may take part in a practice game. In championship contests there are four men, all of whom are skilled horsemen. The two captains agree upon a referee, timer, and scorer.

The American rules provide for four periods of play of 15 minutes each. Two minutes' rest is allowed after each goal secured, and 7 minutes between periods. In the British and Canadian rules, the game lasts for one hour actual playing time, divided into 6 periods of 10 minutes each.

At the beginning of play the referee tosses the ball into the center of the field and between the lines of opposing players who are set waiting for it. Both sides have equal opportunity to hit it, and the play continues until a goal is made, or the ball goes out of bounds, or a period ends. If the ball is driven out at the end lines, the defending side may knock it in again, and it is then placed on the line where it crossed, but not nearer than 10 feet of the goal-posts. When the ball is put in play, each team endeavors to drive it through the opposing line and score a goal. Each goal counts one point.

The four players are respectively the two for-

wards, the halfback, and the back. It is the duty of
the two latter players to support the attack of the
forwards who drive the ball against and through
the enemy's lines, if possible. Meanwhile their supporting players are protecting the ball in play from
the advance of the opponents by blocking them and
in other ways opposing their defence.

The players on the opposite side each have his
man to engage. The two forwards try to block the
efforts of the opposing forwards while the other two
men behind them endeavor to obtain and drive forward the ball. Of course, in mêlés and generally
mixed plays, these original playing positions are
lost sight of, but each player endeavors to keep his
own general duties in mind, and play so as to assist
his team-mates as much as possible, rather than try
for any individual glory, if at the expense of the
team as a whole.

As in other concerted sports, the whole success
of the team lies in its ability to work together in
powerful co-ordination. Players who have trained
together for any length of time seem intuitively to
sense what is expected of them and to fall in naturally
with the group or mass play.

Polo is a game for a man of clear head and quick
action. While the over-impulsive player often
comes to grief, he stands a much better chance of
success than the over-deliberate player. The winning player must be able to see a strategic point at

POLO

A match game between West Point and Virginia Military Institute. A grapple in midfield.

a glance, to dash forward quickly and unerringly, to assume the leadership if such is required, and either to strike the ball while going at full gallop down the field, or else pave the way so that the player behind him may have an uninterrupted field to play.

Much depends upon the training of the pony, and both in match play and practice, the leader must avoid overstraining his horse. He must have a sufficient string so that a fresh mount can be obtained at short notice. Championship contests require from four to twelve ponies for each player. Pastime games do not demand so many.

Above all, the player must so conduct himself as to give no opportunity for criticism on the part of his opponents. While in some involved plays it is almost impossible to avoid fouls, or off-side plays, they should never be intentional, and when the player's attention is called to his error by an umpire, he should be the first to recognize and abide by the decision.

QUOITS

QUOITS

LITTLE is known about the origin of the game of quoits, or its verbal derivative. It has been traced to the old French verb, *quoiter,* to stir up. The earliest resemblance to the game is found in the ancient discus throwing, which has been revived for athletic contests. The discus, however, is solid, and the object is to hurl it as great a distance as possible; while the quoit is a thick metal ring which is hurled at a mark.

Quoits was first taken up as a game, according to the few existing records, in Scotland and England about the fourteenth century. In the reign of Edward III. a royal decree was promulgated against the game, on the ground that it served no useful purpose in the way of military training. Archery was advocated instead. Ascham, a Latin scholar, alludes to it in 1545 in derogatory terms—"quoiting to be too vile for scholars."

It was frowned upon by the gentry as a common sport, but taken up by the laboring classes, as it required little playing equipment, and a court could be set up anywhere, at short notice. Then, as now, horse-shoes were often used instead of quoits.

In this country, there are two separate games,

with different scoring and rules. For example, the quoit pins are sunk flush with the ground; while the horse-shoe pins project several inches, and a prime object of the game is to "make a ringer." The game reached its height of popularity about the time of the Civil War. Official rules were drawn up in 1869.

Both quoits and horse-shoes are healthful and attractive forms of recreation. One great advantage about them is that a playing court can easily be set up in any vacant lot and the tools of the game are quite simple.

While the game as commonly played attracts little attention outside of the immediate circle of contestants, it can be developed into a high degree of skill. The outdoor exercise, the sweep of the arms, and playing conditions generally conduce to good physique.

Perhaps where one game of quoits is played professionally—that is, with strict regard to rules—a dozen are played "go as you please." But who shall say that the latter are not just as enjoyable?

The professional court should be 80 feet long by 25 feet wide. The actual pitching distance from stake to stake is 18 yards. The outside dimensions above given allow the extra space which this game requires.

The ends of the rink are circular and about three feet in diameter. Each end is filled with pottery clay of a stiff-sticking character so that when a quoit

Quoits

lands it is not easily removed by another quoit. Imbedded in the clay at each end are two iron pins, or motts, about forty inches long and one inch in diameter. They are driven into the ground until the head is even with the clay. The nearest point of a quoit to the pin only counts, and the measurement in all instances is taken from the center of the head of the pin.

In tournament games, 61 points constitute a game. Where the contest is close, the playing time often occupies three or four hours.

There is a correct way as well as an incorrect way to pitch a quoit. The poise and attitude of the man, whether or not he is a good pitcher, goes a long way toward benefiting his game.

To deliver a quoit correctly it is necessary to stand erect, with feet close together, the quoit firmly clutched and brought up to almost level with the eyes. After gauging the point to be reached, the arm should be thrown well back, and after getting the full swing, stepping out with the left foot, the "iron" should be sent to its destination. The greatest obstacle in the way of a successful pitcher is the lack of courage. No matter how perfect the position may be, or how correct you may gauge the distance, without courage the quoit is very apt to leave the hand irregularly and land far away from the point aimed at.

A point is scored for the contestant who places his

quoit nearest to the pin, and in no instance can there be more than one point scored on a single pitch. Before established rules were made for the game a quoit encircling a pin was called a "ringer" and could not be beaten unless dislodged. Under the present rules of the game, however, a "ringer," if any part of the quoit should be nearest the pin, counts for but one point.

To determine the winning quoit, measurement must be taken from that part of the quoit lying nearest the pin to the head of the pin, the measurement to be from inside the rim or outside. Frequently quoits are broken during a game by a strongly pitched quoit coming in contact with one that had previously been pitched, and in that event the piece of the broken quoit lying nearest the pin must be considered in the measurement for the point.

The above are tournament rules, however, and not generally applied to every-day contests. The rules most generally recognized are similar to the following Municipal Playground Rules in use in Chicago.

In the playground contests, Spalding Official Quoits shall be used and the weight and size shall be optional with the contestants.

The quoits used in the senior city championship matches shall not weigh less than three (3) pounds.

The distance shall be twenty feet from hob to hob in all playgrounds. The distance from hob to hob shall be thirty feet in the senior contests.

Quoits

The hob shall measure at least twelve inches in length and five-eighths of an inch in diameter.

Delivering Quoits.—1.   No steps shall be allowed ahead of the hob in the act of pitching quoits.

2.   The pitcher may stand astride the hob, provided his feet are back of line drawn at right angles from the center of the hob to a line drawn from hob to hob.

3.   The pitcher may stand back of the hob and take a step forward, provided he does not step in front of the hob.

4.   The person having the lead shall deliver both quoits consecutively.

5.   The quoits must be pitched with convex surface uppermost.

6.   A quoit turned in the act of delivering or by being struck with a pitched quoit, shall count.

Scoring of Points.—Junior contests—Twenty-one points to constitute a game; best two out of three games to decide a match.   Senior contests—Fifteen points for a game, and highest number of points in five games decides winner of series.

Ringers.—1.   A pitched quoit which encircles the hob (ringer) shall count 3 points.

2.   A double ringer shall count 6 points.

3.   A ringer, topped by an opponent, shall count 6 points for person pitching last ringer.

4.   A triple ringer scores 9 points for person pitching last ringer.

5. A ringer topped by two hobbers (both quoits must touch the hob) counts 7 points for person pitching the hobbers.

6. A pitcher placing a ringer and a hobber that may be topped with a hobber by an opponent scores 3 points for his ringer.

Hobbers.—1. A pitched quoit resting on the hob (hobber) shall count 2 points.

2. A hobber topped by another quoit shall count 2 points for quoit nearest or resting on the hob.

3. In case of an "A" and a "B" quoit resting on the hob, they shall both be removed and the nearest of the remaining two quoits count as 1 point.

4. Two hobbers shall count 4 points provided both quoits touch the hob.

Combination Plays.—1. A ringer and a hobber shall count 5 points.

2. A ringer topped by a hobber pitched by an opponent shall count 3 points for person pitching the ringer.

3. In case of a double ringer being topped by a hobber, 6 points shall be scored for person scoring second ringer.

4. In case a ringer is topped with a ringer and then a hobber by an opponent, 8 points shall be scored for person pitching the last ringer and hobber.

Single Points.—1. When neither a ringer nor a hobber is made, the nearest quoit to the hob shall count 1 point.

Quoits

2. If two "A" or "B" quoits are nearest hob, 2 points shall be scored, i.e., one point for each quoit.

3. In case of a tie between "A" and "B" quoits, they shall be removed and the remaining two measured and 1 point scored for nearest quoit.

4. Should three quoits be in contact with the hob, two shall be considered as tied, and remaining quoit scores 1 point for owner.

Holes.—Whenever a cavity six inches deep is dug out at any point around the hob, the hob must be removed to a smooth surface, still maintaining regular distance specified.

Conduct.—The use of improper language or any act perpetrated to disconcert or interrupt the players while in the act of throwing his quoit, is prohibited. Each player to have the privilege of throwing his quoit over again in the event of such having taken place.

HORSE-SHOE PITCHING

This innocent game is played, as its name implies, with regular horse-shoes. It has been familiarly called "barnyard golf" but, as a matter of fact, was played in this country long before the game of golf was heard of in barnyard circles. The official rules as adopted by the National Horse-shoe Pitchers' Association of the United States with headquarters at Akron, Ohio, are as follows:

Grounds and Courts.—The grounds shall be as

level as possible. The pitcher's box shall be filled with potter's clay or any substitute of a like nature; the clay must be kept moist and worked to a putty-like condition and to a depth of not less than 6 inches and at least 18 inches area around the stake.

Pitcher's Box.—The pitcher's box shall extend 3 feet on either side to the rear and front of the stake. Said box shall be constructed of material 2 x 4 inches and shall not extend more than 1 inch above the level of the ground. Where several or more courts are constructed, a 2 x 4-inch shall be laid the full length of such courts 3 feet in front of the stakes.

In delivering the shoe into the opposite pitcher's box, a contestant may stand anywhere inside the pitcher's box. For indoor pitching the boxes shall not exceed 6 inches in height above the adjoining grade.

Stakes.—The stakes shall be of iron, 1 inch in diameter, perpendicular, inclined 1 inch toward the opposite stake and extending 8 inches above the ground in the pitcher's box.

On single courts the stakes shall be set in the center of the pitcher's box. Where several or more courts are constructed, the stakes shall be not less than 8 feet apart, in a straight direct line where possible.

Horse-shoes.—No horse-shoe shall exceed the following regulations: 7½ inches in length, 7 inches in width, 2½ pounds in weight. No toe or heel calk shall measure over three-quarters (¾) of an

Quoits

inch in length. Opening between the calks shall not exceed 3½ inches, inside measurements. No horse-shoe constructed in a freak design will be considered regulation.

Regulation Games.—A standard regulation game shall consist of 50 points, and the contestant first scoring this number after all shoes shall have been pitched, shall be declared the winner.

In all match or exhibition games between two contestants, 11 games of 50 points each shall be an official series, and the one winning 6 games shall be declared the winner.

Pitching Distance.—The standard regulation distance shall be 40 feet from stake to stake, measuring where the stake enters the ground. For women in contests and tournaments, the distance shall be 30 feet.

Pitching Rules.—No contestant shall walk across to the opposite stake and examine the position of his opponents' shoes before making his first or final pitch.

All contestants shall pitch both shoes from the pitching box, into the opposite pitching box, or forfeit the value of 1 point to his opponent.

All contestants having first pitch, after delivering both shoes, shall stand back of a line even with the stake and out of the pitcher's box.

Any contestant failing to comply with this rule shall forfeit the value of such shoes pitched.

Any contestant delivering his shoes outside of the opposite pitcher's box shall forfeit the value of his pitch.

Wrapping the fingers with tape, or the wearing of gloves, shall be permitted in any or all games.

If at any time a shoe is broken, such as by striking another shoe, the frame of the pitcher's box, the stake or other cause, such shoe shall be removed, and the contestant entitled to another pitch.

Ringers.—Any shoe to be scored as a ringer shall encircle the stake far enough to permit a straight edge to touch both heel calks and clear the stake.

Foul Lines.—A foul line shall be established 3 feet in front of the stake, and any pitcher stepping over the foul line in delivering his shoe shall lose the value of his pitch and no score shall be credited to him.

Foul Shoe.—A shoe that does not remain within 6 inches of the stake, in all national tournaments and match contests, shall not be entitled to score. (This does not apply to informal pitching or games where the players decide otherwise.)

If a shoe strikes the frame of the pitcher's box or other object, such shoe shall be considered a foul shoe and shall not score.

Points.—The most points a contestant can score in a single game shall be 50.

A pitcher shall be credited with all ringers pitched.

Quoits

If a shoe when thrown moves another shoe, both shoes are counted in their new positions.

Ties.—All equals shall be counted as ties. If both contestants have one shoe each an equal distance from the stake, or against the stake or ringers, they shall be counted tie, and the next closest shoe shall score. In case of all four shoes being tie or equal distance from the stake, or four ringers, no score shall be recorded and the contestant who pitched last shall be awarded the lead.

Measurements.—All measurements shall be made by the use of calipers and a straight edge.

Coaching.—No contestants during the progress of a game, contest or tournament, shall coach, molest or in any way interfere with a pitcher in any manner, except that in four-handed games, partners shall have the right to coach each other.

First Pitch.—At the beginning of a game the contestants shall agree as to who shall have the first pitch, either in single, three or four-handed games, by the toss of a coin, the winner to have his choice as to lead. At the beginning of the second game the loser of the preceding game shall have the first pitch.

National and State Tournaments.—In all championship tournaments the rotation group method shall prevail. In each group each pitcher will pitch every other game. Same procedure shall prevail in the finals.

All tie games shall be pitched off.

No championship shall be won or lost otherwise than in a legal tournament.

Disputes and Final Jurisdiction.—In case of any dispute, or where the rules do not specifically cover a disputed point, the referee or committee in charge shall have full power and final jurisdiction.

Scoring Rules.—Any shoe that does not remain within 6 inches of the stake shall not be scored or counted in championship contests.

The closest shoe to the stake (within 6 inches) shall score 1 point. If both shoes are closer than the opponent's they shall score 2 points.

A ringer shall score 3 points.

A ringer and a closest shoe shall score 4 points.

A double ringer shall score 6 points and is the highest score a contestant can make.

In case of each contestant having a ringer, the next closest shoe shall score, and all such ringers shall be credited as ringers pitched but not counted as a score.

If each contestant has a double ringer, both double ringers are cancelled and no points scored.

If a contestant shall have two ringers and his opponent one, the pitcher having two ringers shall score 3 points.

In case of a tie of all four shoes, such as four ringers or all four shoes an equal distance from the stake, no score shall be recorded, and the contestants who pitched last will be awarded the lead.

Quoits

Where ringers are pitched and cancelled, they shall be credited to the contestant who pitched such ringers, and no score shall be credited as points scored.

All equals shall be counted as ties and no points scored.

Any shoe leaning against a stake shall have no advantage over a shoe lying on the ground and against the stake; all such shoes are ties. If a contestant has a shoe leaning against the stake it shall count only as a closest shoe.

Three-Handed Games.—In three-handed games, where two contestants each have a double ringer and the third contestant no ringers, the two contestants having double ringers shall score their shoe no count. If all three contestants each have a ringer they shall score the closest shoe. If two contestants each have a ringer and the third contestant no ringers, the two contestants having ringers shall score their closest shoes.

In all three-handed games the contestants having ringers shall at all times score their closest shoes over their opponents who have no ringers, whether it be two contestants with double or single ringers each.

In any and all games the contestant scoring shall have the lead or pitch.

SKATING

SKATING

JUST how far back in the remote past skating ceased to be a necessity and was taken up as a luxury, nobody knows. It is quite probable in those far-off days when Northern Europe was ice bound, that people traveled from one point to another very extensively on skates. These skates may have originally been flat pieces of wood turned up at the end like sled runners, and later perhaps forms of horn, before people learned how to make skates from metal. The Dutch today in winter-time use their canals as such highways of communication both by skates and sled, showing the evolution of this means of transportation from early times.

Undoubtedly there must have been a species of skating in antiquity, for a bone skate, which is the earliest form of skate preserved for us, was dug up in the Moorfields near London, in 1841, and from the soil and other relics it must have dated back to at least the twelfth century.

One of the first recorded mentions of the sport occurs in Evelyn's diary written in 1662, which speaks of skating and skaters more than once. Pepys, a still more famous diarist of the same time, makes mention of the skating costume of the day and especially of "the very short petticoat of the Princess of Orange," as she "did slide upon her scates, first on one foot and then on the other." If Pepys was shocked at the skating attire of the Princess, we wonder what he would think of the knickerbocker suits of the girls of today!

There is very little in early literature referring to skating except brief records of skating events. Addison wrote a poem on the subject in the year 1720, but the other poets generally preferred to write about springtime and flowers and their lady's eyes, rather than a subject so inherently cold as skating.

The first skating club of which we now have a record was organized in Edinburgh in the year 1744. The sport was very little known, however, during the ensuing twenty-five or thirty years, for in the life of Benjamin West, the famous American painter who went abroad and painted royalty, we read that he attracted a great deal of attention by his ability to skate. West came from Pennsylvania and may have learned this accomplishment in boyhood from the Indians, although very little is said in regard to the skill of the Redskins on ice.

In the year 1791, the young man Napoleon Bonaparte while a student at military school had a narrow escape from drowning while skating on the ice. In 1809 the first book on skating was published in England and appeared in the Latin tongue. Why it should have been addressed to scholars rather than

Skating

to the general public, nobody knows. Five years later, another book on the subject entitled "Frostiana" appeared with its hints and suggestions to skaters, who were evidently recognized as being in considerable numbers. One curious recommendation of this book reads that the skater carry a bag of shot in certain pockets in order to assist him in maintaining the correct balance.

While skating was known in America for many years previous to this, as witness the Benjamin West episode, there appears not to have been any formal cognizance of the sport until about the middle of the last century. In the year 1849, a skating club was organized in Philadelphia, and eleven years later one in New York. A skating carnival was held in Brooklyn during the time of the Civil War.

It was about this time that two of the most famous of the earlier skaters in America began to attract world-wide attention. Jackson Haines, pictures of whom represent an extremely handsome man with well-formed legs, won fame in America for his fancy skating and then went abroad where he was the leading figure at skating carnivals and won many prizes. W. H. Fuller, who has been styled the father of figure skating in New England, also attracted wide attention abroad. He is described as a remarkably brilliant figure skater who invented many of the designs which are still dear to the hearts of all fancy skaters.

Sports and Games

From this time on, interest in skating increased rapidly both in America and in Europe. National competitions were held and world records for various events and distances became the features. About the year 1915, interest in skating reached its culmination. It grew overnight into a tremendous fad, theatres, dance halls and restaurants installing small skating rinks as regular features where star performers could entertain with their figure skating in lieu of the usual cabaret song and dance. The Hippodrome of New York converted its huge stage into a rink on which was staged an elaborate ice ballet. At the same time, indoor rinks were opened in cities all over the country, even as far south as San Diego, California. These took the place of the once popular roller skating rinks. Whether or not ice skating will subside as suddenly as that popular craze of a few years ago is still a matter of conjecture, as each winter ice rinks all over the country do a flourishing business.

Like all Gaul, skating may be divided into three parts—pleasure skating, racing, and fancy skating.

SKATING FOR FUN

By pleasure skating we mean, of course, the usual type of skating indulged in by the great American public—those who go in for the joy of the sport at odd moments and do not bother their heads about fancy figures or great speed. But even these ordinary every-day skaters can get some tips from the others that it would be well to follow. It is just as easy to learn to skate properly and gracefully as it is to plod around over the ice awkwardly.

The most common faults of all beginners and many who have skated for a long time are these: (1) Bending over the head too far and at an awkward angle. This is probably done at first in an effort to keep one's balance, but then later to acquire speed. But it is awkward for several reasons. It is liable to pitch one forward, if the skater encounters a crack or other obstacle in the ice; it prevents the lungs from filling with air; and it prevents the skater from looking about him properly as he dashes madly ahead through the crowd. (2) Flourishing the arms. How often do we see skaters go around like animated wind mills! They try to correct every slight loss of balance by wild gestures, first on one side and then the other. (3) Bending the knee joint. This is one of the most common faults of all. It tends to hold the body in an awkward position. The legs especially the one not employed should be thrown out full and free. (4) Swinging from side to side. While a certain amount of rhythm is graceful and adds to ease in skating, any pronounced swaying gives the skater the effect of a ship at sea.

The Natural Carriage.—From the moment when you first set foot upon the ice try to assume and cultivate a natural carriage. Remember that skating is not widely different from walking, and if one learns the wrong way it is very hard to unlearn and cultivate the right way. Hold the head upright as much as possible with the shoulders squared well back so that the lungs can be easily filled with life-giving air. Do not open the mouth or part the lips any more than necessary, as this not only looks ugly but tends to chap the lips. Glance from side to side as you skate just as though you were walking down the street, and try to forget as soon as possible your medium of locomotion. Glance down only enough to watch your step and avoid cracks, rough places and other pitfalls, but only an occasional glance is required to insure you of safety. With this assurance take your glance resolutely away from the ice ahead of you, and look round about you at the moving throng and the wintry landscape. Skating is like any other sport in developing confidence. In this it is somewhat like bicycle riding. Your seasoned cyclist scarcely glances at the ground at all and at times is so supremely confident of what his wheel will do, that he takes his hands entirely off the handle-bars.

With head held erect and naturally, allow the arms to swing freely as you skate. Do not try to hold them rigid any more than you should wish to swing them around unnecessarily. When walking you usually forget about your arms entirely. Do the same thing when skating. Some skaters like to fold

Wide World Photos

SKATING

A professional racer warming up at Lake Placid.

them and hold them this way. Such a pose, however, is likely to look stilted and assumed. Other skaters, especially the speed skaters, prefer to hold the arms behind their backs with the fingers interlaced. This again is an awkward attitude for the ordinary pleasure skater. If it will help you, hold some small object in the hand such as a light hockey stick, but avoid above all things the wild waving of the arms already mentioned. Do not carry any attitude to extremes. If a slight swaying of the arms will assist you, especially in turning a corner, do not hesitate to let them swing, but avoid keeping up such swinging beyond the moment necessary.

Swaying of the body or bending it sidewise from the hips is of course caused by caution on the part of the skater. He may be rounding a corner, or dodging an obstruction, or trying to preserve his balance while on the outer edge of one skate, but such a movement is instinctive and natural and the only caution is to avoid using it so often that it becomes habitual. As to the posture of the legs, Irving Brokaw, the champion figure skater, has this to say: "The 'unemployed' leg must be only slightly bent; excessive hooking gives it a very clumsy appearance, and, moreover, does away with its utility. This 'unemployed' leg is sometimes called the 'balance' leg, which is perhaps a more correct term, because although the skate is off the ice, the unemployed leg has as much, if not more, control in the execution of a movement than the employed, or tracing leg, and it must be used to help the skater and not be repressed. Smoothness and grace in skating are largely due to the proper use of the limbs. The unemployed foot must be carried in such a manner that the toe is always pointing downwards and outwards. Carrying the toe outwards is managed by turning the unemployed leg outwards from the hip. This will be found not easy at first. It is, however, essential that a skater should overcome this difficulty by practice, if proficiency is to be obtained."

To sum up the foregoing, we cannot do better than quote the following concise rules for correct form which have been recognized by figure skaters and are of no less value to the casual skater:

1. Head erect with eyes upon the ice seldom or never during the free-skating, and, in the school skating, no more than is absolutely necessary.

2. Body upright, not bent forwards or sidewise from the hips, shoulders thrown back, and chest expanded.

3. Arms, whether active or passive, should have free play from the shoulders, elbows slightly bent, hands with the palms downward or inward.

4. Skating legs always bent at the knee, to insure a springy rise and dip of the body.

5. Free leg poised or swung entirely from the hip, in the socket of which it should be turned outward and backward as much as possible; always

Skating

separated from the skating leg, knee slightly bent, toe pointing down and out.

We might add to the above that graceful and easy skating is promoted by long sustained strokes. Your choppy skater gets nowhere. Take a full stroke, raising the free foot high and getting the full effect of your momentum before bringing this foot down to the ice for a second stroke.

RACING

After having thoroughly mastered the ordinary skating strokes, the athletic young man or woman will naturally be interested in speed contests. Every year in all of the large cities such contests are held, and hardly a year goes by without some record for short dashes being broken.

The speed skater, like the foot racer, must be guided by certain definite rules. These apply to the start of the race itself and to the finish. A good start can be made by digging the toes of the skates into the ice and poising crouched ready for a quick get away at the firing of the pistol. Other contestants are allowed a flying start and timed as they cross the starting line; as it takes some little effort and time to attain one's full speed on skates, this is really the fairest way to judge speed on the ice. Don't scramble as you go down the fairway. Don't be worried about what the skater on the right or left of you is doing. Keep your eyes fixed on the goal post and head for it with long even strokes, conserving your energy as much as possible for the final dash. Don't open the mouth. Don't swing the arms except to aid the poise of the body at critical times. A forward pose of the body is preferred by some successful skaters, but undue bending looks exaggerated and really handicaps the breathing apparatus.

To illustrate the various types of speed contests together with the time made in some, we will quote from the program and speed records of the International Speed Skating Championship Contests held at Saranac Lake, N. Y., in February, 1922.

Senior, Three-Quarter Mile Race, time, 2.06 1-5. Senior, Half-Mile Race, time, 1.25 3-5. Senior, One-Mile Race, time, 3.15 2-5. Junior (16 years), 800-Yard Dash, time, 1.34 4-5. Senior, 440-Yard Dash, time, 0.41 3-5. Senior, Three-Mile Race, time, 10.03 3-5. Junior, One-Mile Race (16 Years), time, 3.33 4-5. Junior, 220-Yard Dash (16 Years), time, 0.23.

The World's Distance Championships, held at Christiania, Norway, in the same month were reported as follows: 500 metres, 0.43 3-5 (a new Norwegian record); 5,000 metres, 8.21 1-2 (world's record); 1,500 metres, 2.22 4-5; 10,000 metres, 17.37 1-5.

FIGURE SKATING

As soon as the skater has gained confidence and can skate in the ordinary way, he should begin to

Skating

master the art of skating upon the outside edge of the blade. Put upon the ice a small stone, a piece of wood, or any other object to serve for a center. Leaning a little in the direction of this center, and pressing your weight upon the outer edge of the skate, push yourself round and round the center with your left foot. Then practice going round on the outside edge of your left skate in a similar way. Difficult as these movements will be at first, they become easy like other hard tasks by practice, and they open the way to graceful figure skating.

When the two circles have been mastered it is quite easy to cut a figure 3 upon the ice. Begin on the outside edge of the right skate as though you meant to go in a circle, but allow your left foot to hang behind your right foot. There it will act as a kind of weight, your body will tend to swing around, and you will cut out the second part of the 3 traveling backwards, and upon the inner edge of the skate. The impetus gained in cutting the first part of the figure will carry you to the end. Going in the other direction cut another 3 with your left foot, and when you can do these you are on the high road to complete success as a skater.

Says Irving Brokaw, who is an acknowledged authority on this subject: "Striking developments have taken place in the last few years in the art of skating. The theory of the art has been made so simple, and the exposition of the theory so clear and practical, that not only may older people learn to skate from printed instructions, but boys and girls also, if once they think it worth while to try and get over the idea that the hockey skate and the game constitutes all there is in the art of skating. All persons who would like to learn to skate must devote themselves solely to the practice of the art of figure skating and make use of the skate devoted to that purpose, which, instead of having a perfectly flat runner, is curved on the bottom, so as to make it possible to execute curves and circles on the ice, which are the fundamental elements of the art."

The general suggestions already made for correct carriage in regular skating are no less important in figure work. The body should be held easily and naturally with the employed leg slightly bent at the knee and the other leg straight. The skating toe should always be pointed slightly outward unless one has done an evolution and a particular figure which requires an inward curve. Use both arms and legs freely and easily. This not only promotes balance and consequent facility for making figures but also keeps the body from undue strain and weariness.

The elements of figure skating include: 1. The curve down the four edges. 2. Outside and inside forwards. 3. Outside and inside backwards. It is a combination of these three movements which results in all of the intricate figures which are practiced by the finished skater.

Skating

Do not begin by trying to do loops and curves, figure 8's and spread eagles as small as possible. Instead, do them as large as possible. It is a mistaken idea that to become accustomed to doing large figures makes the execution of small figures difficult. The reverse is the case. After one has learned how to execute the large figure involving several loops, he can practice the same figure daily, each time making it a little bit smaller and thus acquiring perfection for figure as well as its small size at one and the same time.

Bear in mind that from the very outset the free and full use of both feet is essential to good figure skating. No skater can succeed if he persistently favors one foot at the expense of the other. With most of us one foot is by nature a little bit weaker or a little clumsier than the other. It is the object of the beginner to discover which foot is the weaker and practice it all the more. If there is a disinclination to use it, that should be a signal to continue to use it until such weakness is conquered. When the two feet are equally efficient, the figure skater is on the right road to success—but not before.

Begin as with plain circles the large size, such as will all point into the well-known figure 8. Learn to do this both forward and backward and on any edge of the skate.

Professional skaters are required to execute such figures through "rest." Thus, if you stand on your right foot, the whole momentum required to complete the figure must be gained by one stroke or thrust from the side of the left skate. There can be no running start in this work, and the stroke must be taken from the side rather than the toe of the skate. This is not easy to acquire, but later the skater will find that there is a certain trick in suddenly throwing the body forward and thus gaining momentum for the desired stroke.

School Figures. The fancy figure skater recognizes certain definite "school figures" which are just as formal and precise as the waltz and the polka to the dancing master. For example, there is a group of elementary school figures which include circles, eights, serpentines, threes, double threes, loops, brackets, rockers and counters. Each of these elementary school figures is made in one of four prescribed ways, depending upon the stroke of the skate, and if made in any other way is incorrectly done. Next come the series of advanced school figures which include one foot eight, change-three, change-double, change-loop, change-bracket, three-change-three, double - three - change - double - three, loop - change-loop, bracket-change-bracket. These also are made in four ways each, in order to follow the prescribed rule. In addition to these school figures, there are at least sixteen others done in America and known by American names such as Forward Cross Mohawk, Forward Cross Choctaw, etc. All these sixteen figures are combinations of the Mohawk and Choctaw. The Mohawk figure is a method of going forward to backward or backward to forward on an edge of the same character. It is effected by spreading the feet and can be easily done by those who have learned the spread eagle. The Choctaw is somewhat more difficult and alludes to the position of the feet by which it is possible to put the unemployed foot down on the inside back tread instead of the outside back. Inasmuch as both of these figures or combinations of figures are made by cross strokes or reverse strokes, they have not been recognized by many skating professors. Cross strokes, in fact, if not well done, are extremely awkward and can hardly be regarded as anything but skating curiosities. For this reason it is not at all probable that they will ever win favor. There seems to be no reason, however, beyond the difficulty of skating them, why the forward Choctaws and Mohawks should not take their place in the regular repertoire of first-class skaters. It is only by means of these steps that inside and outside back threes, emanating from and ending at the center, can be successfully erected.

We cannot, of course, attempt to teach fancy skating in the present article. We are only setting forth some of its guiding principles and we doubt frankly if any book, no matter how explicit and well illustrated, can give the fancy skater the pointers he demands. He should put himself under the guidance of an advanced skater and learn by practical instruction on the ice the proper method of making these figures. Once having mastered them on the ice, it is possible to take a book on the subject and read up still further, as well as to get suggestions for new figures.

DANCING ON THE ICE

A variation of figure skating and especially of such skating in pairs which has become extremely popular among exhibition skaters is dancing on the ice. For this also very definite and rigid rules have been laid down. The skater is taught the waltz, the schottische, the mazurka, and other forms of dances. A few years ago a dancer from Russia known as Charlotte created a furore by her beautiful fancy steps. She has been followed by a school of imitators.

In judging dancing competitions on the ice, the judges often have a ruled score card marked under the heads: A—Carriage; B—Grace; C—Unity; D—Time.

Carriage includes erect carriage and parallel positions, accurate curves and smooth turns. Grace includes suppleness, pliancy, and flexibility. Unity includes striking at same moment, absolutely simultaneous rotation, unity and harmony of movement. Time includes time to the music; rhythmic, undulatory movement.

Skating

Another highly interesting and exciting form of amusement on ice is that of skate sailing. A sail can be improvised from almost any spread or canvas and rigged up by any boy who has ingenuity; and can be so arranged that it can be rolled up and carried to and from the ice under one's arm.

In general, the most satisfactory style of sail is square shaped or rectangular, having a spar at top and bottom and one in the center to hold the fabric rigid. Another popular shape is triangular or kite shaped. Instead of heavy canvas, balloon silk or even unbleached muslin has been found satisfactory. On a straightaway course with the wind behind one, a tremendous speed can be obtained reaching as fast as thirty miles per hour. A skater, however, had better be very sure of his own footing and skill at skating before attempting this tricky sport.

One of the simplest forms of sails is the triangular style which comes about as high as the skater's shoulders. It is formed by a cross spar from six to eight feet long, and a center sprit which comes down to the peak of the sail or about the tip of the shoe of the skater. From this frame is suspended a triangular piece of sail which comes to a point at the bottom. It is held in position by the skater with extended arms and behind him, and by turning slightly to the right or left the skater will be enabled to control his direction to some extent.

SOCCER

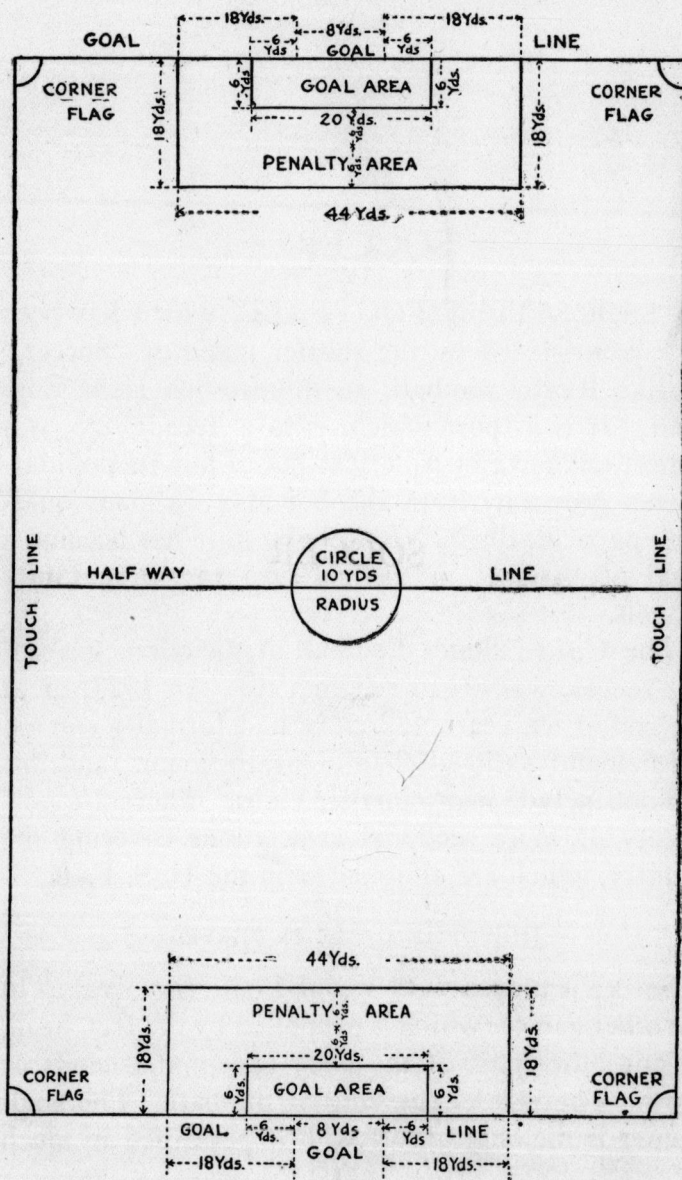

SOCCER

ASSOCIATION FOOTBALL, which has been rechristened by the shorter name of "Soccer," is, like Rugby football, an importation from England. It is a sport which, even a decade ago, was almost unknown in America; but of late its popularity has grown by leaps and bounds. In many quarters, particularly in New England, it has become a rival of baseball in the colleges and preparatory schools.

The United States Football Association, governing soccer, was organized in 1913. In 1923, or at the end of ten years, 132 clubs had formally entered the field for national championship honors, and this did not include many smaller clubs. There are now twenty or more sectional associations covering the country, which are affiliated with the U. S. F. A.

HOW THE GAME IS PLAYED

Soccer is played with a round ball (not oval as in the other game), which is propelled by the feet, head, or any other part of the body except the hands or arms. There is no carrying of the ball. The goalkeeper is the only player who is permitted to touch

the ball with his hands, and that only within a prescribed area. The ball must be not less than 27
inches, and not more than 28 inches in circumference.
Its outer casing is of leather. Its weight is 13 to 15
ounces.

The playing field is not the accustomed gridiron,
but one marked by outside boundaries on all four
sides and bisected by a single line. This field should
be not less than 50 yards, nor more than 100 yards
wide, and not less than 100 yards, nor more than 130
yards long. It is marked by boundary lines, the sides
being drawn at right angles to the ends. A flag with
a staff not less than 5 feet high is placed in each of
the four corners.

As before stated, a half-way line is clearly marked
across the field, but there are no other distance lines.
In the center of this half-way line, and consequently
the exact center of the playing field, a circle with a
radius of 10 yards is drawn.

At each end of the field two goal-posts are erected
8 yards apart, and equidistant from the corner flags.
Across these posts a bar is placed, 8 feet from the
ground. The maximum width of the posts and of
the crossbar is 5 inches.

Each of the two goal areas is indicated by a rectangle, beginning 6 yards from each goal-post on the
goal line, and extending for 6 yards into the playing
field. These two lines are connected by another line
running parallel to the goal line.

Soccer

A larger rectangle, called the penalty area, is indicated by lines beginning on the goal line, 18 yards from each goal-post, and extending into the field 18 yards, being connected with each other by a line parallel to the goal line.

The distance for the penalty kick is indicated by a mark made opposite the center of each goal, and 12 yards from the line.

The game is played between two teams of eleven men each, viz., one goal-keeper, two full-backs, three half-backs, and five forwards. The full-backs are known respectively as right and left full-backs; the half-backs, as right, center, and left half-backs; and the forwards, as outside right, inside right, center, inside left, and outside left.

There are three officials: a referee and two linesmen.

At the start-off of the game the players occupy the following positions:

The goal-keeper in the goal; the two full-backs from 15 to 20 yards from either touchline and just within the penalty area; the wing half-backs almost directly in front of the full-backs, with a space of from 10 to 15 yards between the halves and full-backs, the center half being in the middle of the field, behind the center forward. The forwards, particularly on the side having the kick-off, are placed along the half-way line, with the center forward in the middle, the outside players almost on the touchline and the inside players from 3 to 5 yards distant from the center forward.

The side not having the kick-off cannot approach within 10 yards of the ball, which results in the center forward standing in the middle of the field on the 10-yard circle, the two inside players somewhere on the circle between the center forward and the half-way line. The outside players occupy positions on the half-way line near the touch line. The halves, full-backs and goal-keeper occupy the same positions as the opposing halves, full-backs and goal-keeper.

A blast from the referee's whistle announces the beginning of the game, and at once the center forward who, by toss* has possession of the ball, kicks it over into the enemy's country. He does not, however, send it down the center of the field. Instead, he kicks it either to the left or to the right, and one of his own team runs forward to intercept it and continue its progress down the field.

Of course, the opposing players are not idle, but at once try to intercept the ball and secure it for their own side. If any player is blocked in his own efforts, he endeavors to pass the ball to one of his team-mates —the constant effort being to retain possession of the ball, and propel it to within kicking or "shooting" distance of the enemy's goal.

If a shot at the goal is successful, the ball is

* The winners of the toss have the option of kick-off or choice of goals.

Soccer

brought back to the center of the field, and the game is restarted by a kick, taken by the center forward of the side against whom the goal has been scored.

The duration of the game is 90 minutes, divided into two halves. At the restart after half time, the opposite side to that which had the opening kick-off now takes the ball. The interval at half time must not exceed five minutes.

At any kick-off from the center of the field, the opponents are not allowed to approach within 10 yards of the ball until it is kicked off, and no player on either side is allowed to pass the center line until the ball is in play.

A goal is scored when the ball has passed between the goal-posts under the bar, not being thrown, knocked on, nor carried by any player of the attacking side.

The ball is in play if it rebounds from a goal-post crossbar, or a corner flagstaff back into the field of play. It is out of play when it has crossed the goal line or touch line, either on the ground or in the air.

The goal-keeper is allowed to use his hands to ward off the ball within his own penalty area, but is not allowed to carry the ball.

The rules of the game are particularly stringent against fouls. No tripping, kicking, striking, nor jumping at a player is allowed. An offending player is liable to suspension; and if the player attacked should attempt to retaliate he also may be suspended.

Neither can a player use his hands to hold an opponent. Charging is permissible but it must not be violent or dangerous. A player must not be charged from behind unless he is intentionally obstructing an opponent.

The "free kick" is, as its name implies, the privilege granted under certain conditions for a member of one team to kick the ball in whatever direction he wishes, while it lies stationary on a certain spot. Meanwhile the members of the opposing team must remain at a distance of at least ten yards. The kicker, however, is obliged to propel the ball at least its own circumference, and he may not touch it again before someone else. The "kick off" falls into this category, and has been described above. When the ball is propelled over the goal line of one side by a member of the other side, a "goal kick" is given to the former. This means that a player of that team may have a free kick from within any point of that half of the goal area which is nearest the spot where the ball went out. If, however, the ball on passing over the goal line was last touched by a member of that team whose goal line it is, a "corner kick" is given, which allows a member of the opposing team to kick it from within a yard of the corner staff on that side of the field. The same distance rules hold good, but in the case of this sort of a kick a goal may be made directly, which is not the case with the goal kick.

Soccer

If any one of the personal fouls enumerated above is committed, a free kick is given to the opposing team from the point where it occurred. In addition, the free kick is granted for the offense of playing the ball again before it has touched another player (in the case of throwing in, etc.), offside, carrying by goal-keeper, etc. (To be offside is to be between the ball and the opposing goal when there are not at least two opponents between one and that goal.) In the case of this sort of kick a goal may be scored directly only if the foul is one of personal violence.

"Penalty kicks" are awarded if one of the above-mentioned fouls is committed by a team within its own penalty area. In this case a goal may be scored directly, but only the kicker and the opposing goal-keeper are allowed within the penalty area. The kick, of course, takes place from the specially provided penalty kick mark.

When the ball goes outside the touch line, it is thrown in by a member of the team opposing the team which touched it last. It is usually thrown in by the half-back, and he must keep his heels on the ground, stand back of the touch line, and throw over his head with both hands. If he breaks these regulations a free kick is granted to the other side. A goal cannot be scored directly from the throw-in.

The referee has complete supervision of the playing at all times. Not only must he provide for the infringement of rules, but he is timekeeper as well. He has it in his power to expel anyone from the field for breaking of the rules, and to call the game for darkness or other suitable reason. The referee shall allow for time wasted, lost through accident or other cause, suspend or terminate the game whenever, by reason of darkness, interference by spectators, or other cause, he may deem necessary; but in all cases in which a game is so terminated he shall report the same to the association under whose jurisdiction the game was played. The two linesmen are always subject to the referee, and their sole duty is to determine whether or not the ball is out of play, and by reason of which team. When the ball goes out, they should signify the fact by displaying a white handkerchief.

IN GENERAL

The game of soccer cannot be mastered by any printed book of instructions, but should be taken up under the supervision of a coach or experienced player. It requires strong, alert players of good physique, who can use their heads for other things than to propel the ball.

Footwork is a highly essential factor in the game. The prospective player should learn how to kick or propel the ball with *every side* of the foot. He must master the art of trapping or stopping the ball with his foot; and also know how to dribble the ball along the ground, thus retaining control of it until he has the opportunity to try for a goal or pass the ball along to one of his mates.

Legwork is hardly less important. The knees can be used to fine advantage in propelling the ball, likewise in trapping it.

Passing. The player must learn how to send the ball to a mate by either a long or short pass—and also *how to receive* such passes. Until one becomes experienced, the constant temptation will be to use the arms or hands, which, of course, is out of the question.

The *chest* and the *head* are often used to advantage in stopping the ball and in propelling it. The player should become confident and fearless in using not only the front of his head, but either side as well.

Teamwork is highly important in soccer as in any other concerted game. The most valuable player is not the one who is constantly looking for star or grandstand plays, but the one who always plays with and for his side; the one who is always on the alert to intercept an opponent's ball, but at the same time has the tail of his eye upon one or more of his own side to whom he may pass it to advantage.

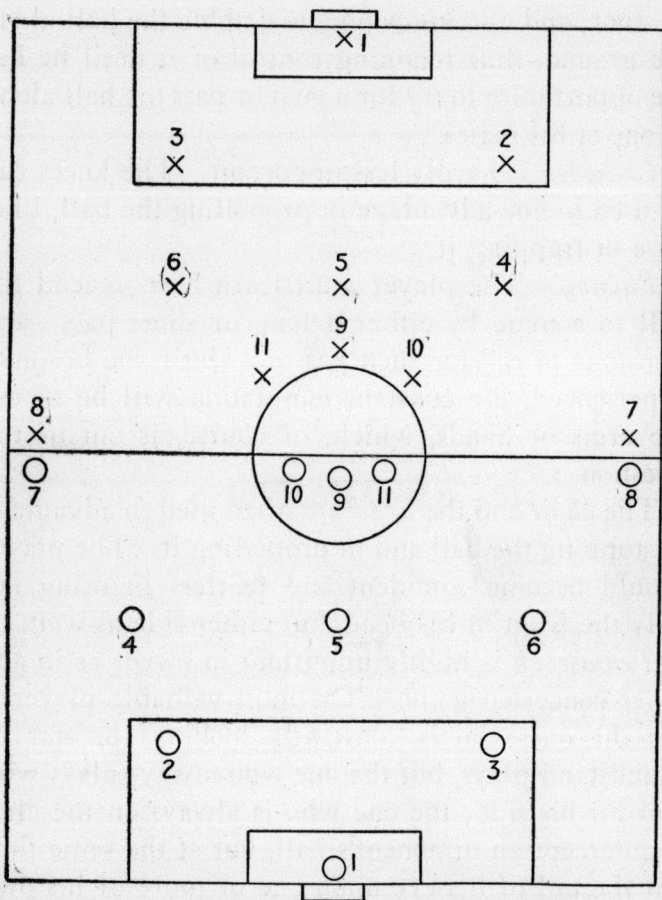

SOCCER: DISPOSITION OF PLAYERS AT KICK-OFF

X—Defending   O—Attacking

1. Goal-keeper   7. Outside Left Forward
2. Left Full-back   8. Outside Right Forward
3. Right Full-back   9. Center
4. Left Half-back   10. Inside Left Forward
5. Center Half-back   11. Inside Right Forward
6. Right Half-back

364

SWIMMING

SWIMMING

A S an exercise swimming is recognized as among
the most beneficial of all. It is enjoyable,
stimulating, and tends to fine physique, good respira-
tion and good circulation. As a means of saving life,
it is even more important. Not only do thousands of
people who cannot swim go in the water as a sport,
but there is also constant travel by water. The ability to take care of oneself when suddenly thrown
overboard, or to act quickly when someone else is in
imminent danger of drowning is of unquestionable
value.

Interest in swimming has steadily progressed of
recent years, due to the fact that as a sport it has been
fostered by military organizations, the Y. M. C. A.,
and other athletic associations, Boy Scout and Girl
Scout troops, and by summer camps and waterside
resorts generally.

While it is undoubtedly true that swimming can
be much more easily taught to children than to
adults, it is nevertheless possible to teach anyone of
any age who possesses enough confidence to trust
himself to the water. The human body when left
to itself cannot submerge completely. It will sink
gently until the mouth and upper part of the face

are exposed, but will go no further if the submerged person does not struggle. The first efforts on his part, if untrained, will splash water into his mouth or nostrils and cause strangulation. When resting on one's back in the water with the chest inflated, the body will not sink further than the chin, and it has a sustaining weight of six or eight pounds.

The first task of the beginner, therefore, is to learn to trust the water—to stretch himself out upon it easily, and to use his arms and legs only as a means of locomotion and not for the purpose of keeping afloat. Of course, these limb strokes will further aid in keeping the body above water, but that is the secondary purpose and not the primary.

The pupil should commence with the leg movement by taking hold of the steps or bar of the tank, supposing it be a tank in which the pupil begins his lessons, with one hand level with the surface, and place the other hand against the side or steps, some 18 inches below the surface. In this manner he readily controls his body. Stretch out the body horizontally to its fullest extent near the surface of the water, and keep the legs closed, toes turned outward, back hollowed and the head turned back.

BREAST STROKE

The easiest stroke to learn and therefore the one used by the majority of swimmers is the breast stroke. While many speedy swimmers disdain to use it, it lends itself to natural and easy locomotion through the water. It has been used in conjunction with other strokes by many long-distance swimmers.

When learning the breast stroke, the first thing to keep in mind is the necessity of conserving one's strength. Do not fight the water and do not take the strokes too hastily. First the arms should be accustomed to the swimming movement, and then the legs. It is the co-ordination of arm and leg movement which makes the careful swimmer. The first stroke for the arms begins with the elbows nearly at the side. The forearms and hands are brought up in front of the chest with the palms facing outward away from the body. The fingers are held straight out and closed together so as to form a sort of paddle. From this chest position, push the arms straight out in front of the body to the full extent with the palms turned slightly outward. Then sweep the forearm entirely around until it is at right angle with the shoulders. Then the elbows are dropped again to the side and the hands brought up in front of the chest ready for the next stroke. While the arms are being straightened out with the full movement, the legs are drawn up at the knee, and the moment the arms are brought down to the side, the legs strike out in a kick or a movement of their own.

The leg movement is really in three parts as follows:

1. Turn the toes outward to the right and left

respectively with the heels nearly touching; draw up the feet gently toward the body somewhat above the level of the back, and as they near the body separate the feet a few inches. When drawn up, the soles of the feet should be at right angles to the surface of the water and just below the surface, while the knees should be turned outward to the right and left, and not drawn up too much under the body.

2. To develop the next movement, the legs must be smartly kicked in the outward direction to their widest extent without straining the thighs.

3. As soon as the legs have been straightened, continue the stroke without interruption by closing them with vigor until they nearly touch each other in line with the body—here is where the toes are turned downward, slashing the water with the soles of the feet—preparatory to bringing them up into the first position.

THE OVERHAND SIDE-STROKE

Many racers prefer the overhand side-stroke to any other, as they claim it allows greater freedom of the body and consequently less strain. But it is a matter of choice as to which side of the body is turned.

Swimming with the left side toward the surface does not impede the action of the heart, and the organs of digestion are kept free from pressure. For the purpose of clear description it will be best to imagine the swimmer is in the water lying on the right side. At the start, the lower arm should be pulled downward toward the hips, in a plane perpendicular to the surface, the fingers being kept close and the hand flat, so as to present a large surface to the water. When this stroke is finished, the hand should be turned quickly, palm upward, so that together with the lower part of the arm it cuts the water sidewise, the arm being almost bent double. Then, as it is shot forward, the hand is gradually turned from palm downward, until, when it arrives at its position in front of the head, and almost at the surface, it is ready for the next stroke. The recovery ought to be effected much more quickly than the "pull," as in the former the water offers resistance only to the upper part of the arm; but during the down-stroke the whole arm and hand have to be dragged through it.

The upper or left-arm stroke is started when the downward stroke of the under or right arm is finished. It begins about half a foot in front of the face. The arm is slightly pointing downward. The pull in most cases is taken with the arm bent a little as it enters the water, but in others the hand is brought under the chest, and then, with the arm bent at right angles, swept back close to the body, the arm gradually straightening as it leaves the water. This stroke should not be made too long, either at the beginning or at the finish, as the effect of the power applied is greater when the hand is opposite the shoulder. At the end of the pull, that is, when the hand is opposite the waist, it should be brought smartly out of the water, and carried quickly forward through the air to recommence its work. In the recovery the fingers are kept near but not touching the surface of the water. As the upper arm enters the water the legs should begin to open for the leg stroke. They should be in the position for beginning the kick when the hand is about six inches from the knee, and the kick should be completed and the legs straightened just as the right hand is pointing toward the bottom. With this movement, called the "alternate movement," the left hand appears to slap the left knee just as the kick is started, but in reality never comes closer than three inches.

The leg movement is described as follows: From the straightened position, the legs are drawn up close to each other and near the body; they are opened and brought together again simultaneously, the left or upper leg being kicked out forward as in running, the knee straightened, and the power applied with the back of the calf and sole of the foot. The right or lower leg is bent almost double, until the heel nearly touches the thigh, the tendon Achilles acting as a cut-water, and the foot swinging as on a hinge, so that there is really very little resistance. The sweep is then made simultaneously with the upper leg, the power in this case coming from the entire front of the leg from the toe to the knee. In the effective part of the stroke the left foot is straightened with a stamp at the same time that the right leg meets it with a vicious kick. As the legs come together, the wash from the upper meets the swirl from the lower, and helps considerably to send the body forward.

In trying to perfect himself in this stroke, the beginner will find that the position of the head requires great attention. He must be able to breathe correctly and at the proper time. About 45 strokes are taken to the minute for a hundred-yard swim, and at each stroke a breath is taken as the upper arm is in the recovery. The exhalation must be going on all the remaining time, the waste air being forced out the nostrils.

THE "TRUDGEON" AND DOUBLE OVER-ARM STROKE

Many forms of this stroke are adopted by sprint swimmers and water polo players. It is a very fatiguing method of progression, and rarely used for distances over one hundred yards; but for short races it is preferred by many to the overhand stroke just described.

Why some long-distance swimmers seem partial to the Trudgeon stroke is not clearly understood, as the overhand side-stroke is much better adapted to longer races. The Trudgeon was first popularized abroad by its sponsor, J. Trudgeon, who acquired his knowledge in the rivers of South America, and later won an English championship race of 100 yards. Many of the swimmers who copied Trudgeon afterward found that a double over-arm stroke was less laborious and equally as fast, as instead of the chest being raised clear out of the water, they were able to keep the body more horizontal and thus use the power which would otherwise be required to raise the chest from water for propulsion. The leg kick is the same as in the ordinary overhand stroke. When the kick is taken, the body is on its side, and as the recovery of the legs is being made, one arm is making a positive stroke while the other is being brought into position out of the water and the body turns on the breast. Meanwhile, the upper hand has gone forward; as it is being pulled through the water and the leg-kick taken, it turns on to the side again.

The double over-arm stroke which is frequently called the Trudgeon is not strictly the original Trudgeon stroke. Trudgeon himself varied the stroke of the double over-arm with a peculiar type of leg motion which is not now in use by swimmers. The modern method is to use the double over-arm with a scissors kick, as it has been found much faster for racing.

In describing the variants on the original Trudgeon stroke, Mr. J. H. Sterrett, the swimming expert, says: "While it would not be literally correct to call the modern Trudgeon stroke a 'double over-arm-

side stroke,' yet that is most nearly what the motions
of the double over-arm approach, for you must first
swim one part of the stroke as a side-stroke movement, and then roll over partly on the breast to get
your other arm out of the water, thus giving you
more positive action and greater speed by getting
both arms out, than you would get from the single
over-arm, in which one of the arms must be pushed
under and through the water, with the resistance such
negative action entails."

The real secret of successful distance swimming
in using the Trudgeon stroke is in acquiring the art
of breathing rapidly. As the face is almost constantly submerged, the beginner will find it extremely hard to time his breathing and his arm
strokes. For a short dash through the water, the
breath might possibly be held for several strokes, but
in the long run this is exhausting. The best method
is to turn the face slightly on the completion of each
stroke for a quick intake of air and then exhale
slowly through the nose while the face is still under
water.

THE CRAWL STROKE

The crawl stroke, like the Trudgeon, was introduced into America from abroad and immediately
sprang into wide favor. It originated in Australia,
the two Cavil brothers being among its first expo-
nents. It is particularly adapted to speed racing and

has been the means of winning the majority of the championship races in the last twenty years.

This stroke is quite different from others. In order to use it successfully, the arms and legs are kept as close to the body as possible so as to offer a minimum of resistance to the water. The upper parts of the legs are kept fairly close together and there is no kicking motion such as is used for foregoing strokes. The swimmer lies as lightly on the water as possible face downward, and the legs from the knee down are alternately raised and dropped with a paddling motion. This amounts to a thrust backward and tends to propel the body straight ahead through the water. The arm motion is somewhat similar to that used in the Trudgeon stroke. As the right foot strikes backward, the left arm which is bent at the elbows is thrust into the water straight ahead and drawn sharply backward for its full length, emerging again from the water at the hips. Meanwhile, the other leg and the other arm are taking up the motion. The result is that some one member is always in the act of propelling the swimmer through the water, and the motion is more continuous than in other types of swimming.

The peculiarity about this mode of swimming is that the work is almost entirely done with the arms; one of the Cavils, in fact, demonstrated that he could win a race with his feet tied together and he did actually do so in a contest with amateurs. Many crawl swimmers use the feet more as a means of steadying the body and keeping their course trimmed, than for any great distance which they expect to make by the use of their feet.

As in the Trudgeon stroke, the matter of breathing is important. It is much harder to breathe properly with the crawl than with other strokes, because the face is continually under water, and in order to get the best value out of the strokes, the swimmer must not turn his body unduly out of line. Since the head and shoulders must be turned slightly in order to get a proper breath, some crawl swimmers prefer to breathe only after every two or three strokes. Experts in the art of swimming, however, breathe after every stroke by a quick half turn of the head just as the arm is thrust forward. The breath is then slowly exhaled under water.

SWIMMING ON THE BACK

The great importance of back swimming has been little recognized by swimmers. Very great attention is paid to the faster methods of progression, championships and ordinary races for every conceivable distance having been promoted; back swimming, however, the knowledge of which is of primary importance in saving life, has been neglected. Fast side-stroke swimming is of small value in saving life unless other methods of progression are known to the swimmer, and it often happens that the speed swim-

mer, who knows nothing else, has had either to re-
lease his hold of a drowning person or else to call
for help himself.

Back swimming can be easily acquired by any
person able to swim on the breast, for the movements
are almost identical.

The best method of learning back swimming is to
stand in water which reaches up to the waist, then
spread the arms out on a level with the shoulder, fall
gently backward on to the water, and as the legs
leave the bottom, take a slight spring so as to impart
impetus to the body. In the first stroke the arms
should be brought round almost to the side, the hands
being kept in such a position that the thumbs are
nearest the surface, and at the same time the leg-
stroke should be carried out in exactly the same manner as in breast-stroke swimming. In bringing the
arms back to first position, the hands should be turned
palm downward, so as to offer less resistance. The
more perfect form of method is to make a sculling
motion with the arms, the hands being brought
toward the sides of the body during the effective portion of the leg-kick, and pushed outward when the
legs are getting ready for the next kick. The tip
of each hand describes a sort of double loop.

FLOATING ON THE BACK

In order to learn to swim easily on the back, one
must of course learn to rest confidently upon the

Swimming

water and at ease. The swimmer who can float will easily pick up the back swimming strokes. To a swimmer who really loves the art as a pastime, there is nothing so enjoyable as being able to float in open sea water. When the breakers are running high the body is at one moment poised on the top of a wave, while the eyes rapidly scan the valley of water beneath and the incoming wave beyond; the next moment the body is sunk in the valley with a high mountain on either side, and the blue sky above.

The essential in floating is plenty of self-confidence. If a man be possessed of this, it will not take him very long to master the art. It is the nervous and impatient who experience so much difficulty. Non-success, even after continued practice, should not be allowed to act as a deterrent, but all the precept in Christendom is often unavailable with the swimmer "who could float if his legs would not sink."

When beginning the attempt to learn, the mouth should be kept closed, as, when the body comes to a horizontal position on the surface, the water will in all probability ripple over the face before the arms are placed accurately beyond the head, and, if the mouth be open, the swimmer forgets all about the need for balancing himself, gasps at the inrush of water, lets his legs sink, and then has to begin again. One of the best methods is to stand on the bottom of the tank, stretch the arms out perpendicularly over the head, and gradually incline the body backward until the shoulders are under water, all this time keeping the legs rigid and the body and arms as far as possible in the same straight line with the legs. The lungs should then be well filled, and a straight push off from the bottom taken. Every movement must be made slowly and carefully; there must be no jerking, or failure will inevitably result. As the legs rise to the surface they should be extended, and, with the arms kept perfectly rigid. The palms of the hands should face upward; the arms themselves should be widened apart if necessary, so as to cover a greater surface of the water, the head should be kept well back. If the body sink for a moment, the limbs should be kept rigid, and the breath held. The mouth and nose, toes and chest, will then rise above the surface, and the swimmer will realize that he is floating. The body will sink slightly at each expiration, but will rise again at each inspiration.

DIVING

Many swimmers enjoy diving more than swimming, and some beautiful forms of diving have been perfected. Diving contests are now a feature at every water carnival. The best method of learning to dive is to stand on a platform or bank, then stoop down until the body is nearly double, stretch out the arms in front of the head, sink the head between them, and gradually tumble over into the water.

DIVING

Three types of fancy high diving, at a summer camp at Peterboro, N. H.

Swimming

The great difficulty is to make the first plunge. Once this is accomplished, proficiency will soon come with practice. Most beginners are nervous, and afraid to enter head first. Their trials are often amusing. They will start for a dive, but change it into a jump; or they will keep their head back and arms up, thus coming down on the water in grand style, with plenty of noise and splash.

A very good plan with a beginner who is learning to dive is to get two other swimmers to hold a towel stretched in front of him. This gives him an idea as to the throwing up of the legs, and as he goes over if the legs are not thrown up, the confederates should raise the towel so as to force the learner to make a clean dive. At his next attempt, he will probably get his legs up properly.

In high diving, which should not be attempted until the learner has thoroughly mastered low diving, the take-off is made either from a spring-board or solid platform. The latter is the safer and more graceful, one of its finest examples being the "swan dive." The diver leaps straight out into midair and the body is then straightened out horizontal with the water. The feet are kept close together, and the arms (in the swan dive) thrown up and back. Then the head is declined toward the water, and the hands brought down together below it in the form of a wedge. The body should enter the water cleanly and without a splash.

A spring diving-board is generally used for running headers by experienced bathers, but should on no account be attempted by beginners. A run of from twenty to thirty feet is made; when the end of the diving-board is neared, a jump is taken, and the body shoots up into the air. Then the experience gained in low diving is brought into service, the body is straightened and declined toward the water. When properly done, this style of diving is very graceful. It creates no splash, and the body enters the water "cleanly." Other fancy dives, such as the "jack-knife," are made from a standing start off the spring-board.

The diver for distance, or plunger, should stand erect on his starting base with the toes slightly overlapping the edge of the tank and the ball of the foot resting firmly upon the diving base. The knees should be kept together. Then the arms should be swung slowly backward and forward and a few short respirations taken, the heels being raised from the ground at each forward swing of the arms. The inhalation should be short and the exhalation long. As soon as the lungs are well cleared, a spring forward is made, and a deep inspiration is taken. As the feet leave the diving base the hands are thrown above the head in line with the body, which in the spring forward should be directed so as to enter the water as far as possible from the starting point. The actual angle to be observed can only be arrived at by continual practice, but at no time should the body be more than two or three feet below the surface of the water. When the body has once entered the water, the palms of the hands should be flat, the fingers kept perfectly straight, and thumbs locked. The feet should be turned well back, with the soles as nearly as possible facing upward. At the same time the body must be kept rigid in as straight a line as possible, and perfectly motionless. If these directions be observed, the body will move from twenty to thirty feet under the water, then gradually rise to the surface, and float onward in a straight line; the plunge terminating when the swimmer finds the air in the lungs exhausted, and is thereby compelled to raise his face. When the body is rising to the surface after the dive, care should be taken that the head and arms do not come too far out but remain on the surface; otherwise the impetus gained by the dive will be greatly lessened, and the distance of the plunge curtailed.

In order to "hang on," or otherwise expend to the greatest advantage the progressive power which has been gained from the dive, it is essentially important that the management of the breath should be made the subject of careful study, as it is the principal difficulty with which the plunger has to contend. There is, of course, a great strain on the respiratory organs when a long plunge is being taken, and it will therefore be evident that immediately before the dive the lungs should be fully inflated with pure air, so as to allow the plunger to enter the water under conditions which will enable him to make the longest stay, with his mouth and nostrils below the surface, without undue strain.

In order to effect a good plunge, many of those who take part in competitions "hang on" an inordinate time, until the respiratory center becomes affected, and the head painful. We have known two or three instances of plungers sinking, face downward, in a state of insensibility; but such cases are rare, as the face being close to the surface can be quickly raised when the feeling of strain becomes noticeable. It will, however, be recognized that in deep water the danger is one that should not be overlooked, and when such competitions are in progress both the plungers and officials should be on the alert for possible accidents.

TENNIS

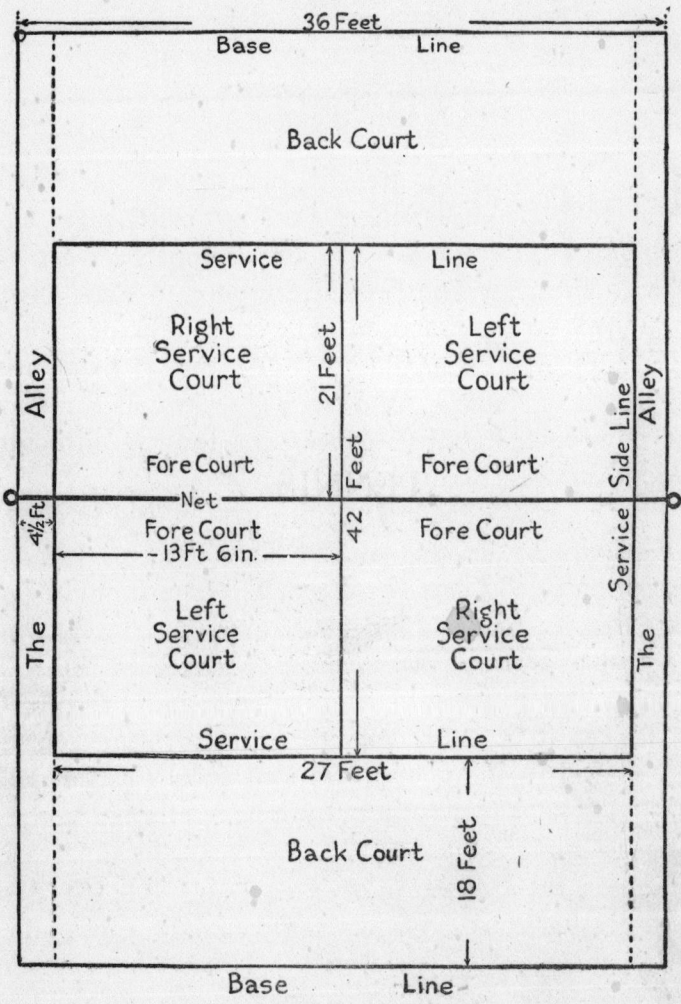

36 Feet

Base   Line

Back Court

Service   Line

Right
Service
Court

Left
Service
Court

21 Feet

42 Feet

Fore Court   Fore Court

Alley   Service Side Line   Alley

Net

4½ Ft

Fore Court   Fore Court
─13 Ft 6 in.─

Left
Service
Court

Right
Service
Court

The   The

Service   Line

27 Feet

Back Court

18 Feet

Base   Line

386

TENNIS

TENNIS—or to give it the proper technical name, Lawn Tennis—is a sport with royal antecedents. There has been an attempt to trace it back to antiquity and find a reference to some such game in Homer's *Odyssey*. The sixth book describes a Grecian princess as playing at a game of ball with her maids of honor. While the Greeks and Romans did have such handball games, it would be difficult to connect them with tennis.

The French were among the first of the modern nations to take up this sport. Several terms still in use are derived from the French. It is thought by some that the name of the game itself is derived from the French word *tenez,* meaning "seize it" or "play."

After the fourteenth century, we find frequent references to a game something resembling tennis and played in the court circles of both France and England. Chaucer is thought to have alluded to this game in his reference to "playen racket to and fro."

Among the French monarchs, Louis XI, Charles V and Charles VI all were devoted to this game which they termed *La Boule*. In still later years in France during the reigns of the various Louis, there are frequent references to the sport. From the sixteenth century on, it was widely played both in France and England. Shakespeare makes a direct allusion to tennis in his play *Henry V*, Act I, Scene 2, in a passage beginning "When we have match'd our rackets to these balls." *1500-1612*

The tennis there alluded to, however, was indoor, or what we now call Court Tennis. It was played either within doors or within enclosed garden walls. There were usually long galleries erected along the side walls for the benefit of the spectators.

Lawn tennis as such can hardly be traced further back than 1870. While in earlier times the game was probably played by the indoor devotees of the sport on any outdoor court that might be available, it had still been regarded as an indoor game. In 1874, however, a Major Wingfield of England took out a patent for a game of outdoor or lawn tennis which speedily became popular. The court as devised by him was of a pattern termed "The Hour Glass." A few years later this type of court gave way to the familiar rectangle as we now have it.

From 1880 on, this outdoor game grew in popularity by leaps and bounds both abroad and in America. Two of the first clubs in this country were the Boston Athletic Club and the New York Racquet and Tennis Club.

Tennis has, however, been regarded as a game for a few rather than for the masses. The fact that only a few players can participate at a time—either two,

miss Mary Outerbridge (1875)

three, or four—and that it does not lend itself well as an amphitheatre spectacle has restricted its popularity. It has not been until recent years, that tennis has assumed prime importance among outdoor sports, partly due to the fact that our American champions were victorious in international contests for several years in succession and won the titles of champions of the world. With the rise of such players as Malcolm D. Whitman, William A. Larned, Holcombe Ward, Beals C. Wright, William J. Clothier, Maurice E. McLaughlin, R. Norris Williams, II, William M. Johnston, Vincent Richards, William T. Tilden, II—to say nothing of other players of high order—America presented an impregnable front to the rest of the world.

The Davis Cup Contests are participated in by a dozen different countries and are played abroad as well as at home. In 1900, 1901, and 1902 successively the United States won this coveted prize. Then for a period of ten years it went to other hands. In 1913, an American won again, losing the next year to Australia. During the years of the war, there were no competitions. In 1919, playing was resumed with Australia as winner. For the next seven years America was the victor, but in 1927 France wrested the cup away.

Tennis for women has attracted almost as much attention as that for men, and again our country has produced extremely strong players, such as Mrs. May Sutton Bundy, Miss Mary K. Browne and Miss Helen Wills of California, and Mrs. Molla Mallory of New York. The contest between the latter and Mlle. Lenglen of France in 1923, won by the French player, attracted world-wide attention. England also has produced some brilliant women players. "Mixed doubles" by the foremost men and women players are a feature at all international contests.

HOW A COURT IS LAID OUT

A tennis court may be either a dirt surface, i.e., scalped of turf, or a grass surface. Tournament games are played on the latter, but the majority of players prefer the dirt court as they think it a faster game. Furthermore, this type of court is more easily kept up.

In choosing a site for the court, have it run if possible from north to south. Facing a court east and west results in one or the other player, on clear days, having to face the sun, which is a serious handicap. It is also best, if possible, to lay out a doubles court, on which four players can take part, rather than a singles, which is limited to two players. The doubles court may include the extra bounds for single players, and thus be used for either type of game.

The accompanying diagram illustrates the manner of laying out both courts, with the standard dimensions.

Tennis

The singles court is a rectangle 78 feet long and 27 feet wide. It is divided across the middle by a net, the ends of which are attached to the tops of two posts, standing 3 feet outside the court on each side. The height of the net is 3 feet 6 inches at the posts. It should be pulled taut between the posts but retained at a height of 3 feet in the middle by a strap called the center strap, which should be not more than 2 inches wide. There is a band at the top of the net, from 2 to 2½ inches in width.

At each end of the court, parallel with the net, and 39 feet from it, are drawn the base lines, the ends of which are connected by the side lines (see diagram). On each side of the net, at a distance of 21 feet from it, and parallel with it, are drawn the service lines. The middle points of the service lines are joined by the center service line which divides the space on each side of the net between the service line and the side lines into two service courts. The places where the center service line, if extended, would meet the base lines are indicated by 4-inch marks immediately inside the base lines, called center marks. All lines and marks should be not less than 1 inch or more than 2 inches in width, except the base lines, which may be 4 inches in width. As one faces the net from each base line, the right and left halves of the intervening court are the right and left courts, respectively.

In the doubles game the court is the same length

as in singles but is 36 feet wide. The service courts are the same as in singles. If necessary to avoid delay, the singles side lines may be allowed to remain marked in their entirety, instead of only where they coincide with the service side lines.

IMPLEMENTS OF THE GAME

The playing implements are light, resilient, hollow balls which are struck or volleyed back and forth by means of rackets. The balls should measure more than 2 8-16 and less than 2 10-16 inches in diameter; and should weigh not more than 2 1-16 ounces. The rackets, which are used to propel or bat the balls back and forth across the net, are made of wood strung with lambs' gut; or if metal with metal stringing; but wood is preferred. They are of varying weights depending on the size or strength of the player.

Mr. A. E. Beamish, the English expert, has this to say with regard to the racket: "When the novice chooses his racket, if he hasn't an expert friend to help him in person, he must remember certain points and hints as well as he can, or he will be sure to get something quite unsuited to him." Generally speaking, he should be guided by the strength of his wrist and muscles, the size of his hand, and other physical details, which vary with everyone and consequently render any arbitrary rules for selection of the racket quite impossible. In the writer's opinion there are three points at least which every good racket must possess, besides those which are demanded by the individual characteristics of the selector:

"1. The racket must be well strung, i.e., have an even tension of gut all over the playing surface.

"2. It must be well balanced, i.e., when swung back and downwards, swing easily without drag at any point. This quality is very difficult to find, except by contrast. The writer knows from the 'feel' of the racket that 'comes up badly' how the well-balanced article should behave.

"3. The racket's head should be long rather than round in shape, with a concave block in the shoulder. This last detail is most necessary, for the sound reason that thereby about one-quarter inch more length is obtained in the main strings, which will thus have a correspondingly increased power of drive.

"In addition to these vital points, the characteristics of a good racket, which the beginner should learn to look out for and recognize in the selection of his racket, there are other points, more individual to his own peculiarities, which he will have to find out for himself. He must exercise his judgment as to the size and shape of the handle, point of balance, style of stringing and thickness of gut, as well as upon other small details not so important to the quality as to the appearance of the racket itself.

"The beginner is advised to choose a racket of from 13½ to 14½ ounces in weight, never less and

never more, if for use by a man; and one from 13 to
13½ ounces, never more than this weight, if for use
by a woman. The racket should be tightly strung
(never play with a loosely strung racket at any cost),
of medium gut, as having the best qualifications for
wear, with a long head, and a concave block (for
reason given above) at the shoulder. The size of the
handle is so absolutely a matter of individual choice
that no opinion can be given on the question; the
beginner, however, should remember that the ills
attendant upon the use of too big a handle are greater
than the penalties that wait upon the users of one too
small. In the first instance, by giving the fingers
too much to hold, the player will lose flexibility of
wrist, and probably strain his muscles; in the second
case, the racket will twist in the hand, more often
than not, and the stroke be spoiled. In the first case
downright damage will probably be done, in the
latter merely some lost games. From this the beginner should know that his best course is to get a handle
that exactly suits him, and avoid both evils."

HOW THE GAME IS PLAYED

The game may be played by two, three, or four
persons. Where there are two on a side the doubles
court is used, as previously described. In a three-
handed game a single player plays in a single court,
while the two others must cover a doubles court.

Tennis

In a four-handed game both courts are, of course, double courts.

The choice of sides and the right to serve in the first game shall be decided by toss; provided that, if the winner of the toss choose the right to serve, the other player shall have the choice of sides, and *vice versa;* or the winner of the toss may insist upon a choice by his opponent. If one player choose the court, the other may elect not to serve.

The opposing players take positions on opposite sides of the net. The player who first delivers the ball is called the server, and the one to whom he serves, the receiver. The object of the game is to deliver or return the ball successfully within the bounds of the enemy's court.

At the end of the first game the receiver becomes the server, and the server the receiver; and so on alternately in subsequent games.

The server takes a position with both feet behind the base line, and between the limits of the center line and the side line. He delivers the service from the right and left courts alternately, beginning from the right, and endeavors to hit the ball in such a way as to cause it to drop into the service court, diagonally opposite.

It is a fault if the server fails to strike the ball, or if the ball served drop in the net, or beyond the service line, or out of the court, or in the wrong court.

After a first fault, the server is privileged to serve again from the same court from which he served that fault, unless it was a fault because he served from the wrong court.

The server must be sure that the receiver is ready. If the latter attempt to return the service, he shall be deemed ready.

A service or fault delivered when the receiver is not ready, is called a "let," and does not count. Also a served ball which strikes the net, even though otherwise good, is a "let" ball.

The service must not be volleyed; that is, taken, before it has touched the ground. After the first return, however, it may be either volleyed or returned from the first bound. A ball is in play on leaving the server's racket, if no fault has been committed, and it remains in play till the stroke is decided in favor of one or the other players. It is a good return if the ball is driven back into the proper court, even though it may touch the net.

For other rules and decisions governing the play, the reader is referred to the Official Rules.

On either player winning his first stroke, the score is called 15 for that player. On either player winning his second stroke, the score is called 30 for that player. On either player winning his third stroke, the score is called 40 for that player. The fourth stroke won by either player is scored *game* for that player, except as follows: If each player has won

Tennis

three strokes, the score is called *deuce;* and the next
stroke won by either player is scored *advantage* for
that player. If the same player win the next stroke,
he wins the game; but if he loses the next stroke, the
score returns to deuce, and so on, until one player
wins the two consecutive strokes immediately following the score of *deuce,* thus winning the game.

The first player who wins six games wins the set,
except as follows: If both players win five games
the score is called "games all"; and the next game
won by either player is scored advantage game for
that player. If the same player win the next game,
he wins the set; but if he loses it, the score returns to
games all; and so on, until one or the other player
wins two consecutive games immediately following
the score of games all, when he wins the set.

The players shall change sides at the end of the
first, third, and every subsequent alternate game of
each set. In many friendly games, however, the
change occurs at the option of the players.

In all contests the play is continuous from the first
service till the match is concluded; provided, however, that at the end of the third set each player is
entitled to a rest which shall not exceed 10 minutes;
and, provided, further, that in case of an unavoidable
accident, a cessation of play which shall not exceed
two minutes, may be allowed between points; but
this proviso shall be strictly construed, and the privi-

lege never granted for the purpose of allowing a player to recover his strength or wind.

The above laws, which are simplified from the Official Rules, also apply to the three-handed and four-handed games, except as follows:

In the three-handed game, the pair who have the right to serve in the first game shall decide which partner shall do so; and the opposing pair shall decide in like manner for the second game. The partner of the player who served in the first game shall serve in the third, and the partner of the player who served in the second game shall serve in the fourth, and the same order shall be maintained in all subsequent games of the set.

The players shall take the service alternately throughout the game; a player cannot receive a service delivered to his partner; and the order of service and receiving once established shall not be altered, nor shall the receiver change courts to receive the service, till the end of the set.

THE PRINCIPAL STROKES

"In the game of Lawn Tennis," says Mr. Beamish, "there are practically only three primary strokes, upon which the others are founded. The rules and methods governing the production of these strokes are fundamental, and apply in a more or less modified degree to them all. Thus the beginner should first of all understand the principles which affect the

TENNIS

Tense moment in the Davis Cup Matches of 1923, at Forest Hills, Long Island.

production of these strokes; then he will be better able to appreciate their value, and the part they play, in the other more difficult shots he afterwards attempts.

"Finally, he will obtain, in this way, a good grounding in the first principles of the general strokes of the game, which will help him very considerably in his more mature efforts later on.

"Every stroke in the game of Lawn Tennis (as of Golf) can be divided into three separate and distinct actions, which should be in practice, however, so harmoniously blended into one movement that no single one should appear more conspicuous than the other.

"1. The first movement, or the preparatory part of the stroke, is the swing back of the racket.

"2. The second movement, or the working part of the stroke, is the forward swing of the racket, to meet the ball, and the blow itself.

"3. The third, or the finishing part of the stroke, is the end of the racket's swing after it has met the ball; this controls the balance of the striker and regulates the power and strength of the shot.

"Upon the first of these depends the accuracy of the second, and the correct production of the third. The third, again, has a considerable power of affecting the second, in proportion to the amount of attention that is paid to it.

"Thus all these movements are interdependent and

affect one another to a considerable extent. Upon the manner in which they work depends the success of the whole series of which the stroke as a whole is comprised.

"Now, any golfer will tell you, and treat the thing as a truism, that the swing back of the club regulates the length of the shot. Very few tennis players have applied this to their own game, consciously at least, and are not aware that the racket's backward swing should be long or short as the stroke intended is to be deep or short. Neglect of this fairly obvious fact is one of the most frequent causes of mistiming, loss of power, and 'snatching'—that complaint of the beginner, whose eagerness to hit the ball hurries the backward swing into the actual stroke itself and ruins the timing of the shot.

"Again, upon the unimpeded finish of the racket's swing after the ball has been hit depends the power of the stroke and the balance of the player's body, as well as the smooth production of the stroke without jerk or check.

"And once more, as with the golf club, this free follow-through of the racket after the ball has been struck has a kind of retrospective value on the stroke itself. For as a general rule, when the follow-through is freely made the player's balance is sustained, and the stroke then gets every single atom of value from the swing of the racket and the transference of the player's body weight from one foot to the other.

"Play the shot with a checked follow-through and the tightening up of the muscles that will nearly always precede this fault—if it is not a reason for it —will cause the ball to be mistimed and the stroke spoiled.

"Thus, if beginners would appreciate the fact that each of these three actions that comprise the stroke has its value in the whole movement, they would give more care to them severally and successively, and so be enabled to make each shot as perfectly as their skill and capacity to put them into practice will permit."

Service. The game is always begun with the service—so this will be the first stroke described. On picking up your racket, you will notice that your hand instinctively covers the flat part of the handle. This natural grip is all right for some forms of service, but not for all. If you wish to make a long, clean hit across the net—and this is the only kind of service to learn in the beginning—you should grasp the handle with the center of your palm a little to the right of the center of the narrow part of the handle itself. The fingers can then close round the narrow part of the handle with a firmer grasp. Any other kind of grip will result in a service with a cut ball.

Take up your position with your feet and shoulders in the same line and in such position that this line would cut directly across the court in which you intend to serve. The service runs diagonally from the right to the left or from the left to the right. If you are a right-handed player, grasp the racket in your right hand and the ball in the left and raise the two simultaneously, tossing the ball lightly into the air in such a way, if it were not struck by the racket, it would fall back and strike you on the left shoulder. At the same time throw your shoulders and head well back and draw the racket back with a slow easy sweep as far back as you can conveniently bring it. This, of course, comes only from practice. Mr. A. E. Crawley says: "The height at which the ball is hit is where the arm in hitting is straightening at the elbow. Service is a throw, and in throwing a cricket ball the ball leaves the hand just as the arm is straightening. Therefore, and in all strokes, the arm must be fairly well bent at the start. Then it goes up, bends down behind the head, comes up and then down on the ball, as your shoulders come round from their original diagonal position and your right leg swings with them. The ball should be thrown up a couple of feet higher than the point at which you hit it; you have more time to watch it, and it is easier to hit when descending.

"Don't throw the ball before your racket swings up. It is easier and more rhythmical to throw both up together. Here comes a difficulty, and to most beginners this throwing of the ball to the right place with the left hand is very difficult. Practice throwing up and atching, without using the racket. Now, the special difficulty is that you are facing more or less the right-hand net-post, and your left hand is about just in front of your left hip, your racket in front of your right hip. Therefore, to throw the ball so that it would drop on your left shoulder, you must throw it in a curve from your front to your left shoulder. There is a further reason for this, namely, that the two arms must, throughout the stroke, keep the same distance apart, neither stretched backwards nor turned in like scissors."

In service, as in all full strokes, the golfing rule of "slow back" applies to tennis. The motion of the arm as it comes to the ball should be hastened, and still more so after hitting. This is the secret of the follow-through, so important also in the golf stroke. Any check on or after impact is fatal. Therefore, when you *see* the ball, aim carefully, watch it hard, and get on to it with *increasing* speed.

Return Shots. Immediately the ball is in play, any number of other strokes will be needed by both players. The return play depends entirely upon the speed and location of the served ball. The kind of return shot to use must be decided instantly. Many players serve their first ball so fast that it is almost impossible to return it, at any rate with any degree of accuracy. But in the ordinary game, the first stroke frequently lands in the net, and the player does not dare drive the second with the same speed for fear of committing a double fault. He will consequently deliver an easy ball which the opposite player should be able to return, and also to place at some advantage.

The Smash. This is the name given for overhead balls which are sent back with considerable force into the opposite court. As in the service, the movement of the body itself is all important for accuracy. The same grip should be used as in the straight service. This stroke is difficult to learn but can be used with deadly accuracy when once acquired. For smashing, the player may make use of the same grip as that of the straight fast service. The full arm swing reminds one of the lusty blows of an axe. High balls are more easily handled with a smash stroke than lower ones; although many players have developed both forehand and backhand shots with great power.

Forehand Strokes. The secret of a successful forehand drive is a short swing back and a long follow-through. This with practice results in such accuracy that the hand and the racket seem to be guiding the ball back to its exact position in the opposite court. Do not bend the arm or turn the wrist, as the least deflection will spoil the aim. Do not swing the racket further back than the shoulder, and an even shorter swing is better. The stiff wrist

Tennis

which is so essential is maintained by tightening the grip of the fingers. Do not grasp the handle at right angles or straight across, but slope your fingers forward, along it. This insures better leverage and consequently better control.

The Volley. In every game of tennis there is the constant temptation to volley the ball—that is, return it before it has struck the ground. This is more difficult than it looks, and results in many wild smashes out of bounds. One has less time to judge of the ball's flight or trajectory. Furthermore, excessive volleying quickly tires out all the players. Many of the best players only volley certainties. Mr. Crawley says of this stroke:

"The best grip is that for a chopper. Holding comfortably, with the head of the racket well up, you can slide your hand a fraction round, before hitting, to the right for a forehand volley, to the left for a backhand. Sometimes it is unnecessary even to do this. Further, when waiting, hold the racket straight out in front of you like a rapier. If you hold it across your chest, you may be too late for a forehander; if you hold it down by your right side, you will be too late for a backhander. The intermediate position is the best. Again, if you hold the racket well up, you can easily protect your face from being hit, a not uncommon accident which has frequently caused the loss of an eye.

"Most of the quick-firing volley-plays in doubles,

is not hitting the ball, but just meeting it, and the angle at which the racket meets it decides its direction. Other volleys are hit with a bent arm, half-arm shots these. For low volleys you must, of course, stoop. It is possible to volley a ball, which is only two inches from the floor, by grounding the racket behind it, with (as in all low volleys) its head laid back. Such a ball may be cut if it is almost out of reach. Again, you may drive the ball as if you were playing a full drive from the floor. In this volley only need the wrist be stiff; though in all volleys which are more than taps, the wrist is stiffened as you follow through. The lob-volley is easy, and very useful when the opponent is coming forward rather rashly. Make it quickly at the last moment and only just high enough to be out of his reach. If too high, he will have time to run back and return it. Lastly, there is the drop-volley. When the opponent is well back and you are close to the net, it is a certain winner. Meet the ball slowly and gently, drawing the racket down and under it, thus putting on back-spin and letting the ball, so to say, roll off the racket. The drop-shot off the ground is executed in the same way, but is best made with the racket well up so as to come down and under the ball. To alternate long drives with short drops is a useful principle of tactics."

Backhand Stroke. Many a good tennis player in the making has failed to achieve distinction because of his or her inability to master the backhand stroke. It is the most difficult of all, because the most complex and unnatural; and as soon as an experienced player on the opposite side discovers this weakness in an opponent, he is merciless. While many players can return a ball by the backhand stroke after a fashion, comparatively few of them can place it with accuracy; consequently, if it falls within bounds it can be easily returned.

The beginner can master this stroke, however, if he takes it up naturally and without being "afraid of it." Grasp the racket as you would a small hand-mirror and hold it up in front of you in order to look straight through the strings. Then let it drop slowly to your side until the racket stops in a horizontal position. You will note that the handle is extending diagonally through the palm, with the fingers clutched lightly but firmly around it. Now separate the forefinger slightly from the rest and crook it. You will find that the control of the handle lies between this arched forefinger and the thumb, while the other fingers merely act as supports.

Now practice meeting gently driven balls with the backhand sweep, held in this manner, and note how the slightest change of angle or undue pressure on any part of the racket affects the direction of the ball. The perfection of this fine and necessary stroke only comes through practice, and any player can acquire it if he is only patient and not afraid.

Ground Strokes. One of the most important of strokes is the half-volley. This can be practiced and mastered by oneself. Drop a ball and hit it the moment it reaches the floor. Aim not at the ball, but at its point of contact with the floor. Strike with an upward swing which will tend to raise the ball and get it over the net. The easiest half-volley is when the ball is close beside your foot. The hardest, when it comes directly at your foot.

"If you expect a forehand stroke," says Crawley, "you can wait for the ball with this grip on your racket, and the racket held in front. If you expect a backhand, you can wait with the backhand grip, racket again in front. But it is wiser to wait with the intermediate grip—that for an axe—and shift it as you go to meet the ball.

"Before the ball reaches the ground, you must, of course, be more or less in a position suitable for returning it. Step into the sideways moving stance with your last-but-one step before hitting. Meanwhile, what about your racket? As with the other implements for hitting a ball, you should take aim. When you hammer a nail, you first *aim,* by putting the hammer on the nail; then you swing back and smite. So, before the ball reaches the ground, your racket should be pointed forward, to the place which, as you will have judged, is appropriate for the impact. Then, 'come back with the ball,' and then forward to it, accelerating as you get on to it

Tennis

and your arm straightens. At the end of the follow-through the head of the racket should be as high as your shoulder and pointing to the place where you sent the ball. These two things mean that you have hit upwards and in a line with the proposed direction of the ball. It is only in cut- and spin-strokes that the racket moves across the direction or obliquely to it."

DEFINITIONS OF PLAYING TERMS

Net. The netting placed across the middle of the court.

Post. One of the wooden or metal uprights supporting the net.

Band. The strip of canvas attached to the top of the net.

Base Line. The back line at either end of the court.

Side Line. The line at either side of the court that marks the outside edge of the playing surface.

Service Line. The line 21 feet from the net that bounds the back of the service courts.

Centre Service Line. The line dividing the service court into halves and separating the right and left service courts.

Center Mark. The mark bisecting the base line, defining one of the limits of the service position.

Side Service Line. The line forming the boundary of the service courts at the right and left side lines.

Sports and Games

To Serve. To put the ball into play.

Service, or Serve. The act of putting the ball into play.

Server. The player who serves.

Receiver. The player who receives the service.

Toss. To spin or throw up the racket for choice of service or court.

Fault. A served ball that does not strike in the proper court, or is not properly served.

Foot Fault. During service the lifting of both feet at once, or stepping on or over the base line.

Volley. A stroke made by hitting a ball before it has touched the ground, except in serving.

Racket. The implement used to strike the ball.

Let. A served ball that touches the net and yet goes into the proper court. Also any stroke that does not count and is played over.

Stroke. The act of striking the ball with the racket.

Permanent Fixtures. The umpire, linesmen and spectators, and their chairs or stands, net, posts, back- and side-stops, and many other objects situated around a court.

In Play. A ball is "in play" from the instant it leaves the server's hand until the point has been decided.

Point. The smallest unit of the score. Four points scored win a game, unless both sides have won three points, when the score is "deuce" and one side must gain a lead of two points to win the game.

Game. The unit of scoring next higher than the point, scored when either side has won four points, unless the other side has meantime won three; in that case the side first gaining a lead of two points wins.

Set. The unit of scoring next higher than the game, scored when either side has won six games, unless the other side has meantime won five; in that case the side first gaining a lead of two games wins.

Umpire. The official in charge of the match, whose duties are defined in the Regulations.

Referee. The official in charge of a tournament, whose duties are defined in the Regulations.

Linesman. An official of a match, whose duties are defined in the Regulations.

Tournament. An official competition.

Tournament Committee. The committee in charge of a tournament.

Challenge Cup. A trophy placed in competition under stated conditions, which must be won more than once.

LAWN TENNIS ETIQUETTE

In addition to the rules of the game which every player is presumed to know, there are unwritten laws covering the game which it would be well for the player to keep in mind. The following recommendations, compiled by a member of the National Rules Committee, are worth remembering:

Return all stray balls that come in your direction as promptly as possible. You appreciate this favor in return.

"Thank you," is an appeal, not an acknowledgment. Comply by returning the stray ball quickly and good-naturedly.

When returning the balls between strokes to the server, look first to see where he is standing, and return the ball as near to that part of the court as possible. Roll them along the ground and under the net if you can.

If you touch the net while the ball is in play or commit any other infraction of the rules that loses the point for you, instantly announce the fact of your doing so.

Do not leave it to your opponent to keep the point or game score. It is your job as much as his, and it makes the game run smoother and faster.

Do not call a ball that you have hit "in" or "out." That is for your opponent to do.

Do not serve until your opponent seems to be ready; a glance at him will tell whether he is or not. It is not fair to hurry your service.

When a service is a fault, let it go by you and do not hit it, as it is very apt to annoy the server as he is delivering the second ball.

Your opponent will call the balls on his side of

the court, and, no matter what you think, play on his call; the breaks will even up during a match. There are very few players who will knowingly call them wrong.

The spectators are bound by laws of etiquette no less rigid. They should remember that tennis is played strictly as an amateur sport for its own sake and not for profit. To seek to influence a play by expressions of approval or disapproval is bad form. Restrict yourself to applause for good shots made by either side and after the play is over.

Do not applaud errors; by that is meant that your approval should be given to good strokes only. Do not applaud a shot that goes out of court or into the net, even if it gives a point to the player you want to win.

Do not coach the players. Never call "Good," "Out," "Let it go," "Hit it," etc., because thereby you are influencing a player's judgment, which is a factor in the outcome of the match. Coaching interferes with the fair playing of a match and may become extremely disconcerting by causing doubt as to whether some particular call came from a spectator or was an official's decision.

If you do not agree with the decisions as they are given, withhold your disapproval; remember that the linesmen and umpires are in a better position to judge the play than you are.

Do not throw a stray ball into the court while play

Sports and Games

is on; wait until a stroke is finished and then roll it in.

Refrain from talking loudly while a match is on, as a player may hear you and take it as a call from a linesman, and thus not play a good ball.

Under no circumstances walk or stand so near a court that you obstruct a contestant; this is inexcusable.

LACROSSE

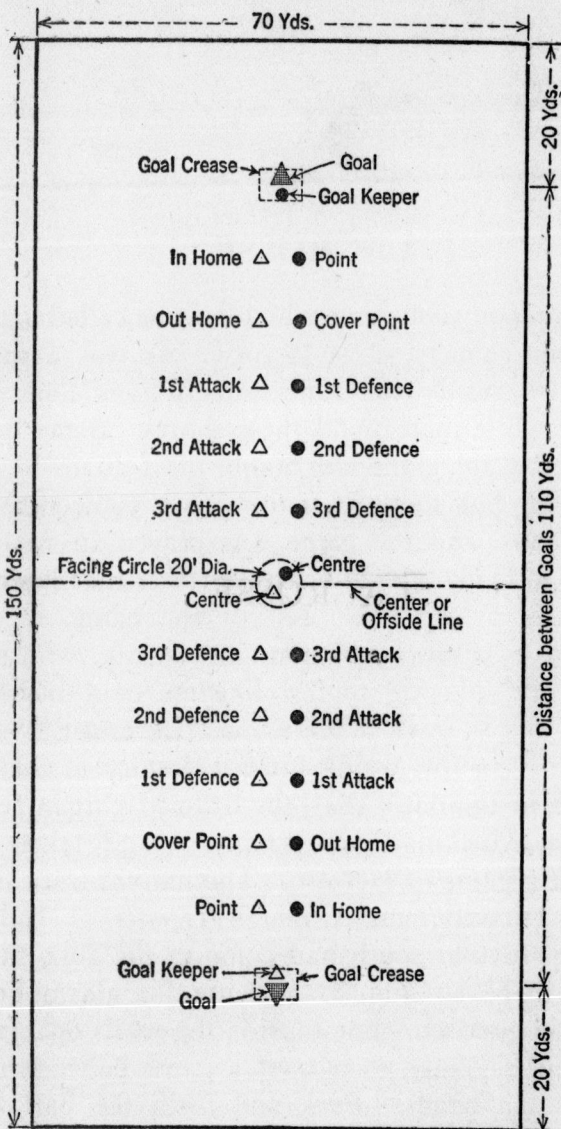

Goal Crease → Goal
Goal Keeper

In Home △ ● Point

Out Home △ ● Cover Point

1st Attack △ ● 1st Defence

2nd Attack △ ● 2nd Defence

3rd Attack △ ● 3rd Defence

Facing Circle 20' Dia. ● Centre
Centre → Center or Offside Line

3rd Defence △ ● 3rd Attack

2nd Defence △ ● 2nd Attack

1st Defence △ ● 1st Attack

Cover Point △ ● Out Home

Point △ ● In Home

Goal Keeper → Goal Crease
Goal →

70 Yds.

20 Yds.

150 Yds.

Distance between Goals 110 Yds.

20 Yds.

LACROSSE

IF there is any one game which may be called native to this country, it is lacrosse. It was a game played by the North American Indians long before the white man found these shores. Some have thought that the game was taught the Indians by the Norsemen, but there is nothing but conjecture to support this, and the game was played in various ways by so many widely scattered tribes that it seems indigenous to the soil. As for the name, it was bestowed by French colonists in Canada, who saw in its chief playing tool a likeness to a bishop's crozier, and so gave it the name, "La crosse."

There is an interesting historical story to the effect that, in Pontiac's War, the little Michigan frontier post, Mackinac, was surprised and taken by means of a game of lacrosse. The natives were supposedly friendly, and although reports of Indian uprisings further south had come to the fort, there seemed to be no immediate cause for alarm here. The little garrison came outside the walls one June afternoon, as usual, to witness a game between two rival Indian bands. Back and forth the ball was volleyed, until one extra long shot sent it bounding

417

inside the walls. After it swooped the yelling contestants, but once inside their game was forgotten, and a savage war whoop resounded. The fort was seized, and the garrison overpowered before a blow could be struck.

As a matter of fact, the Indians played the game in a more warlike manner than their white brothers of today. The goals were often placed a long distance apart—perhaps a mile or more—and the whole intervening distance was the scrimmage field. The contest was one calling for the utmost courage and endurance, and often a skull was cracked, or an arm broken. The ball was a good-sized spheroid stuffed with feathers and covered with moss or buffalo hide, and was driven along pretty much as in the present game. The Choctaws used two poles six feet apart, with a crossbar, like our football, for their goal; but some tribes used only a single post, tree, or rock, and goals were scored by hitting the post with the ball. The net used in the present game was a paleface invention. In the Indian game the goal would be surrounded by a throng of painted, nude figures, and the attacking party had to force its way through. At times several hundred players were engaged and it resembled a battle more than a game.

As now played, the game occupies a field of about the same size as a football gridiron. Near each end is a goal, something like that in ice hockey—a frame six feet square, with a net coming to a V-shaped point behind it. The goals are 110 yards apart, and are located in a "crease," which is 18 x 12 feet, and can be occupied only by the defending side.

The field is a quadrangle, measuring 150 yards long by 70 to 85 yards wide (see diagram). The goal creases, therefore, are not at the extreme end,

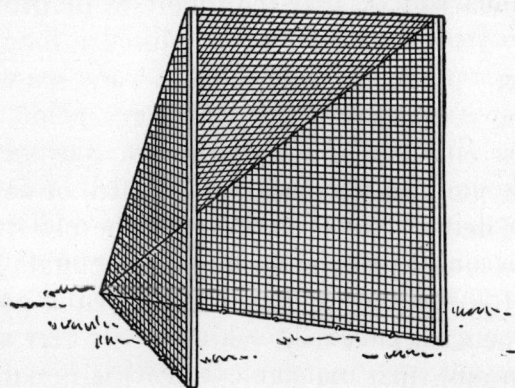

GOAL

but are placed far enough up the field to allow some 20 yards playing space behind them. The game starts from a circle in the center of the field, which is 20 feet in diameter. Between this center line and each goal stand the two teams, made up in part of attack and of defense. At the extreme end on each side is the goal-keeper, whose job it is always to defend his own goal. There are 12 players on each side, and their line-up is much the same as in basketball.

Sports and Games

The game usually consists of two halves of 30 minutes each, with an intermission of 10 minutes; but where there is a tie an extra 10-minute period may be allowed. The game is started by one of the two centers in the circle. The "draw" which begins the hostilities is made by placing the ball, a solid white rubber sphere, between the backs of the sticks of the two men who confront each other in the circle. When the referee's whistle sounds, each man jerks his stick swiftly away in the endeavor to deflect the ball in the direction of his own team. The moment the ball bounds on one court or the other, that team begins to drive it toward the enemy's goal. This may be accomplished in several ways—by carrying in the net at the end of the stick, thrown to another player, bounced, knocked, or kicked. It may be advanced in any such manner except that it must not be touched with the hands by anyone save the guard at the goal.

The two teams each have players for attack and defense. The duties of the defense are always to keep the attack of the other side from advancing the ball. They do this in several manners, such as intercepting a pass, or body-checking a runner, the latter corresponding to a football tackle. Such a tackle is allowed only when the opponent is in actual possession of the ball, or about to seize it. The most important member of the defense squad is the goalkeeper, who has great responsibility, and who may

Lacrosse

make use of his hands as well as his weapon to keep the ball away from his coveted goal.

The following is an abridgement of the Rules for 1930, as approved by the U. S. Intercollegiate Lacrosse Association.

The crosse may be of any length to suit the player, and shall not exceed one foot in width. It shall be woven with cat-gut. ("Cat-gut" is intended to mean rawhide, gut or clock string; not cord or soft leather). Metal of any kind shall not be allowed upon the crosse; splices must be made either with string or gut.

The ball shall be India-rubber sponge, not less than 7¾ nor more than 8 inches in circumference and 4½ to 5 ounces in weight. In matches it shall be furnished by the home club, and shall become the property of the winning team.

Each goal shall consist of two poles 6 feet apart, and 6 feet high out of the ground, joined by a rigid top cross-bar. The poles must be fitted with a pyramid-shaped cord netting of not more than 1½ inches mesh, which pyramid shall extend and be fastened to a stake in the ground at a point seven (7) feet back of the center of the goal, and the said netting shall be so made as to prevent the passage of the ball put through the goal from the front, and the bottom of the netting must be held close to the ground with tent pegs or staples. The goals shall be placed at 110 yards from each other, with from 20 yards to 35 yards of clear playing space behind each goal. In matches, they must be furnished by the home club. The width of the field shall be at least 70 yards and not more than 85 yards. The boundaries of the field shall be marked with white lines, and a white line shall be drawn through the center of the field perpendicular to the side lines.

The Goal crease shall be a marked line, 18 x 12 feet, and the goal poles shall be placed 6 feet from the front and back lines, and 6 feet from the side lines.

A white circle with a radius of 10 feet shall be marked in the center of the field.

Twelve players shall constitute a full team; they shall be regular members and in good standing, of the team they represent.

The players on each side shall be designated as follows: "Goal-keeper," who defends the goal; "Point," first man from goal; "Cover-Point," in front of "Point;" "First, Second and Third Defense;" "Center," who faces; "Third, Second and First Attack," and the players nearest the opponents' goal shall be called "Outside Home" and "Inside Home."

Captains shall be appointed by each team previous to the commencement of a match. They shall be playing members of the team for which they act.

The Referee shall be a disinterested party, and shall not be a member of either of the contending organizations, unless agreed upon by both teams. The authority of the Referee shall commence from the time of the appointment, and shall continue until the end of the match.

There may be a Judge of Play who shall assist the Referee in the control of the game, and whose authority shall be of the same duration as that of the Referee. His duties shall be to follow the play from the side lines and watch for fouls, reporting to the Referee those which are committed behind the Referee, or which by reason of his position can not be seen by the Referee.

There shall be two Umpires, one at each goal. They shall be disinterested parties, and shall not be removed during the progress of the match, except by order of the Referee.

Two Timekeepers shall be appointed, one by each Captain, before the commencement of the match, whose duty it shall be to keep an accurate account of the time of each half and of the intermission, deducting time for stoppages in the actual play resulting from injuries to players, ball out of bounds, or disputes. They shall also keep a record of all time lost between goals. They shall immediately report to the Referee any variance in their time, and the matter shall be decided by him. He shall be guided by them as to the duration of the halves and match, but the same shall not end until the Referee actually calls "time."

Time shall not be taken out by a player except for injury, and then for a period not longer than two minutes.

Play shall be started at the beginning of each half and after each goal is scored, in the center of the field, by the Referee placing the ball between and touching the reverse surfaces of the crosses of the players facing and resting, not on the ground, but supported by the reverse surfaces of the crosses, and when both sides are ready the Referee shall start play. This is known as "facing."

The crosses shall rest upon the ground at right angles to a line connecting the two goals. The players facing shall stand on the same side of the center line of the field as the goal they are defending, and when the Referee shall start play, each player may attempt to direct the course of the ball by a movement of the "crosse" in any manner he desires.

When the ball is faced in any other part of the field, except center, the crosses shall be placed at right angles to a line running from the ball to the nearer goal. The defending player shall stand between his crosse and his own goal, so as to face away from his own goal. The attacking player shall face toward the goal and take a position on the opposite side of his crosse.

In all cases where the ball is faced, no player shall be allowed within ten feet of those facing the ball until it is in play.

Lacrosse

Goals in all cases must be scored by putting the ball through the goal from the front side.

After the end of the first half the opposing teams shall change goals.

Should the ball be accidentally put through a goal by one of the players defending it, it shall be a goal for the team attacking the goal. Should it be put through a goal by any one not actually playing, it shall not count.

The Goal-keeper, while defending his goal within the goal crease, although not allowed to catch and throw with his hand, may bat away with his hand or stop and block in any manner with his crosse, hand or body.

A player with the ball in his possession, or within the reach of his stick, may be stopped by a body-check. A body-check shall be understood to be the stopping or checking of an opponent (who is in possession of the ball or about to receive the same) with the checking player's body; provided—

(a) The check is not made from behind;

(b) The player making the check does not hit with his stick the body of the player checked;

(c) The player making the check does not hurl his body through the air, but keeps at least one foot on the ground;

(d) The player making the check does not fall or throw his body against the player being checked in such way as to strike him below the knees and trip him.

Sports and Games

No player, while attacking his opponent's goal, shall for the purpose of shooting, passing, receiving or retrieving the ball, go within the goal crease, nor shall he at any time interfere in any other way with the Goal-tender while the latter is within the crease.

426